WALTER HEAPE, F.R.S.

WALTER HEAPE, F.R.S.

A Pioneer of Reproductive Biology

John D. Biggers & Carol Kountz

Jamestowne Bookworks, Williamsburg, Virginia

John D. Biggers, Ph.D., D.Sc. is Emeritus Professor of Cell Biology at Harvard Medical School, Boston, and Carol Kountz is Associate Professor Emerita of Writing at Grand Valley State University, Allendale, Michigan.

Jamestowne Bookworks, Williamsburg, Virginia
Copyright © 2016 by Jamestowne Bookworks.
All rights reserved. Published 2016

ISBN: 978-0-9975990-0-8 (print edition)
ISBN: 978-0-9975990-1-5 (digital edition)

Walter Heape, F.R.S. by John D. Biggers & Carol Kountz
Biography of Walter Heape
Marine Biological Laboratory, Plymouth
The Royal Society of London
Breeding cycles and behavior in animals
Classification of estrous and menstrual cycles
Reproductive technology (embryo transfer and artificial insemination)
Sex determination
New Elkhorn Mining Company
High speed cinematographic photography

Jamestowne Bookworks LLC
107 Paddock Lane
Williamsburg, VA 23188

Front cover: Walter Heape, by Walter Stoneman, taken in 1918, NPGx44318. Copyright © The National Portrait Gallery, London.

Dedicated to Anne McLaren, Donald Michie and Betsey Williams for years of encouragement to finish this book

The Authors

John Biggers, Ph.D., D.Sc. is Emeritus Professor of Cell Biology at Harvard Medical School, Boston. He was born in Reading, England on 18 August, 1923. He graduated with degrees in Veterinary Science and Physiology at the University of London, and was later awarded the degrees of Doctor of Philosophy and Doctor of Science. In 1971 he was appointed Professor of Physiology, Harvard Medical School, and later Professor of Cell Biology with the renaming of Departments. Formerly he was Professor of Population Dynamics at the Johns Hopkins School of Public Health and King Ranch Research Professor of Reproductive Physiology at the University of Pennsylvania School of Veterinary Medicine. Before immigrating to the USA he held Faculty Appointments at the Universities of London, Sydney, N.S.W., and Sheffield. From 1954 to 1955 he was Commonwealth Fellow at St. Johns College, Cambridge. He has taught courses and seminars in several areas of physiology and reproductive biology and has frequently been an invited speaker.

John Biggers has received several awards including the Hartman Award of the Society for the Study of Reproduction, Pioneer Award of the International Embryo Transfer Society, and the Marshall Medal of the Society for the Study of Fertility (UK). He is a Fellow of the American Association for the Advancement of Science, an Honorary Member of the Society for the Study of Fertility, and a Life Member of the New England Fertility Society.

John Biggers is a Former President of the Society for the Study of Reproduction and an Editor of the Biology of Reproduction. He has been a consultant to the National Institutes of Health, the National Science Foundation, and he was Chief Scientific Advisor to the Ethics Committee of the US Department of Health, Education and Welfare that made recommendations on human in vitro fertilization and embryo transfer. He is a consultant to LifeGlobal Group LLC, Guelph, Canada.

John Biggers has published over 250 papers in such fields gametogenesis, fertilization and early embryonic development, placentation, infertility, sperm preservation and statistics. He continues to maintain these interests during retirement.

Carol Kountz, Ph.D. is Associate Professor Emerita of Writing, Grand Valley State University, Allendale, Michigan. In addition to teaching, writing, and lecturing in an academic setting, she has also served as managing editor for Plays Inc., Publishers and *The Writer* magazine.

Table of Contents

Preface

My attention was drawn to Walter Heape in the 1950s when I was working with the late Dame Anne McLaren on the culture and transfer of preimplantation mouse embryos. That he was able to transfer rabbit preimplantation embryos from one mother to another in the 1890s, which he reported in the *Proceedings of the Royal Society*, seemed remarkable. It was not until I wrote about Heape's paper on the centenary of its publication that I discovered he had made other important contributions to mammalian reproductive biology, so that when he died in 1929 he was regarded as one of the fathers of reproductive biology. I decided to write this book because his works are largely forgotten except in the field of human in vitro fertilization.

Walter Heape was a gentleman with private means. His father made a fortune in Australia and after returning to the UK became a director of the Union Bank of Manchester and Vice-Chairman of the Board. Walter initially worked in business, but then decided to pursue science. He worked at Cambridge University assisting Francis Balfour, the founder of comparative embryology. Although Heape never read for a degree he was eventually appointed an Instructor and was awarded the prestigious Balfour Scholarship, which enabled him to do independent research for three years. For his contributions he received an honorary M.A. degree from Trinity College. He went on to have a distinguished career in which he played a key role in the founding of reproductive biology and applied animal science. Eventually he was elected a Fellow of the Royal Society of London. He was also a man of many talents—as an administrator supervising construction of the Plymouth Marine Laboratory, as a businessman directing the Elkhorn Mining Company in Colorado, and as an inventor in the Great War designing a high speed cinematic camera for ballistic research.

The reproductive sciences we know today are very different from the days when Heape was in his prime. What did biologists know about reproduction at that time? It was described largely in terms of natural history, morphology and development.[1] Two fields central to understanding reproduction in mammals, genetics and endocrinology, were still in their infancy, and textbooks on physiology available to Heape made no mention of these subjects. In a major textbook of physiology published in the United Kingdom in 1898, Sir Edward Sharpey-Schafer wrote:[2]

> The subjects of generation and reproduction have been omitted in this textbook, because, although strictly speaking appertaining to physiology, they are studied almost entirely by morphological methods, and are more conveniently treated in connection with morphology.

Heape's work can only be appreciated in terms of the intellectual environment in which he functioned, which we have described in some detail. We hope that the publication of this book will restore his recognition.

John D. Biggers (March 2016)

---

[1] For example: Carpenter WB (1876) Principles of Human Physiology. 8th ed. Lindsey, Philadelphia; Dalton JC (1871) A Treatise on Human Physiology. 5th ed. Lea, Philadelphia.
[2] Sharpey-Schafer ES (1898) Textbook of Physiology. 2 vols. Macmillan, New York.

Acknowledgments

Walter Heape left very few letters and unpublished notes. There are, however, a number of letters he wrote about scientific questions which are preserved in several archives. The most valuable are the archives of Anton Dohrn, the founder of the Stazione Zoologica in Naples, because he systematically kept hand-written copies of all letters he wrote as well as those he received. Other valuable archives are at the Plymouth Marine Laboratory, the Galton Archive at University College in London and the British Archives at Kew. Other letters are preserved in various collections at the University of Cambridge Library, Imperial College London, the University of Edinburgh, The Royal Society Library, and Queens University, Canada. We are indebted to the helpful librarians at all these institutions. Heape's extant letters have been transcribed in detail because they are largely unknown, having been read by very few people.

John Biggers (JDB) also had interviews with two family members who knew Walter Heape. Alexandra Heape, the wife of Walter's youngest son allowed him to read Heape's diary from his voyage and records after 1877, and he consulted Patricia Mulcahy-Morgan, daughter of Barbara, Heape's daughter. We thank Professor Henry Leese who arranged for JDB to meet with Mr. Eric Cussans, a former apprentice at Thomas Cooke where the high speed cinematic camera was constructed and who remembered seeing the machine being tested.

We are indebted to Professors David Whittingham, Catherine Racowsky, Jay Baltz and Dr. Michael Summers for critically reading a draft of the manuscript. We are also indebted to Steven Heape, great-grandson of Walter Heape, who made family photographs available to us. Dr. Betsey Williams (wife of JDB) was particularly helpful in searching for obscure documents on the Internet and in libraries, and for criticism of some of the early drafts.

The book would never have been completed without the help of Dr. Carol Kountz, who joined as co-author after the project began.

Publisher's Note

This book is the life story of a gentleman-scientist and businessman who worked with some of the greatest names in the natural sciences during the late Victorian-Edwardian eras, including Francis Balfour, Anton Dohrn, Michael Foster, James Frazer, E. Ray Lankester and William Bateson. Walter Heape's career spanned a period of revolutionary progress, with pioneering contributions to reproductive biology and animal breeding which had hitherto been under-investigated and hobbled by superstition. It is lamentable that he is not better known, but this first biography fills an important gap in scholarly detail.

There are two other, more personal, reasons for welcoming the book. I was familiar with Heape's research while a graduate student in Cambridge where he also worked, and I even cited his 1890 paper in my dissertation. But until I read this book I had no idea of just how rich and accomplished his life had been. The second reason is that I can think of no authors better qualified for this project than John Biggers and Carol Kountz. John's eminent career in reproductive science has spanned six decades from Cambridge to London to Johns Hopkins and finally to Harvard. I admired his research throughout my own career and encourage everyone in our field, and anyone with a bent for the history of science, to enjoy this fruit of his endeavors.

We normally follow American spelling and punctuation styles in our books, but since the subject and senior author of this book are British we have adopted some of the common practices of the UK, and have strictly preserved them in the many quotations and correspondence.

Roger G. Gosden
Jamestowne Bookworks

FAMILY TREE

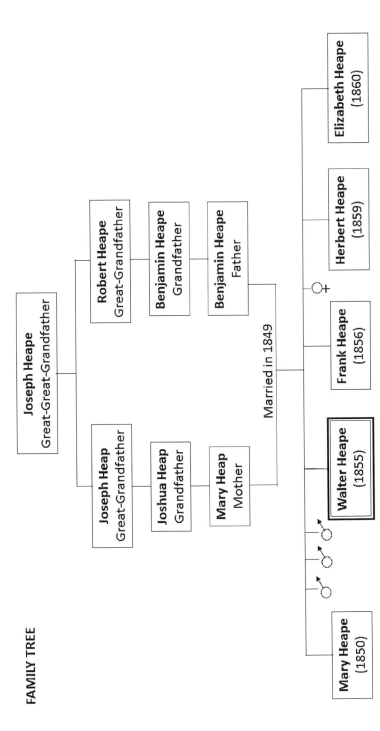

Sex symbols: Died as infants or children.

1

FAMILY BACKGROUND AND EARLY LIFE

WALTER HEAPE, who was destined to become a scientist, entrepreneur and inventor, was born at number 10, "The Boltons," Brompton, a sub-district of Kensington in London on April 29, 1855 to Benjamin and Mary Heape.[1] His father, a devoted Unitarian, was a highly successful businessman who had made a fortune in Australia. From the age of fourteen years Benjamin worked in a cotton spinning mill at Vicar's Moss in Rochdale, some fifteen miles north of Manchester, England, owned by the firm of Butterworth & Heape (dissolved in 1842).[2] Benjamin found his relatives running the mill to be slow, and when an economic depression hit the cotton industry in small towns around Manchester they lost money. In 1837 his thoughts drifted to the possibility of making a career in a new country. After two years, during which the economic depression and attendant social unrest worsened, the 21-year-old man left on 22 May 1839, embarking in Liverpool on a small 212 ton migrant wooden barque called the *Alice Brooks*, and arrived in Adelaide, South Australia, on 23 September 1839.[3]

Benjamin travelled to Australia with Richard Grice and his family from Bootle in Cumberland with whom the Heape family had business and social connections. They were accompanied by two shepherds.[4] Soon after arriving in Adelaide they left to begin their enterprise in the new town of Melbourne, operating out of a tent on the Yarra River. The objectives of the firm of Heape & Grice were to act as general merchants, to own sheep or cattle stations and to advance money to squatters in exchange for produce. The business rapidly became a huge success, and within six years they were operating two ships, one named *Benjamin Heape*, which among other things imported timber from the Baltic. When gold was discovered in Australia, Messrs. Heape and Grice operated as intermediaries, making more large profits from its sale to the Bank of England.

Benjamin married his second cousin, Mary Heap, the daughter of Joshua Heap of Liverpool, during a visit to England in 1849. Although Benjamin and Mary had a common great grandfather, Joseph Heape, she spelled her name without a final "e", the reason being an agreement made between two of Joseph Heape's sons, Robert and Joseph. Early in life they "…agreed that one should retain the final "e" to the name, and the other drop it, in order that thereafter the families might be better distinguished."[5] It was Joseph who founded the Liverpool branch of the family and whose surname is spelled Heap.

After their marriage, Benjamin and Mary returned to Melbourne, and on 22 February 1850 a daughter, Mary, was born, followed a year later by a son, Benjamin, but he only lived for seven months. In 1852 Benjamin and Mary and their baby daughter returned from Melbourne to London where they remained for four years, at first in Highgate and then in Brompton. During that period another four sons were born but only Walter survived childhood.

In March 1856 Benjamin moved the family to "Polefield House," Prestwich, close to his earlier home outside Manchester where the economic and social turbulence of the 1830s and 1840s were past and the region was prospering from the manufacture of cotton goods, giving the town the nickname Cottonopolis. A chemical industry had also grown up alongside for dyeing cloth. Despite progress, there was considerable unemployment and pollution of both air and water as the city industrialized. The watercolor painting "View of Manchester from Kersal Moor" by William Wyld commissioned by Queen Victoria in 1852 depicts a maze of smoky chimney stacks.[6] After five years in Prestwich, the family moved to "Northwood" in another district of town, Sedgley Park, where Benjamin lived the rest of his life. Early in this period a second unnamed daughter was born, but she lived less than a year. A second surviving son, Frank, was born in 1856, followed by another daughter in 1858 who also died soon after birth. A third surviving son, Herbert, was born in 1859 and the last child, a daughter named Elizabeth, was born in 1862. "Northwood" was not only a family home but a substantial estate, having been purchased for the sum of £19,000. Benjamin's ample fortune from Australia together with appointments as Director of the Union Bank of Manchester and Vice-chairman of the Board allowed a comfortable living for the family and for Walter and his brothers and sisters to grow up.

The family was strictly Unitarian following a decision made by his paternal grandfather Benjamin Heape around the year 1800 to leave the Methodist Church where he was a member in Rochdale. By revoking belief in the Holy Trinity he was taking a risk because at that time it was considered blasphemy and punishable by loss of British citizenship and imprisonment until the 1813 passage of *The Doctrine of the Trinity Act* by the Houses of Parliament. Even then Unitarianism continued to have detractors. According to Charles Darwin, his grandfather Erasmus said that "Unitarianism was a feather-bed to catch falling Christians."[7] Nevertheless, Unitarianism rapidly expanded because it appealed to many thought leaders who were to transform the intellectual life of England.[8] It emphasized the search for knowledge, particularly in basic and applied science, and applying it for the benefit of society.[9]

Not surprisingly, Grandfather Benjamin's decision was made in the face of strong family opposition, which lasted many years. His brother, the Rev. Richard Heape, recorded in his diary on 4 January, 1820:

> *I feel much concerned for my brother Benjamin; his present views of the Gospel are such as I believe will ruin him eternally if they are not changed. Oh! That God would direct me what to say, and enable me to say it in such a manner as will bring conviction to his mind.*[10]

On 28 January, 1820 Richard wrote another emotional appeal to his brother:

> *... all that painful anxiety was felt respecting you by a departed mother, and I know is still felt by a living father, and I believe is still suffered by all your brothers and sister.*[11]

Grandfather Benjamin's father, Robert Heape was distressed for the rest of his life about his son's religious beliefs, as revealed in a letter to his clergyman son, Richard, dated 26 December 1827:

> *Am very ill over him [Benjamin]. I beg you most sincerely will join me in your prayers for him. I cannot, no, I will not give over praying for him. I believe if any good is done it must be by importunate faith and prayer that the Lord would be pleased to convince him of his great error.*[12]

4

On his conversion to the Unitarian Church, grandfather Benjamin became identified with a chapel in Blackwater Street to which he gave generously, and in 1840 he and his five sons, including the absent Benjamin, and his son-in-law were made trustees of the chapel.

Before migrating to Australia, Benjamin was from an early age an active member of the Unitarian Church, particularly in its educational mission and taught at the school in Rochdale. By the age of 16 in 1833 he was a founder member of the Rochdale Literary and Philosophical Society,[13] and for the four years before leaving for Australia he was its treasurer.[14] At one of its first meetings he introduced a debate on whether painting, poetry, or music gives more enjoyment to mankind. Music won.

Young Benjamin valued membership of the church, as he pointed out in correspondence with Harriet Martineau about whether he should emigrate. Martineau is considered the first woman sociologist and was a radical reformer on behalf of the poor. A fiercely independent woman, she was "the darling of the Whigs, a one-woman advertising agency, whose soap-opera novellas popularized and explained the reforms." She frequently corresponded with young men seeking her advice, who she recruited to Unitarianism. But she disapproved when promising men decided to forsake England in a time of economic crisis for, in reply to Benjamin's first letter, she wrote:

> ...*Why should you leave England? You say you have kind parents. Will they not suffer by your going? You say you have good prospects; why deprive your country of the blessing of a prosperous citizen? You are a republican. You are the more wanted here, where the great battle for free institutions has begun to be fought, and every man has a solemn duty to perform in choosing his part and acting it well. You are an Unitarian. In the present miserably depressed state of our sect we can ill spare one who 'glories in the Creed.' These are very*

serious considerations, and I can hardly conceive of any inducement to emigration which can counterbalance them.[15]

Benjamin Heape was asked to promote the circulation of the Unitarian periodical *The Christian Teacher* in return for her advice. But Martineau's appeal had no effect on Benjamin, who chose to emigrate.

After returning from Australia he used his wealth to support the Unitarian cause, and contributed £250 in 1856 to the building of a new chapel in Rochdale. He became a trustee of several chapels, two of them in Rochdale and three in Manchester. His children were presumably raised to share his faith, and both Elizabeth and Walter were married in Unitarian chapels.[16] Walter's keen interest in later life in the practical applications of science in commercial fishing, animal breeding and fertility may well have been instilled by this upbringing.

Walter did not attend school but received his education at home from a private tutor, as did many wealthy households in those days. The zoologist E. Ray Lankester, with whom he later had many professional dealings, had a governess who stimulated his interest in natural history through lessons and visits to the British Museum.[17] Some private tutors were clergy-men and some were hired from overseas, such as Germany.[18] The classes they taught included Latin because pupils would need that language to enroll at a university. But not every notable scientist in those days had the advantage of private education. T. H. Huxley, for example, taught himself chemistry, history, Latin, Greek, algebra, and geometry while he was apprenticed to a doctor in London's East End.[19] At the age of seventeen years Walter entered the relatively new Owens College which was founded in Manchester in 1851 with the strong support of local industrialists. In a break from the traditions of Oxbridge the benefactors decreed that "... the students, professors and teachers, and other officers and persons connected with the said institution, shall not be required to make any declaration as to, or submit to any test whatsoever, of their religious opinions."[20]

Walter seemed destined for a business career for at the age of 18 in 1873 after one year at Owens College he left to join the firm of Joseph Heap & Sons of Liverpool, a rice milling company probably run by his relative Richard Rankin Heap. An impression of this business can be gleaned from the Articles of Association prepared at the time of the company's sale and incorporation in 1899:

> To carry on the business so to be acquired, and develop and extend the same, and generally carry on business in the United Kingdom and abroad as rice millers and dressers, factors, brokers and merchants, also general millers, manufacturers of oil and feeding cakes, grinders and dressers of flour and meal, farmers, ship owners, carriers by land or sea, agents for insurance companies, and underwriters, and manure manufacturers; and to obtain, get, buy, sell, produce and prepare for market, and deal in paddy and rice of all descriptions, grain of all descriptions, and all other substances of any other description, printers and publishers of decorative, illustrative or literary prints, upon goods or for publications contributive to the interests of the trades or businesses above referred to, and to manufacture and sell, either by wholesale or retail, every description of goods and provisions, whether made wholly or in part from rice or any other substance, and generally to carry on any or all of such businesses in all its branches and any businesses of a character similar thereto, or which contribute to or facilitate the same or any of the objects aforesaid, or which by the advances or increase of knowledge, or exigencies of labour may be substituted therefor.[21]

Walter did not remain with this company for long because he soon moved to the merchant firm of John Carver Darbishire of Manchester, and was stationed in Gibraltar. He moved again in 1875 to the cotton-spinning mills of Richard Harwood and Sons, probably run by George Harwood of Bolton near Manchester.

Although still a young man, he was often afflicted with ill-health and decided to embark on a voyage around the world to recuperate.[22] According to his diary it was a life changing experience. He left Liverpool on 29 July, 1877, on the sailing ship *Cassiope*, an iron clipper of 1,559 tons built in 1875 for Messrs. Heap and Sons of Liverpool. This was a much more comfortable vessel than the one in which his father sailed to Adelaide nearly forty years earlier. Ocean voyages were sometimes dangerous and seven years later the *Cassiope* left Rangoon for Falmouth but was never seen again. An official inquiry into its loss concluded that it had probably foundered in the Indian Ocean during a cyclone.[23]

His health apparently improved on the voyage because 68 days after setting sail from Liverpool he wrote in his diary on 5 October:

Can go about the rigging in most places easily enough now. As soon as one has confidence to rely on your hands instead of feet everything is easy. A little exercise practice gives one sufficient strength in grasp and arm. I am improving in strength a great deal ....

Walter arrived in Melbourne after 81 days at sea on 19 October 1877. Before setting off he had been given many introductions to people in Melbourne and the State of Victoria, and it was presumably through his father's former partner, Richard Grice, that he met its governor Sir George Bowen. Less than a week after arriving in Melbourne he attended a large ball for Mrs. Jeffray's daughter, and later attended the Melbourne

Cup races for three days. His diary was very forthright in opinions about some of the people he met:

Oct 24. Saw [?] Seemed a conceited snob - thought him an arrogant ass.
Attended a ball on October 25 for Mrs. Jeffray's daughter 250 guests. Some
very pretty girls but dancing abominable.
Oct 28 Heard Unitarian lady preacher—she gave an earnest, clear,
thoughtful sermon—never heard a woman speak so well, and was surprised to
see so much power with a certain amount of gentleness. But certainly do not
like to see a woman in the pulpit.
November 1 went to Mrs. Coates for tea—made themselves very agreeable.
The two girls very nice. The men unbearable. Mrs. Coates very kind.

One of his major expeditions out of Melbourne included visits to Woods Point, 120 kilometers east-northeast of Melbourne, and Walhalla, 184 kilometers east of Melbourne. Both were productive gold-mining townships located at the southern end of the Great Dividing Range. Excerpts from his diary describe in detail how uncomfortable it must have been to make this journey by horse-drawn coach over exceedingly rough terrain. His enthusiasm for the unfamiliar landscape and its flora and fauna was undiminished, however, and his affinity for accurate terminology emerges as well. The following record anticipates the course of his future life:

Started at 8 o'clock by coach of four for Fernshaw, first stage of about 14
miles very monotonous and uninteresting, scattered gum trees over flat
plains—lunched at Sillydale which is about 20 miles from Melbourne: five
miles of this stage regular bush road, or rather track and very rough. We
gradually get nearer the hills. A few miles from Sillydale change coaches and
take a three horse coach, on to Fernshaw: part of the road rough but much of
it good. Passed Mr. Harker's place, to whom I have a letter from his brother.
He has some very good grazing land, 2,500 acres about and a good sized
house. As we approach Fernshaw which is among the hills, the scenery

becomes prettier. The hills are thickly wooded and the trees increase in size as we go on, until they become very gigantic—the giant trees are mountain ash, they use them for fencing, etc. Wood split very easily, trees evergreen and cast the outer skin of bark, the driver said annually. We heard locusts in the trees as we came along. They are 3 inches long about, green or brown, and make a very loud chirp. They were in very great numbers, and made a loud noise.

Changed coaches at Fernshaw and went on in a two horse car to Maryville. Passing over the black spur mountains. Went through some splendid forest scenery—and along the edge of many very beautiful fern gullies, which are very beautiful, the fern foliage looking so delicate and graceful. Enormous trees standing, and lying on the ground, many burned still more half burned by bush fires—the outer bark hanging in shreds from many trees, many feet in length (20-60 feet). The utter chaos of trees and ferns, and brush wood I never saw before—immense trunks of trees and ferns, and brush wood—immense trunks some decayed through, others just fallen, nearly hidden by ferns, grasses and scrub. Enormous trees standing, some alive, some dead; some dead ones whole, others supported only by their outer wood the inner wood decayed away. The line of trees with long shreds of bark hanging down, and blowing about. Large tree ferns, with decayed brown fronds handing against the trunk, newer fronds spread out, and young ones of fresh green just openning [sic] out. Bracken, [illegible], i.e. sapplings, as thick as sugar canes, grasses … Corduroy roads, i.e. roads made of logs of wood put crosswise, and a little soil thrown over. Several parts of the road made this very uncomfortable, frequently jumped right off one's seat, coming down with a bump in fact every few yards this happened. Arrived at Maryville about 8. Having had 12 hours coaching. What in England would be called very rough coaching.

As the diary continues, Heape writes a crisp and precise description of the native animals, again with a traveler's verve for unexpected sights, such as the small, powerful bear:

Nov. 13. Went with 2 policemen on foot, 3 miles about, part way through the bush to the falls—on the way thro' the bush, saw a kangaroo rat, and the dog a powerful greyhound caught a native bear, a short, lethargic, clumsey [sic] (on the ground) animal size of a spaniel much thicker, very hard to kill, cry like a human being, claws very long and sharp, will tear the flesh if it catches you, stupid and slow in movement on ground, very helpless. Saw a dead snake— looked for some wallibi [sic] but did not get any.

Bush travelling on foot very fatiguing, every few yards large fallen trees to clamber over, grass long! Thick and dried sticks, bracken and tree bark knee deep and making ground very uneven and slippery. Where the earth visible it is stony in many places. Falls very fine: three, one on top of the other, large body of water falling over—one of the police and myself bathed, water very cold, got a short way under the falls and had a shower bath, felt like an immense weight dropping on ones shoulders ...

Saw bullock drags with six and eight bullocks. Laughing jackass—bird eats snakes. Kills them by carrying them high in the air and letting them drop. Saw ants about one inch long—black. Locusts, caught one, and found the noise which is very shrill and exceedingly loud to be made thro' two holes on the back where wing cases join neck, apparently by action of air on stretched parchement [sic], since by holding finger over holes no noise could be made ...

His clear description of mechanical and chemical operations at the gold mine reveals someone who was well-informed and inquisitive.

November 19. Went down Walhallla Long Tunnel Mine, one of the most renowned in the colony. We went down at 8 o'clock 500/600 feet along a tunnel we walked, at the end was a large chamber with two engines (worked by air, supplied by engine outside) one for pumping, one for raising quarried ore—went down 500 ft, and then walked along a tunnel say 1000 ft to where men were working: climbing about to several places, saw the quartz reef, and on close inspection the gold in some pieces. This is said to be very rich quartz, and owing to the manner and direction in which it lies they know it will last for a long time.

... Quartz sent up, and crushed by machine into pieces of uniform size, then pounded into dust, and water washes this sand over mercury which amalgamates with gold and is separated from gold again in retort by evaporating mercury. The strata outside the lode contains gold united with

other metals, the amalgam not uniting with mercury is collected by delicate washing, calcined in retort, again submitted to crushing, and washed over mercury which as before unites with the freed gold particles.

After mainland Australia, he sailed to Tasmania, and then to New Zealand where he visited Milford Sound and Haven, recording in his diary, "This is the most magnificent scenery for grandeur I have ever seen." The tour continued to Invercargill, Dunedin, Christchurch, Wellington and Auckland. He then took a steamer to Sydney from where he sailed for England on 16 June, 1878, onboard *HMS Shamon*, taking the easterly route via Cape Horn. The vessel docked in England on 28 September, 1878. A diary entry dated 18 August on the voyage home depicts him as a hardy youth learning to box:

Took boxing lessons. Do me a great deal of good. At first I felt the hitting a good deal, and suffered from headache but now I do not suffer that way. And am getting on I believe pretty fairly. I enjoy the exercise and am very anxious to be able to box.

During the long sea voyage he studied a botanical textbook to learn more about the Australian trees and ferns he had seen. Another indication that his life goals were changing was a note after reading essays by Herbert Spencer, whom he observed was "a supporter of Darwin and Wallace."[24] By the end of the voyage Walter Heape may have already made a decision to abandon business for the pursuit of science.

On his return in 1878, he resumed his former association with Owens College, but this time to work in the laboratory of Professor Arthur Gamgee. The college was to become Manchester University three years later and had changed radically since he left five years earlier. There was a new emphasis on professionalism in science and Gamgee had been appointed the first Brackenbury Professor of Physiology with the mission "to combine teaching the elements of science to beginners and to ordinary students, and fostering a spirit of research among older men."[25] The professor's first task was "organizing the present physiological laboratory, and placing the teaching of physiology in Owens College on a proper basis as one of the regular studies in a liberal scientific training, and not merely as one of the subjects of the medical curriculum."[26] In this endeavour he became one of the three pioneer physiologists in England, alongside Michael Foster at Cambridge and Burdon Sanderson at University College, London, and established physiology as a science in its own right and independent of the medical curriculum. The trio attracted students by making physiology a laboratory subject underlain by chemical and physical methods.

Gamgee offered lectures and laboratory classes on basic physiology, physiological chemistry and histology.[27] He also encouraged students to participate in his research which focused on blood chemistry, including the mechanisms of blood clotting. Unfortunately we know nothing of the arrangements that led him to recruit Heape to his laboratory apart from a bibliographic note that he studied histology. The opportunity to work with Gamgee may well have been a fortuitous start to Heape's scientific career in biology because as a member of a distinguished academic family the professor could have introduced him to some of the most famous figures in the biological sciences in late Victorian England. Gamgee's reputation was highly esteemed by Michael Foster and Francis Balfour at Cambridge University, and both of those men soon had a large influence on Heape's career.

After less than a year in Manchester, Heape studied botany at Oxford University for a brief period with Marmaduke

Lawson, not a taxonomist of the first rank.[28] He moved on to Cambridge at the end of 1879 to attend lectures by three eminent men—Michael Foster, Sydney H. Vines and Francis Balfour, who had the most influence on his future career.

2

THE INFLUENCE OF FRANCIS BALFOUR

SOON AFTER ARRIVING in Cambridge in 1879, Walter Heape came under the influence of Francis Maitland Balfour, a short-lived but nonetheless towering Professor of Animal Morphology. Although Heape was not formally registered as a student, Balfour called him his pupil and allowed him to work in his laboratory and attend courses taught by him and Professors Michael Foster and Sydney Vines in the areas of animal physiology, botany, morphology and embryology. He was particularly attracted to the last two, and chose to work directly under Balfour's supervision, a man only four years his senior. What was the intellectual and social environment for Heape in Balfour's laboratory?

Born into a wealthy and influential family in 1851, Francis Balfour "belonged to what is perhaps the rarest social class to be found among university teachers, the aristocratic."[1] His eldest brother, Arthur, became the Prime Minister of England following his uncle, Robert Gascoyne-Cecil, the third Marquess of Salisbury.[2] After schooling at Harrow, Balfour entered Trinity College, Cambridge, in 1870 where he came under the influence of Michael Foster, the man who had laid foundations for what blossomed into the renowned Cambridge School of Physiology.[3]

Michael Foster was Fullerian Professor of Physiology at the Royal Institution in London when the Fellows of Trinity appointed him Praelector in Physiology in 1870. Their decision reflected and bolstered a revolutionary promotion of biological sciences in British universities.[4] In Cambridge his duties included teaching embryology which was often considered under the heading of "Generation" in the 19th century and occupied large parts of courses and textbooks of anatomy.

Foster soon recognized Francis Balfour's brilliance and invited him to help prepare his lectures in embryology for publication. The first edition of what became a classic was published in 1874 under the title *Elements of Embryology*.[5] The following year, Balfour taught a short course for Foster on embryology because his academic potential and contributions to research were already recognized by his election to a fellowship at Trinity. Two years later he was appointed by the college as Lecturer in Animal Morphology, and launched a course on the subject which attracted 10 to 12 students at first,[6] but was quickly oversubscribed. In another two years he was elected a Fellow of the Royal Society of London at only 27 years of age.

Henry Fairfield Osborn has left an impression of Francis Balfour in 1879 when Heape joined the laboratory. Osborn was one of Balfour's distinguished students who became the director of the Museum of Natural History in New York City.[7] He wrote:

> Never shall I forget my first impression of Francis Maitland Balfour as I met him in the great court of Trinity College of Cambridge in the spring of 1879 to apply for admission to his course in embryology. At the time he was twenty-eight years of age and I was twenty-one. I felt that I was in the presence of a superior being, of a type to which I could never possibly attain,

and I did not lose this impression throughout the spring months in which he lectured on comparative embryology at Cambridge and in which we enjoyed many long afternoons of bicycle riding on the level roads of the Fens. I always felt that Balfour lived in a higher atmosphere, in another dimension of intellectual space. Not that he was aloof—far from it, for he was always in closest and most generous touch with the minds of his students; he made you feel that you had a mind and that your opinion and observation were of value, although you knew all the while that your mind was still embryonic and your opinions of the most tentative order. His was by far the most balanced mind among all the English biologists. He was at the time absorbed in embryology, which was the reigning biological discipline of the day ... The other great lesson taught by Balfour was that of the balanced daily life: the morning lecture and tour of the laboratory, the five quiet hours devoted to his own writing and research, the vigorous afternoon exercise, and the delightful care-free and shop-free evening. At the time Balfour was turning out the great volumes of his "Comparative Embryology", a monumental work, I asked him how many hours a day he gave to writing. He replied: "Never more than five hours."

By the time Walter Heape arrived in Cambridge, Balfour had completed research on the development of elasmobranch (cartilaginous) fishes that brought him fame. The work was done in part at the Stazione Zoologica in Naples where Balfour occupied one of the Cambridge University Research Tables during 1874 and 1877. Back in Cambridge he devoted most of his energies to writing a compendium summarizing current knowledge about animal development. The two volumes of this monumental work *Comparative Embryology* were published in 1881 and 1882.[8] Before their publication embryology research was neglected in Britain, and leadership was in Europe, particularly Germany, and much of it unread by British scholars. That Balfour's book became quickly recognized as a major contribution is indicated by a review in *Nature* by a doyen of British biology, E. Ray Lankester at University College, London:

> The present volume is illustrated by about four hundred wood-cuts, and consists of more than six hundred pages of royal octavo size. The first volume was of very nearly the same size, and as copiously illustrated. Together they form a contribution to that science of Biology which our countryman, Charles Darwin, has refounded and reformed, of which English men of science may feel justly proud. No work of the kind exists in any foreign tongue, and probably no such work would have been undertaken had not Mr. Balfour given himself to the task. Translations of Mr. Balfour's book are at this moment in course of publication both in Germany and in France. The thoroughness with which he has carried out the revision and incorporation of a few more than a thousand scattered memoirs by contemporary writers, and the excellence of his critical remarks and original observations and drawings, are all the more remarkable when it is remembered that only three years have passed since the work was commenced, and that during that time Mr. Balfour has been actively engaged in lecturing and teaching in his laboratory at Cambridge, has published several original memoirs himself, and has superintended the production of as many more by his pupils.[9]

The book was also acclaimed in non-scientific circles and by his former student Henry Osborn for its coverage of a scattered literature.[10] The London literary magazine *Saturday Review* commented on the book's important contribution to understanding the ancestry of life on Earth,[11] and mentioned the youthfulness of its author: "… the scientific world, both here and on the continent, was moved to no slight astonishment when it became known that the author had not yet passed the age at which men are usually learners rather than teachers."

Balfour's students remembered his gift for precisely communicating knowledge and encouraging listeners to think critically. Osborn again:

> In teaching he combined manly force with a delicate regard for the feelings of his pupils. From the writer's personal impressions of him as a lecturer, he did not aim at eloquence, but to be understood in every step; rarely looking at his hearers, he spoke rapidly and with intense earnestness, crowding a vast deal into the hours. The main qualities of his character shone forth in his lectures— energy, which he infused into his hearers; truthfulness, which soon gave implicit confidence in his statements; modesty and sympathy, which inspired effort and free exchange of thought.
>
> Balfour's love of truth came constantly to attention during laboratory instruction. While looking over a student's shoulder, he would sometimes say with a laugh, "You must interpret that specimen with the eye of faith;" but this was very far from being a serious injunction, for he urged his students to take the greatest caution when interpreting observations under the microscope. However tempting a certain interpretation might be, Balfour never accepted it until it rested on sound evidence. An instance of this sort was recalled by the writer which related to the much disputed origin of a well-known embryonic structure: A number of sections had been prepared seeming to confirm the view that Balfour himself had advocated some time before; it required considerable self-control not to attach a somewhat forced meaning to them: this was, however, forbidden; and it was not until several days afterwards that fresh sections established the fact beyond question.[12]

When Walter Heape joined the Balfour laboratory he may have signed up to a series of demanding courses taught by his mentor, which were announced in the Cambridge University *Reporter* for April 6 of 1880:

Mr. Balfour gives notice that he will deliver during the Easter Term a course of Lectures on Vertebrate Embryology at the New Museum on Mondays, Wednesdays and Fridays at 11 o'clock beginning on Wednesday, April 14. The lectures will be accompanied by Practical Work on the Amphibia, Aves and Mammals.

The academic diet for the twenty lectures in 1880 was recorded by one Balfour's other students, George Bond Howes, whose notebooks are deposited in the archives of the University Library.[13] The first ten lectures featured comparative embryology in a range of model species. Lecture 11 covered mammalian generation and preimplantation development, but these subjects were only known for the rabbit, and Lecture 12 included embryonic envelopes and placentation. The remaining eight lectures considered the development of organs and systems, closing with the urogenital tract.

Heape may have attended other courses given by Balfour because the October 5 issue of the *Reporter* contained the following announcement:

Mr. F. M. Balfour gives notice that he will deliver two Courses of Lectures on Morphology with practical work at the New Museums. Each Course will extend over two terms.
The Elementary Course on the Invertebrata on Mondays and Wednesdays at 9 A.M., commencing Wednesday, October 13. The Advanced Course on the Invertebrata on Tuesdays and Thursdays at 11 A.M., commencing Thursday, October 14.

Continuation of these courses was announced for the following Lent Term in the January 25 issue:

Mr. F. M. Balfour gives notice that he will continue his two Courses of Practical Morphology at the New Museums.

The Elementary Course is the Vertebrata on Mondays and Wednesdays at 9 A.M.

The Advanced Course on the Invertebrata on Tuesdays and Thursdays at 11 A.M. commencing Thursday, February 3.

Heape would have interacted with several individuals influenced by Balfour who would later distinguish themselves with contributions to biology made in their own right. Among them were Adam Sedgwick, William Bateson, A.E. Shipley, W.F.R. Weldon, D'Arcy Thompson, and Richard Assheton, some of whom Heape encountered again later in his professional life.

One of Balfour's major influences on his students was a philosophy about the role of embryology in biology. By the time Heape arrived in Cambridge, Balfour was convinced that embryology could help fill gaps in the fossil record to uncover the genealogy of all life forms—a subject that was fashionable after the publication of Darwin's *Origin of Species*. His interest in the subject was initially stimulated from working on the development of sharks at the Stazione Zoologica in Naples during 1874 as well as his interactions with Lankester, who was working in Naples at the same time on molluscs. At that time there were two major explanations for evolutionary history: Haeckel's biogenic law, which is often identified by the sound-bite "ontogeny recapitulates phylogeny,"[14] and von Baer's laws of development. Haeckel's theory is best summarized in his own words:

The History of the Evolution of Organisms consists of two kindred and closely connected parts. Ontogeny, which is the history of the evolution of individual organisms, and Phylogeny, which is the history of organic tribes. Ontogeny is a brief and rapid recapitulation of Phylogeny, dependent on the physiological functions of Heredity (reproduction) and Adaptation (nutrition).

The individual organism reproduces in the rapid and short course of its own evolution the most important of the changes in form through which its ancestors, according to the laws of heredity and adaptation, have passed in the slow and long course of their paleontological evolution.[15]

Karl von Baer's four laws of development were originally published in 1828 and translated by Thomas Huxley as follows:

(i) … the more general characters of a large group appear earlier in the embryo than the more special characters.

(ii) From the most general forms the less general are developed, and so on, until finally the most special arises.

(iii) Every embryo of a given animal form, instead of passing through the other forms, rather becomes separated from them.

(iv) Fundamentally, therefore, the embryo of a higher form never resembles any other form, but only its embryo.[16]

Both Bowler[17] and Hall[18] have argued that Balfour tended to favor the general to specific views of von Baer instead of the recapitulation of ancestral traits proposed by Haeckel. Soon after Heape joined his laboratory, Balfour listed what he considered to be the main tasks of embryology:

(a) Testing how far comparative embryology can reveal ancestral forms common to the whole of Metazoa.

(b) Revealing whether a particular embryonic larval form is constantly reproduced in the ontogeny of different animals, and whether that form represents the ancestral type of those groups.

(c) Determining whether larval forms agree with living or fossil adults, an agreement that would imply that the adults were closely related to the parent stock of the group in which the larval form occurs.

(d) Understanding how some organs can atrophy or become functionless in some groups but persist in others.

(e) Determining to what extent organs in development pass through a condition permanent in lower forms.

Balfour believed that formation of the germ layers gave rise to an important ancestral stage which he had studied in many species but never in mammals. He asked Heape to help fill this knowledge gap by studying the formation of germ layers in rabbits, and thereby introduced his student to the research enterprise.

The three germ layers are called ectoderm, mesoderm and endoderm, and their respective synonyms are epiblast, mesoblast, and endoblast (hypoblast). Over the years these terms have been used interchangeably. The terminology arose from studies of morphology in adult invertebrates, and later adopted for describing embryonic stages. While serving as a surgeon on the British naval vessel, *HMS Rattlesnake*, Thomas Huxley wrote a paper in 1849 describing his extensive studies on jellyfish,[19] noting that many coelenterates consist of only a specific type of inner and outer cell type. By 1853 the names ectoderm and endoderm were coined by George Allman for these two layers.[20] Huxley pointed out that they are comparable both morphologically and physiologically to the two germ layers in the embryos of higher animals. In 1873 Lankester proposed "planula" as a generic name for two-layered embryonic stages, identifying the layers as ectoderm and endoderm, and if a third layer was sandwiched between them he called it either mesoblast or mesoderm.[21] Haeckel had already adopted the term "gastrula" for planaria where an orifice connects an internal cavity with the outside,[22] and almost simultaneously described the three germ layers. In the translation of his work from German Lankester's usage was adopted.[23]

Long before these advances Cruikshank recovered cleavage stage embryos from the oviduct of female rabbits in 1797.[24] Several other investigators in continental Europe studied mammalian development in more detail up to the blastocyst stage and formation of germ layers, so that a considerable amount of information had accumulated by the time Walter Heape began his research. The rabbit was widely adopted to represent early mammalian development, although Balfour had warned in his *Treatise on Comparative Embryology* that the rabbit was not necessarily a reliable model for other mammals.

Balfour challenged Heape to resolve the differences between competing theories of the origin of germ layers in rabbit embryos proposed by two eminent biologists, Edouard van Beneden from Liège in Belgium and Albert von Kölliker from Würzberg, Germany. When a mammalian blastocyst forms it consists of an outer layer of cells, now called the trophectoderm, enclosing a cluster of cells, or inner cell mass.[25] Van Beneden, who was the first to describe the process of fertilization in mammals,[26] believed that the epiblast which gives rise to body cells develops from the trophectoderm while the hypoblast and mesoblast derive from the inner cell mass.[27] He claimed, moreover, to have observed a blastopore like that in Haeckel's gastrula and present in many non-mammalian embryos, including frogs and some invertebrates. Von Kölliker, on the other hand, believed that the outer cells disappear and the inner cell mass is the origin of the epiblast.[28] In fact, the layer of cells called epiblast by von Kölliker separate from the inner cell mass to occupy a superficial position which is called the germinal plate. The outer cells that are destined to disappear form Rauber's layer.[29] He also believed that the hypoblast too separates from the inner cell mass, and then the mesoblast develops as a layer between the epiblast and hypoblast.

Heape probably carried out his research in the newly constructed New Museum site of the Fawcett Building, but because biology was rapidly expanding at the university he must have worked under very crowded conditions. Everyone engaged in scientific work was male, and any women present were occupied with other essential work for running a department.[30] His project required the preparation of histological sections of rabbit blastocysts to which he later added mole embryos. Embedding embryos in paraffin wax before sectioning was a routine technique in Balfour's laboratory, and there is a detailed description of the protocol in the appendix to the second edition of Foster and Balfour's *The Elements of Embryology*. It was slow and tedious work requiring either a small, hand-held microtome incorporating a razor blade or the more sophisticated Jung sledge microtome. Both instruments required every section to be handled separately. Only a short ribbon of consecutive sections could be produced at once, instead of complete serial sections which are so desirable for studying the structure of embryos.[31] Heape worked on the project three years before the first fully effective microtome was invented by Richard Trelfall at the Cavendish laboratory, which Caldwell showed was capable of generating a complete series of sections. Trelfall later founded the School of Physics at the University of Sydney, Australia, while Caldwell continued after Balfour's death to work in the Laboratory of Animal Morphology where he was a student.

Heape confirmed von Kölliker's theory, but Balfour was not so easily satisfied, as revealed by his summary of the controversy in the second volume of his *Treatise on Comparative Embryology*:

The history of the stages of the rabbit immediately following, from about the commencement of the fifth day to the seventh day, when a primitive streak makes its appearance, is imperfectly understood, and has been interpreted very differently by van Beneden on the one hand and by von Kölliker, Rauber, and Lieberkühn on the other. I have myself in conjunction with my pupil, Mr. Heape, also conducted some investigations on these stages, which unfortunately not as yet led me to a completely satisfactory reconciliation of the opposing views.

A few years later, Richard Assheton joined the Morphological Laboratory where he completed extensive studies of early rabbit embryos that he had nearly finished in Gamgee's department at Owens College.[32] He confirmed von Kölliker's and Heape's work, as did Hubrecht soon afterwards,[33] and van Beneden eventually agreed and withdrew his original views.[34]

Meanwhile Heape began a detailed investigation of the embryology of the European mole (*Talpa europea*), a species that had been studied shortly before by Lieberkühn.[35] Neither Heape nor Lieberkühn explained why they had chosen such a difficult species which could not be kept in the laboratory. It is tempting to imagine Heape in the spring doing daily rounds of setting traps in the immaculate lawns in and around Cambridge where moles were regarded as pests. It must have been frustrating work because the probability of collecting early stages of development from wild animals is very low, and the mole breeding season in England lasts only from March through May for a gestational length of 30 to 40 days.[36]

Interest in moles may have been due to its classification because, as Thomas Huxley had pointed out in 1872 and 1880, insectivores share common features with diverse groups and were therefore potentially useful for characterizing ancestral forms, which was a primary objective of Balfour's laboratory.[37]

26

Heape reported his findings in four papers beginning with an overall summary communicated to the Royal Society by his mentor.[38] Publishing a preliminary note to the Society was a common practice in those days. The second paper was devoted to a detailed analysis of germinal layers in mole embryos,[39] and the other two were published three years later about the segmentation of ova and later stages of development.[40] It was the second of those papers and earlier work with Balfour on rabbits that attracted most attention, eventually being quoted in textbooks of mammalian embryology.[41] It also compared the germ layers of rabbits and moles with those in house mice, field mice and guinea-pigs which had been described by other investigators. Heape noted that the gastrulae formed a sequence according to the degree of involution (inversion) of the germ layers. The germ layers in rabbits do not invert but form a flat germinal disc on the surface of the gastrula, which he called the normal pattern. In the mole the germ layers begin to invert and then return to the plate form seen in the rabbit. And in the other three species the germ layers undergo different patterns and degrees of inversion. He commented:

A consideration of these facts ... leads me to believe that the difference in the development of normal animals and those in which the so-called inversion of the layers takes place is one of secondary importance, and, in fact, that no such fundamental differences exist as was supposed by the older observers; the temporary inversion of the layers which occurs in the mole connecting the two types very closely.[42]

Heape was making an "evo-devo" interpretation of embryology.

Meanwhile, Balfour's reputation for setting very high academic standards was coming to the attention of the authorities at Cambridge. On 27 March, 1882, the Council of the Senate made the following report:

> The successful and rapid development of biological teaching in Cambridge, so honourable to the reputation of the University, has been formally brought to the notice of the Council. It appears that the classes are now so large that the accommodation provided but a few years ago has already become insufficient, and that plans for extending it are now occupying the attention of the Museums and Lecture-Rooms Syndicate.
>
> It is well known that one branch of the teaching, viz. that of Animal Morphology, has been created in Cambridge by the efforts of Mr. F. M. Balfour, and that it has grown to its present importance through his ability as a teacher and his scientific reputation. The service to the interests of Natural Science thus rendered by Mr. Balfour having been so far generously given without any adequate academical recognition, the benefit of its continuance is at present entirely unsecured to the University, and the progress of the department under his direction remains liable to sudden check.
>
> It has been urgently represented to the Council that the welfare of biological sciences at Cambridge demands that Mr. Balfour's department should be placed on a recognized and less precarious footing, and in this view the Council concur. They are of opinion that all the requirements of the case will be best met by the immediate establishment of a "Professorship of Animal Morphology" terminable with the tenure of the first professor.[43]

The recommendation was approved by the Full Senate on 12 May 1882, and Balfour was elected to the chair on 31 May, 1882.

Tragically, Balfour had less than two months to enjoy his new status. An avid mountaineer, a popular sport of exercise-minded Victorians, he set out with a guide on 18 July to climb the Aiguille Blanche, part of the Mont Blanc massive which no one before had scaled on the route he had selected. When they failed to return within two days a search began and five days later their bodies were found in a couloir on the Italian side of the mountain. He was only thirty years old.

His death left a major void in the School of Animal Morphology, whose role in the university was rapidly expanding and had gained an enviable reputation for its teaching.[44] At his memorial in Cambridge on October 21 Adam Sedgwick, whom Balfour had appointed Demonstrator, declared: "To the School of Morphology here his loss, I need hardly say, has been crushing."[45] Balfour's efforts were held in such high esteem that several senior faculty members persuaded the Vice-Chancellor to encourage his program to continue under Sedgwick's supervision.[46] It must have been hard for Sedgwick to undertake this role as he had only recently earned his master's degree and was scarcely older than some of the senior students. Nevertheless, he gave notice in the University *Reporter* on 10 October that he would deliver two courses of lectures on morphology and offer practical exercises at the New Museum site:

> An Elementary Course on the Invertebrates ... This course will extend over two terms.
> The Advanced Course on the Invertebrates ... This course will be in conjunction with Mr. W.H. Caldwell and will extend over three terms.[47]

Sedgwick appointed Walter Heape, W.F.R. Weldon and W.H. Caldwell as demonstrators for assisting a professor with classes. And on October 17, 1883, he gave notice that he would repeat a course of lectures that had last been given by Balfour:

A course of Lectures on the Embryology of Mammals and Birds
accompanied by practical work on Aves and Mammals.[48]

The practical experience the students received is described in
an appendix prepared by Heape and Sedgwick to a second and
enlarged edition of *Elements of Embryology* (1883) by Foster and
Balfour.[49] It included the recovery and observation of living
rabbit preimplantation embryos, and seems very likely that
Heape drew from experience to contribute this appendix and
help to design the practical course. The methods were described
as follows:

> With the aid of a lens it is frequently possible to distinguish the
> ovum or ova through the wall of the oviduct. In this case cut a
> transverse slit into the lumen of the duct with a fine pair of
> scissors a little to one side of an ovum; press with a needle upon
> the oviduct on the other side of the ovum, which will glide out
> through the slit, and can be with ease transported upon the point
> of a small scalpel, or what is better a spear-headed needle. In case
> the ovum cannot be distinguished in the oviduct by superficial
> observation, the latter must be split up with a fine pair of scissors,
> when it will easily be seen with the aid of an ordinary dissecting
> lens.[50]

The organization of this laboratory class must have involved
borrowing microscopes from Foster's laboratory since Sedgwick
had none available for teaching. It was not until the end of 1884
that the University purchased 100 Zeiss microscopes for student
use.[51]

Five years had passed since Heape's visit to Australia and
New Zealand when, in August 1884, he decided on another
foreign tour. He spent the long vacation at the Eastern Cape of
South Africa, shooting in the infamous Addo Bush which Major

P. J. Pretorius, a renowned hunter, described as a jumble of under-growth consisting of thorns and spikes of every description and which he called "Hunter's Hell."[52] Heape shot a large bull elephant standing 9 ft. 6 in. whose skeleton he brought home and placed in the Zoological Museum at Cambridge. It is still on display there. He also collected live specimens of *Peripatus*, an odd-looking arthropod found in damp tropical forests, for Sedgwick's evo-devo research in Cambridge. Some specimens contained early stages of *Peripatus* embryos without which research would have been incomplete.[53]

Heape's contributions as a university assistant must have been exceptional in the years after Balfour's death because following his return from South Africa he was advanced to Senior Demonstrator with special responsibilities similar to a post that had existed for some time in the Physiology Department. A Report of the Special Board for Biology and Geology dated 12 March 1884 contains the following proposal:

> The large increase in the numbers attending the course of Elementary Biology indicated by Mr. Sedgwick and Mr. Vines (the class during the present term numbers 194 students), which is due in great measure to the recent changes in the regulations for the examination for medical degrees, renders urgently necessary the appointment of a Senior Demonstrator who should have special charge of the practical work and general management of the class in Elementary Biology, whilst also superintending the financial details of the Morphological Laboratory. The post would be of great responsibility and labour, as is shown by the experience of Mr. Heape who for some time past has been discharging duties of this kind, and in view of the stipend assigned to the analogous post in the Physiological Laboratory, the Board are of the opinion that the remuneration of this post should be not less than £200 a year.[54]

The General Board of Studies did not approve the proposal because of insufficient funding,[55] but a year later on 10 December, 1885, Heape was awarded an honorary M.A. degree by Cambridge University (*Admissus ad titulum Magistre in Artibus, honoris causa*)[56] and, soon after, on 12 February the Council of Trinity College approved his becoming a member of the college. This was an unusual way of joining a college and may have been facilitated by his contributions to teaching and friendship with Michael Foster.

When he returned to Cambridge in 1884, plans to establish a new marine biological laboratory at Plymouth were well under-way under the guidance of E. Ray Lankester, Thomas Huxley, and others. Recognition of Heape's administrative and academic abilities were likely responsible for his being chosen to superintend the proposed laboratory and supervise its construction. He may have welcomed a new challenge, having become disillusioned along with his colleagues Sedgwick and Bateson with the evo-devo approach to evolutionary biology. He became a pioneer in mammalian reproductive biology and its practical applications, but only after leaving so-called animal morphology and finishing his work at Plymouth.

3

LAUNCHING THE MARINE BIOLOGICAL LABORATORY AT PLYMOUTH

IN 1885 Walter Heape, then 31 years old, left the University of Cambridge where he was a Demonstrator in Morphology to become the first Resident Superintendent of the Laboratory of the Marine Biological Association in Plymouth. He held this position until he left in March 1888, shortly before it was officially opened. It was a brief tenure but he succeeded in supervising the construction of the first marine biological laboratory in England, as well as initiating a research program and proposing some long-term objectives for the institution.

To place Heape's role in proper perspective for the enterprise, the influence of two major 19th century biologists, Anton Dohrn and E. Ray Lankester, and movements that encouraged the study of marine biology in England must be understood. Anton Dohrn was the founder of the Stazione Zoologica in Naples, Italy, and Lankester became the Director of the Natural History Departments of the British Museum and Vice-President of the Royal Society of London. They met early in their careers when Dohrn was a docent studying with Ernst Haeckel at the

University of Jena in Germany and Lankester was a recipient of a Radcliffe Traveling Fellowship from Oxford University.

Dohrn was working at Messina, Sicily, in the winter of 1868-69 on the embryology of crustaceans when he realized the advantages of a zoological station on the Mediterranean coast.[1] Professor Carl Vogt of Geneva and others had dreamt of creating such an institution, but found no way of financing the project. But a year later Dohrn hit upon the novel idea of building an aquarium with an associated laboratory for conducting research on marine organisms. Revenue to support the laboratory would be obtained by opening the aquarium to the public.[2] Dohrn chose Naples because it was a major European center of commerce and tourism, and by 1872 he had persuaded the mayor to set aside a plot of land on the waterfront. The foundations of the Stazione Zoologica were laid in April of the same year.

Dohrn was not content with a single laboratory for he had visions of a series of laboratories for studying marine life in several geographical areas. In 1870 he had attended the Annual Meeting of the British Association for the Advancement of Science in Liverpool where his proposals were so persuasive that the General Committee established a "Committee for the Foundation of Zoological Stations in Different Parts of the Globe."[3] Anton Dohrn was elected its secretary with the membership of Professor Rolleston of Oxford and Mr. P.L. Sclater, Secretary of the Zoological Society of London. At a meeting in Edinburgh the following year they recommended to form a committee with the aim of building a zoological station at a suitable location on the south coast of England, like Torquay, and requested funding for the project either through a single grant or a series of annual grants.[4] Sclater offered to lay the proposal before the full committee of the Section of Zoology and Botany.

Meanwhile Dohrn had raised enough funds to begin construction of the Stazione Zoologica, and later in the year Lankester visited him in Naples. Lankester spent the winter of 1871-72 working on the development of molluscs, lodging with a small circle of friends in the Palazzo Torlonia on the Margellina. It was from there that building of the Stazione was being supervised, so he was able to observe the planning and building of the new facility. This experience enabled him at the British Association meeting in Brighton in 1872 to describe the progress being made in Naples in detail six months before it was scheduled to open. Lankester's enthusiasm is transparent in the final paragraph of his paper on the Mollusca:

> I cannot conclude this summary without pointing out how great an advantage will be gained by zoologists in the station, now nearly ready for work, which my friend Anton Dohrn has erected on so magnificent a scale, by the devotion of his private fortune and much energy and patience. It stands in the Villa Reale, on the sea's edge; and there the naturalist will not have to dispute and bargain with the intelligent but rascally fishermen; all will be managed for him by the employees of the station. Further, he will have the use of a splendid library, he will be able to keep his specimens with ease in the tanks of the station, supplied with streams of sea-water, and will have constantly the means of contemplating, even when he may not wish to study minutely, those exquisite forms which came in hundreds through my hands, but of which I said nothing, with which the waters of the Bay are teeming.[5]

Raising funds for a marine laboratory in England was frustrating, and in 1880 Lankester pointed out there were other marine laboratories going ahead along the lines of the Stazione

Zoologica, including one founded by the Johns Hopkins University on the Chesapeake Bay. He wrote:

> These things cannot be done without money, and at present the public in England and America will not subscribe so handsomely towards the erection of the first zoological station as they do to that of the fifty thousandth church. They were taught long ago to subscribe to church-building by the examples of states and princes. It requires some initiation to render the subscription lists of zoological stations popular.[6]

Lankester's lament would soon be answered in England through a turn of events originating in the commercial world with the opening of a Fish and Fishing Exhibition in Berlin in 1879. The exhibition was a great success, yet without any significant contribution from England, which prompted the following comment from a correspondent covering the exhibition:

> It is a great pity that England sends almost nothing. As far as I can hear, the entire blame rests with the English Government, which refused to give and support or encouragement to the affair ... I believe this is the first time that England has been last on the list in an International Exhibition ...[7]

The response to this criticism was a flurry of British fisheries exhibitions, which had a significant effect in bringing together leading representatives of the fishing industry and the scientific community. When the first exhibition opened at Norwich in April, 1881, Thomas Huxley gave a lecture on the biology of the commercially important herring,[8] and the same year he was appointed H.M. Inspector of Fisheries. The following year he presented a paper at the Royal Society on the so-called "salmon disease" which was causing large losses in some English and Scottish rivers.[9]

A month before the second exhibition in Edinburgh in April 1882, a gathering under the presidency of the Prince of Wales agreed to host an International Fisheries Exhibition in London the following year. Huxley was appointed to the committee for managing the organization, along with Dr. Albert Gunther, who was an international expert on fish biology and Keeper of the Zoological Department of the British Museum. At an exhibition conference on 27 July C.E. Fryer (a future Inspector of Fisheries) presented a paper entitled "A National Fisheries Society" in which he envisioned an organization that embraced all aspects of the industry.[10] It was named the National Fish Culture Association. Lankester presented a paper that day proposing to build a similar laboratory to the Stazione Zoologica somewhere on the coast for supporting research on marine organisms. He received encouragement from the well-known ichthyologist Francis Day who urged that the work be done by competent, knowledgeable naturalists.[11]

On 31 March of the following year, 1884, Huxley held a meeting in the rooms of the Royal Society at which the following resolutions were approved:

(i) That in the opinion of this meeting there is an urgent want of one or more laboratories on the English coast similar to those existing in France, Austria and America, where accurate researches may be carried on leading to the improvement of zoological and botanical science, and to an increase of our knowledge as regards the food, life, conditions and habits of British food fishes, and molluscs in particular, and the animal and vegetable resources of the sea in general. (Proposed by the Duke of Argyll, seconded by the Right Hon. Sir Lyon Playfair).

(ii) That it is desirable to found a Society, having for its object the establishment and maintenance of at least one such Laboratory at a suitable point on the coast, the resources of the Laboratory, its boats, fishermen, working rooms, etc., being open to the use of all naturalists under regulations hereafter to be determined. (Proposed by W.B. Carpenter F.R.S., seconded by Sir John Lubbock F.R.S.).

(iii) That the following gentlemen be requested to act as a provisional council, and report to an adjourned meeting, to be held on Friday, May 30th, as to the constitution and organization of the Society, and other matters, and in the meantime have power to admit suitable persons to the membership of the Society: further, that Professor Lankester be asked to act as Secretary, and Mr. Frank Crisp as Treasurer *ad interim*. (Proposed by Sir Richard Bowman F.R.S., seconded by Mr. Georges J. Romanes F.R.S.).[12]

There were careful preparations for this important meeting for it became supported in a very major way by many public figures and the Royal Society.[13] The London *Times* leant support by announcing the foundation meeting with a long article.[14] It is not surprising, therefore, that very distinguished representatives from business, science and politics were named to the provisional council.[15]

The new society expressed a commitment to build a financially self-sustaining laboratory, but still faced a major challenge to raise funds. At the end of the foundation meeting Lankester announced:

... that it was hoped that they might raise a fund of from £6,000 to £10,000 for the purpose of starting one laboratory, and it would now be possible for individuals who took an interest in the proceedings of the Society, to send to the Treasurer, Mr. Frank Crisp, cheques for £100 or £1,000 to start the fund. If those who believed in the utility of the Society, and its projected Laboratory, were prepared to subscribe generously to the Laboratory Fund, the anticipations of those who had spoken so hopefully of the work taken up by the Society would be speedily realized.[16]

In accepting the role of honorary secretary Lankester was making a major commitment, which he immediately embraced. A laboratory site had to be selected and negotiations undertaken to secure the site and finance the building.

There were several sites under consideration, among them Citadel Rock on the water front offered by the Corporation of Plymouth. In August 1884, Lankester and Charles Stewart visited Plymouth to consider the prospect. Lankester was well-informed about the challenges ahead for building a marine laboratory after watching the construction of the Stazione Zoologica. He knew that one of the critical engineering problems was to ensure an adequate supply of good quality sea water, and consulted Anton Dohrn about the Citadel Rock site in the following exchange of letters:

7 August, 1884

Dear Dohrn,

I have come down here with Charles Stewart to inspect the sites offered to us for our laboratory. A difficulty has arisen on which I shall be glad of your advice. On the top of the Citadel Rock there is a splendid level site—we can have an acre of ground. It is close to the sea—overhanging it in fact—but it is 110 feet from high-water mark. To get nearer to the sea, say 20 to 15 feet from high water mark we should have to blast the rock and we should be in a cramped narrow space.

Now I want you to tell me whether 110 feet high is a disadvantage in regard to the supply of sea-water. If we wished to have a continuous supply from the sea—pumped in every day and run through and out of our tanks back to the sea—the height of 110 feet would be fatal. But if we have a large tank in the basement of our building as you do (or used to do) at Naples we should only require to replenish this tank every now and then—say once in six months. The expense of this pumping for one day up to 110 feet would not be very serious.

I am anxious to know if you still use the system of a reservoir tank, and whether you would advise me to use the system or to endeavor to get a fresh supply pumped up every day from the sea. Everything depends on what you consider best.

I should say that for special purposes requiring large volumes of the purest sea-water (such as hatching fish eggs in quantity) we propose to have a hull anchored about a mile out in the sound—over the sides of this various tanks could be floated to—and visited every day.

I am very much pleased with the looks of things here. The Sound is a noble piece of water and contains a very rich fauna. Beyond the Eddystone [lighthouse] we can get to the deep water of the mouth of the Channel—forty fathoms and upwards.

When you write to me as to the method of supply of sea-water which you recommend, will you also give me your advice as to the disposition of our space—supposing our building to cost £5,000—apart from fittings. I find that we must occasionally (perhaps twice a week) open the room on the ground floor to the public—at a small fee—I suppose we could place our bigger experimental tanks in such a way on the ground floor that the public may come in and see them (just to keep up the local interest) and yet they could be made thoroughly accessible for workers.

How would you arrange the laboratories now? And how manage the sea-water supply for the upstairs department.

I propose to have working accommodations for ten persons in all.

The money is coming in. I see £4,000 now and the way to £4,000 more. I shall be immensely obliged if you could give me a detailed sketch of what we ought to do, as your experience suggests: and I shall lay it before the Council early in October—if you can spare the time to write before then.

With kind regards. Sincerely yours, E. Ray Lankester[17]

Dohrn replied immediately:

My dear Friend,

By all means accept the site on top of the Citadel Rock. I know it quite well and I think it is the very best you can find in Plymouth. I have worked 3 weeks in Pl. at the house of dear old Spence Bate; please remember me kindly to him and tell him that I am glad that an offspring of my own doings shall now be under his wings at Plymouth.

As to your arrangements for this your coming laboratory I find it rather difficult to give you any special indication knowing so little about the price of work and material and possible complications. What I can say in regard to tanks is this. Even if you had a site on low water mark you never could pump the water directly from the sea into the tanks, especially as in Plymouth Sound there are very strong tides which cause a great deal of impurities in the water. Besides the water after circulation in your tanks is better aerated and filtered for breeding purposes than the sea-water itself. Only mind one thing: when you pump the water up the hill you must have large tanks, let us say two tanks of 20 × 10 meters and at least 1 mt. deep, the first tank to receive the water, pumped directly from the sea, to give it a chance for depositing all solid matter in it. The second tank for the overflow from the first to contain the necessary amount of clear water for feeding your working tanks.

I don't know whether you could have a windmill on top of your mountain for pumping purposes. I suppose this would be the cheapest thing for this purpose, and as far as I remember there is more than enough wind and rain in Plymouth. Besides you want a gas engine for pumping the water from the second tank into the working tanks. Can you have no windmill then I think it wisest to have a gas-engine strong enough to work from the sea into the tanks and at other leisure doing other duties.

As to working tanks and showing tanks, of which you speak in your letter, all depends on the amount of money you can spend. When you are settled about this estimate of the house itself, brickwork, etc. let me know what will remain for such work as tanks, pipes and pumps, and I give you an adequate idea of what I think must be needful for you, always considering that you will at the highest have ten workers.

I have been a little frightened at the exposition in "Nature" when I saw that your whole staff would consist of two people, one with £150, one with £100 a year. Fancy that our "personnel" consists now of 37 people, and will because of the laboratory and the new ship most likely be augmented up to 50 persons or more. But I suppose that the reason of your statement is not to frighten people who might fall into fits when they hear of anything being contemplated like the Zoological station of Naples. But depend on it, when your place will be anything worth having you will have an annual outlay of at least £2-3,000.

    Goodbye for today. I am rather in a hurry, in spite of August heat.

    Anton Dohrn[18]

The problem of an adequate water supply must have continued to occupy Dohrn's mind, for a few days later he wrote again to Lankester:

Dear Lankester,

    As far as I remember the Citadel rock is vertical, and in this case I think one machine on top of the hill would be sufficient by means of transmissions, as well for circulating the water in the building, as for filling the reservoirs. Such an arrangement can be made vertically, but it would be rather difficult and expensive if the slope were gradually declining towards the sea. The best material for pipes and pumps would be iron and for the tubes conveying the water to the aquaria enameled iron.

    Without knowing the size of your reservoir and aquaria it is impossible to tell the size and expense of the machine. We use an engine of 4 hp which supplies the aquarium with abt. 15,000 liters per hour, feeding besides the little aquaria in the laboratories.

    As the filling of the reservoirs will only be necessary perhaps every 3 or 4 months, it would be extremely costly to have a special machine for this purpose on level of sea. Did you think of using a windmill for filling the tanks? In this case a very small gas-engine would be sufficient for circulating the water.

    Kindest regards to Hubrecht, yourself and Macintosh.

    Ever yours, Anton Dohrn[19]

Finally the decision to accept the Plymouth Rock site for a laboratory was confirmed, if not plain sailing to acquire it. Although it was offered by the Corporation of Plymouth, it was very soon discovered that the land did not belong to the city of

Plymouth but was the property of the War Office. Consequently, new negotiations had to be opened for leasing the land from the British Government.

The response to Lankester's appeal for funding, however, was rapid. By June 1885, when the society held its first annual meeting, £8,000 had been subscribed, and this sum grew to £15,000 a year later, which was sufficient for constructing the laboratory. Walter Heape himself contributed 15 guineas as a life member.[20] Lankester soon realized he needed assistance. Thus at a council meeting of the society on 13 May 1885 it was resolved:

> ... that the Chairman, Hon. Secretary and Treasurer be empowered to appoint an Assistant Secretary whose duty shall be to collect subscriptions for the Association, the said Assist. Sec. to receive a fixed salary not exceeding £50 and a percentage of 10% on all monies received through his individual exertions as shall be agreed on with him by the above named officers.[21]

It was at this time that Heape became involved with the affairs of the society, and at that meeting he was appointed assistant secretary. The unusual way in which he was to be compensated for his efforts based on the amount of money he raised did not fare well with some members of the society. At the next council meeting held on 12 June the resolution passed at the previous meeting was rescinded and replaced by a new one:

> ... that Mr. Heape be appointed assistant secretary at a salary of £100 a year, the arrangement to be terminable by 3 months' notice on either side.[22]

Heape set up some of the money he raised in a so-called Cambridge Fund as an investment account.[23]

During the summer of 1885, he travelled to the United States of America where he saw some of the activities of the US Fish and Fisheries, then led by Commissioner Spenser F. Baird.[24] He was particularly interested in the recently completed laboratory for the investigation and production of lake and saltwater fish at "Woods Holl" in Massachusetts.[25] He attended the opening, but it is not recorded whether he was officially representing the British Marine Biological Association or going privately.[26] He visited two other stations, one at Bucksport, Maine, which worked on the production of the eggs of the Penobscot salmon, and the other at Northville, Michigan, which was culturing the eggs of whitefish, trout and other freshwater species. Both stations at the time were exporting fish eggs to the National Fish Culture Association in England.

On 27 October the Marine Biological Association's council lobbied the British Treasury to support the building of its laboratory with an annual grant.[27] Surprisingly quickly, the Treasury awarded a grant of £5,000 on 14 December towards the construction of the building and an annual operating grant of £500 for five years. These awards combined with the Association's own funds were sufficient for construction of the Plymouth laboratory to go ahead.

During the 15 months since he first inspected the site, Lankester was probably overworked as both the Jodrell Professor of Zoology in London and editor of the *Quarterly Journal of Microscopical Science*. A letter written on 8 December to Huxley shows that he had begun to lean on his assistant secretary, Walter Heape, for more than fund raising:

I want at Monday's Council meeting to appoint Heape of Cambridge Resident Superintendent at a salary of £200 a year. He will at once take up his residence at Plymouth and look after the building as it progresses, and at the same time commence some general exploration of the Sound, and

44

prospecting in various directions. He will be able at once to collect fish statistics and familiarize himself with the fishermen, and get to know what there is accessible in the Sound and immediate neighbourhood. He is an invaluable assistant in this work and gives up his berth at Cambridge to take it. He has superintended all the details of the plan and contract so far.[28]

Lankester also wrote a letter to Sir William Thistleton-Dyer, Director of Kew Gardens, outlining the proposal with the suggestion that "He [Heape] can then visit Naples to learn some tips as to management …"[29]

Heape was appointed Resident Superintendent of the laboratory in a letter from Lankester on behalf of the Association:

Dear Mr. Heape,

I am directed by the Council of the Marine Biological Association to inform you that they have this day appointed you to be Resident Superintendent of the Plymouth Laboratory of the Association at a salary of £200 a year to which a residence will be added (on the completion of the building). The appointment is to take effect from Jan. 1st 1886 on the understanding that you resign the post of Assistant Secretary which you at present hold before that date. The appointment is to be terminable by six months' notice on either side. Six weeks' vacation is suggested by the Council, but this is understood to mean actual vacation and does not apply to absences from Plymouth undertaken on behalf of or on the business of the Association. The Council has made no stipulation as to the details of your duties; having been informed that you are thoroughly interested in the enterprise of the Association and will undoubtedly do your best for its success.

I may however state that it is expected that you will for the present continue to act as Assistant Secretary and will take up your residence at Plymouth with a view to superintending the erection of the building and the commencement of an enquiry into the Fauna of Plymouth Sound.

It is hoped that you will be able to enter into relations with fishermen and others so as to acquire some detailed knowledge of the Sound and its living products which will enable the Laboratory to be effectively worked as soon as it is completed.

E. Ray Lankester

P.S. The question was raised as to whether the Resident Superintendent should have a seat upon the Council of the Association, but it was decided that for the present such an arrangement was not desirable (though the question of making such an arrangement at a future date [was?] left unprejudiced). The Council understood that you will act in concert with and under the direction of [the?] Secretary of the Association. At a future date (when the building is complete) it [will?] be necessary to have a detailed agreement as to [the?] powers and duties of the Resident Superintendent.[30]

Walter Heape was now the first paid employee of the Marine Biological Association. The tone of the latter part of the letter of appointment makes clear that Heape's activities were to be strictly controlled by Lankester and that his ability to make independent decisions would not be allowed. He evidently regarded Heape as an assistant because in a memorandum to the council on 28 January 1886 he stated:

It [the Association] will also have the services of Mr. Heape, but this gentleman's time will be clearly occupied by details of administration.[31]

Lankester's desire to utilize Dohrn's experience of setting up the Stazione to the full was clear, for at the time Heape's appointment was approved a leave of absence was granted for him to spend April and May in Naples.[32] This visit was facilitated by appointing him to one of the Cambridge Tables, research spaces that external institutions rented for their members working in Naples.[33] The purpose of his visit was made clear in a letter Lankester wrote and Heape delivered by hand to Dohrn on his arrival:

This letter will be given to you by my friend Mr. Walter Heape M.A. of Cambridge who has been appointed Resident Superintendent of the Laboratory of the Marine Biological Association at Plymouth and is now about to occupy the Cambridge Table at Naples in order to learn as much as he can which will be of service to him in the discharge of his duties at Plymouth.

I would therefore ask you as a favour to the Council Association, which numbers many of your personal friends in its ranks, to give Mr. Heape special opportunities for seeing the management of your aquarium, or the laboratory and of dredging and other collecting work. Also if you would let him be instructed in some of the arts of preserving specimens which you have carried to such perfection at Naples—it would be a great benefit to us which would be duly appreciated by the Council ...

Ever yours sincerely, E. Ray Lankester[34]

Heape got along very well with Dohrn and their friendship lasted for many years.

While he was in Naples, the Council requested Lankester at their meeting on 19 March to prepare a memorandum for the objectives of the Plymouth laboratory. It turned out to be a lengthy document with a summary of objectives:

(a) A biological and physical survey of Plymouth Sound, embracing a complete knowledge of its Fauna and Flora and of the exact conditions under which the various species therein included exist. This will necessarily occupy some years, and may be gradually extended beyond the limits of Plymouth Sound.

(b) The study of the food, habits, and reproduction of specially selected food fishes and commercial shell fish. This should not be delayed but undertaken simultaneously with the general survey, since it is in this direction that public interest is keenest, whilst, moreover, the Council definitely pledged to the Government to aim at results in this direction.

(c) The investigation of anatomical, embryological, and physiological problems for which the Fauna of Plymouth Sound offers opportunity. The Association should aim at promoting the studies of volunteer observers from the Universities and elsewhere in this direction. It would not be desirable that the Association should spend any portion of its general funds directly upon this class of investigations, but it should aim at giving every facility to men of science who desire to engage in such work on their own account.[35]

Lankester also noted that: "The results obtained under these three heads will form the subject matter of the reports which the Council of the Association is pledged to issue."

Heape did not resign his existing post immediately and only transferred the money in the Cambridge Fund to the Marine Biological Association in December 1886.[36] Nor did he move to Plymouth before going to Naples, and the resulting delay became a concern for Lankester and the Council because of the conditions of the grant from the Treasury, which included the preparation of reports on the fishing industry at Plymouth and the fauna and flora of Plymouth Sound. Soon after his return to England on 7 June the Council requested him to take up his quarters in Plymouth immediately and, in addition to supervising construction of the building, to start preparing the reports.[37] Heape's move remained tardy for a letter to Alfred Newton shows that Heape was still resident at 17 Fitzwilliam Street in Cambridge on 18 July,[38] but by 9 October, 1886, he was occupying 5 Holyrood Place in Plymouth.[39] One of the first things he became engaged in was how to breed sole in ponds, but the naturalist J. T. Cunningham was appointed to take over this project the next year.

Heape had to focus his mind on the key question of securing clean seawater for the aquaria. He compared the pros and cons of ten different methods of pumping water from the sea into the main reservoirs and the kind of pipes needed, garnering advice from seven foreign aquaria and his own experiments. He sought Dohrn's advice about the choice of pipes.

My dear Dr. Dohrn,

    Will you be kind enough to give me your opinion upon the following matters?

(1) It is probable, is it not, that under these circumstances it will not be necessary to change the water oftener than once in three months at any rate?

(2) Do you consider that if iron pipes be used to convey the sea water from the sea to the reservoirs, that the water will be damaged in transit? I don't mean of course the first time of using but after the first time.

(3) If you do not advise the use of iron pipes will you suggest what should be used?

    You were kind enough to say you would help us so I do not ask you to forgive me for troubling you.

    Yours sincerely, Walter Heape[40]

Anton Dohrn replied:

Dear Mr. Heape,

    It is with great pleasure that I answer the questions you made by your letter of 20th inst.

    It is probable that the water in the reservoir will keep quite well, if changed once in three months, provided however that the water is quite clean and without organic matter. You will most likely cover the reservoir by vaults? Our reservoirs are covered and dark.

    You will best use enameled Iron or Cast Iron Tubes. The Tubes (not enameled) would only occasionally be filled with water and therefore be damaged by rust in an extraordinary manner. Before pumping into the reservoir it would be necessary to "ward" them. We have enameled tubes connecting the aquarium with the sea, and I recommend that you also make use of them.

    How far have your works proceeded? I shall be very glad if you will drop me a line on this subject, when you have some minutes to spare, for I understand you must be very busy ...

Have you got any information about Pennington in Bolton and Ward in Manchester? As you kindly promised to help us, we shall be very glad for your news.

With kind regards, Anton Dohrn[41]

On 2 December 1886, Heape replied:

Dear Dr. Dohrn,

I am much obliged for your note and the information contained. In reply to your queries,

(1) We have done something towards one building, the excavation is complete and materials are ready for building—I am led to hope that the roof will be on by the end of April.

(2) The people that I promised to enquire about for you, Pennington and Ward, are still in ignorance of my mission.

I have only been in Manchester about 2 days since I returned from Naples and had no time to see them. You will remember it was considered better that I should see them myself rather than put the matter in the hands of anyone else. I have not forgotten your commission and hope I can send you word of these men after Xmas. I shall be in Manchester during Xmas.

With kind regards, yours sincerely, Walter Heape[42]

Lankester reported to the Council on 27 May 1887:

… a Government Grant Committee of the Royal Society voted £250 to a Committee consisting of Professor Huxley, Moseley, Lankester and Mr. Sedgwick for the investigation of the Fauna and Flora of the Plymouth Sound in connection with the Laboratory of the M.B.A. (Marine Biological Association).[43]

The first report written by Heape, "Notes on the Fishing Industry of Plymouth," was a detailed description of the fishing industry including several statistical tables. The report was comprehensive as seen by the list of contents:

I. Methods of fishing, localities fished, and fish caught. There are 11 methods of fishing carried on at Plymouth: 1. Beam trawling. 2. Drift-net fishing. 3. Moored net fishing. 4. Seine fishing. 5. Bultering or long-line fishing.[44] 6. Hand-line fishing. 7. Eel spearing. 8. Mullet trapping. 9. Crab and lobster fishing. 10. Prawn and shrimp fishing. 11. Oyster, mussel and cockle fishing.

II. Industries connected with the fishing trade carried on in Plymouth: 1. Boat building. 2. Sail making. 3. Rope making. 4. Fish-line making. 5. Net breeding. 6. Fish curing. 7. Fish skin curing. 8. Fish oil manufacture. 9. Ice manufacture.

III. Methods of ownership, wage, apprenticeship, insurance, and sale of fish: 1. Payment of trawlers. 2. Payment of drifters. 3. Payment of hookers. 4. Systems of payment compared. 5. Insurance of trawlers. 6. Insurance of drifters and hookers. 7. Methods of buying and selling fish.[45]

To compile this report Heape consulted several books and pamphlets available at the time including several publications associated with the International Fisheries Exhibition of 1883. He also acknowledged the help of a variety of people: fishermen, a fish salesman, the Superintendent of the Mercantile Marine Office, the Sutton Harbour master and a ship builder. The style of this report was written through the eye of a businessman. An example is the following analysis of the cost of bait for long-line fishing or "bultering", which is used to catch conger, ling, ray, skate, cod and pollack.

Bait. The bait used by bulterers is chiefly squid (*Loligo*); but they also used pilchard, mackerel, herring, garfish (*Belone vulgaris*), whiting (*Gadus merlangus*), gurnard (*Trigla*), chad (the young of *Pagellus centrodontus*), bream (*Cantharus lineatus*), and dogfish (*Scyllium canicula*); according to the season and in case of scarcity of squid. During the spring—about Lent—when many trawlers are fishing in Mount's Bay, and there is but a small supply of squid and great competition for what there is to be sold, the bulterers fall back on "fish baits", and pilchard is perhaps the best of these. At this time of year the long-line fishermen even go as far as Falmouth, Mevagissey, Looe, and other ports along the coast to buy bait.

Price of bait. The price of bait varies very widely. Squid, when plentiful, may be as low as 6d a maund.[46] Pilchard, in the same way varies from zero to 5s per 100.

Amount of bait used. Some idea of the amount of bait which might be used may be gathered from the fact that it takes 1,000 pilchards or six maunds of squid to bait a long bulter. A maund of squid will weigh say 56 lbs. Say sixty boats average 2,000 fathoms of line, i.e. 1,333 hooks per boat. They will consume 288 maunds of squid or say 144 cwt (over seven tons) in baiting their lines.

Value of bait used. This amount represents in value at 6d a maund £7 4s 0d. It represents in value at 12s a maund £172 16d 0d. Or, they will use 48,000 pilchards, which represents in money: £12 0s at 6d, or £120 0s at 5s. In the case of a single boat, when squid are cheap it costs 3s. To bait a long bulter with 1,666 hooks, when dear £3 12s, whereas pilchards cost from 5s when cheap to 50s in the dearest times, to bait a long bulter.

An average is not easy to calculate, but from the accounts of two hookers which have been very kindly submitted to me, it appears that about £100 a year per boat is spent on bait; that is to say, for sixty boats of the same size for the year would cost £6,000. Making allowance for boats laid up at various times, the smaller size of some boats, and the fact that certain of them do not use their lines all the year round, the sum spent on bait for the year by Plymouth boats may be estimated at not less than £4,500. The bait question is therefore a serious one.[47]

At a council meeting held 27 May, 1887, it was resolved that, subject to recommendations made to the chairman and secretary, Heape's report should be printed for all members of the Association, with an explanatory statement. The report was published as the opening article in the first issue of the Journal of the Marine Biological Association with the following explanation:

> Mr. Heape's notes are intended to furnish information which will be useful as a preliminary to the investigations to be carried out in the Plymouth laboratory when it is completed. They are necessarily not the result of original observation, but are compiled from various sources. They have not been published in any shape before the present date, August 8th, 1887. E.R.L.[48]

The report immediately came under criticism for infringing the activities of the National Fish Culture Association,[49] which was expressed by the ichthyologist Francis Day in no uncertain terms in the Association's journal. He also pointed out errors and that Heape's knowledge of fish biology was deficient, which was a major disqualification in a superintendent.

Heape published asecond report soon afterwards in August, entitled "Description of the Laboratory of the Marine Biological Association of Plymouth."[50] It was a detailed description of physical features and floor plans of the new laboratory.

In 1886 Heape also started to find ways of breeding sole in ponds and continued this work until August 1887 when a naturalist, J.T. Cunningham, was appointed who took over the project.[51]

Serious conflicts began to surface between Heape and Lankester culminating in Heape giving him six months' advance notice of his resignation as Superintendent in September 1887. Heape also wrote to Huxley, presumably to defend himself against charges that Lankester had made against him. That letter, which is lost, prompted Huxley to contact Sir Michael Foster who was then a council member.

September 30, 1887

My dear Foster,

I found Heape's letter among a heap of others (I wrote 17 answers the next morning and have not done yet) when we returned last Friday evening.

Ex parte, it looks a tolerably complete answer to Lankester's charges—I have expressed no opinion on that point in my reply to Heape, but assured him that it should be fully and fairly considered by the Council. What is at the bottom of it all?

Heape's appointment was warmly urged by Lankester and backed by all Cambridge representation that hitherto veered and tacked pretty much as L. has bidden them. You know that my faith in our Hon. Secretary is a negative quantity—and I shrewdly suspect some dirt at the bottom of this present action. If I can help it the Council shall not be made his catspaw for doing any injustice to poor Heape. On the other hand, unless Heape is a much stronger and better man than I take him to be it would be the ruin of the Association to keep him on.

L. is an executive officer and he could throw the whole blame of any complication that might arise on the Council if we kept on a subordinate against whom he had reported. The position is abominably difficult and I hope you will think seriously over what is to be done on the 7th.

When are you coming up? Could we have a talk any time before the meeting?

Ever yours, T.H. Huxley[52]

Huxley's response to Lankester's unknown charges is not surprising because he had strong reservations about the man's interpersonal behavior. They came to the forefront in another letter he wrote earlier to Foster refusing to nominate Lankester for membership of the prestigious Athenaeum Club in London. Huxley wrote:

The Athenaeum is a body the members of which rather pride themselves on being bound by the tradition of gentlemen and the proposing a new member rending himself bail for the latter on that particular. Now I have done good deal for Lankester as a man of science in my time, and I am prepared to do more—but I cannot reconcile it with my conscience to say that he has the remotest conception of what the word "gentleman" means—or that you are ever safe from his turning around upon you with the manners and the actions of a thorough cad.[53]

Although Lankester sensed Huxley's coolness towards him he could not understand why, and expressed his unhappiness to Anton Dohrn. Dohrn replied at length:

12 December, 1886

My dear Lankester,

Your letter has given me a good deal of thought of an unpleasant character. I see from it that you are suffering under a nervous depression; a state of mind has taken hold of you, which is not healthy. I have been suffering too often by the same, not to understand that it is useless to try and persuade you of its passing character. But as long as it lasts, all your ideas are tinged with black and you cannot form a right view of anything.

I do not know what the wrong may be that Huxley has operated on you; but I am sure it has not the character which you impose to him. He has grown old and old people are likely to be obstinate. That Edinburgh business has done you wrong, and has placed him in an awkward situation: perhaps it has irritated him in a way to supersede other considerations.

Tell me, if I could be of any use in cementing the breach between you. You know, I continue on excellent terms with him, and our good relations are not only scientific but really personal, only the other day I had a charming and friendly letter from him. I would be good to do anything in that direction. As to you taking the Plymouth business in your hands ... you have promoted the thing. You cannot possibly aspire at its directorship before you are appealed to, otherwise all sort of misinterpretations would come to the front. Have you reflected on that?[54]

Heape's resignation was accepted for political reasons by the council despite Huxley's concerns about foul-play. Lankester wanted Heape to leave Plymouth immediately which Heape refused to do, staying until the full six months' notice had expired. Lankester's anger over Heape's refusal was conveyed to Huxley by letter of 10 January 1888:

> *I am very sorry that you will not be able to come to the meeting on Wednesday of the MBA Council. I will read your letter to the Council and a day will be arranged to suit your convenience. I gather that you think it is not desirable to postpone Heape's communication until the next monthly meeting and I myself shall be glad to hear what form it takes and to be rid of it. Heape wrote me that he had sent a statement to you. The position is a vexatious one for me, because I had had the most friendly relations with Heape, until step by step arrived at the definite and final conclusion that it would be an injury to the prospects of success of the Association and a fraud upon its supporters to keep him in the position of Resident Superintendent. I was obliged to take steps to throw him overboard. I thought the matter was settled, my only further trouble in the matter being that Heape was so little sensitive to hints and even direct suggestions that he continues to stay his full six months at Plymouth after he has resigned, and after I have told him that it would be convenient to the administration if he would terminate his official duties at once. It is of course not possible that Heape should be of much use to the Association now that he is about to leave his post, and I have not the least idea what he is doing all this time at Plymouth.*[55]

Conflict seemed to be inevitable because of Lankester's views on Heape's role, and there seems little doubt that he wanted total control over all decisions about the laboratory, perhaps expecting one day he would be its director. Heape was not allowed to attend council meetings so that his opinions only reached the members after being filtered by Lankester. His irritation is revealed in a written remark to Dohrn: "I have resigned my post here as you advised me. Committees are the devil to deal with ..."[56] As a man of independent means and strong personality Heape was not slow to express his opinions or leadership. He also had another take on personal sphere of influence as secretary of Section D (zoology) of the British

Association for the Advancement of Science from 1882 to 1887. The stress that Lankester was suffering at the time made matters worse for Heape with a man who was well-known for his intemperate speech.

Some of Heape's fertile ideas for projects at the marine laboratory appear in the first report:

(a) That a diagram should be prepared showing the relation of the weather to the products of the Plymouth fishery, and the financial relations of capital, expenditure, and profit in certain instances.

(b) That an experiment of putting live soles into a pond of salt water, which had been placed at the disposal of the Association for that purpose by Mr. Thomas Bulteel, of Radford, should proceed.[57]

(c) That endeavours should be made to induce fishermen of this port and the neighbourhood, both trawlers, hookers, and drift fishermen, to assist the work of the Association, by recording daily details of the ground fished and the fish caught. The outline of a plan for this work was suggested, and it was urged that the information so gained should be published regularly in the Journal of the Association, and the opinion expressed that these results, when considered in relation to weather reports of the district, would be likely to throw much light upon the movements of fish, especially of non-migratory fish.

(d) That a similar experiment should be carried out in Plymouth Sound, in order to compare the results obtained within the Sound, it being suggested that some idea might be gained of the influence of sewage and of traffic, etc., upon the movements of both migratory and non-migratory fish.

(e) That certain persons in Plymouth and the neighbourhood, having recognized qualifications, should be requested, and in certain instances employed, to write accounts of what they know about fishes and the fishery of the district.

(f) That investigations of the Fauna and Flora of the Sound, and of the Fishing Industry of the District, should be continued.

(g) That investigations should be made upon and preserving and curing squid for bait.

(h) That the Admiralty should be approached with a view to the lending of dredging and other instruments used in the "Challenger" expedition.[58]

There may have been problems with the delayed reports for the Royal Society, and particularly for the report on the fauna and flora of Plymouth Sound. It was required by the terms of the Royal Society grant for constructing the laboratory, yet Heape had not produced it by 27 May, 1887, when Lankester reported to the Council that another grant had been awarded by the Royal Society:

> ... a government grant committee of the Royal Society had voted £250 to a committee consisting of Professors Huxley, Moseley, Lankester and Mr. Sedgwick for the investigation of the Fauna and Flora of the Plymouth Sound in connection with the Laboratory of the M.B.A.[59]

Heape finally produced a "Preliminary Report upon the Fauna and Flora of Plymouth Sound," but it was not published until August 1888, about five months after he had relinquished his post at the laboratory. He acknowledged that it was only a catalogue, assembling observations that had already been made by other naturalists for what is the largest estuarine system in southwest England. Boswarva had published an extensive list of marine algae in the Plymouth area which was reproduced in Heape's report.[60] Other local naturalists included Edward Parfitt,[61] whose extensive publications on the natural history of Devon were quoted, and C. Spence Bate, F.R.S. on the Crustacea. Spence Bate was a distinguished naturalist who published the volume on shrimps from the Challenger Expedition. Help was also obtained from fishermen on the less common species of fish in Plymouth Sound. The report was, however, a useful guide for more detailed studies in the future of the organisms, and particularly fishes, inhabiting the Sound.[62]

In his final report Heape volunteered suggestions about the role of the future director of the laboratory:

(i) The Superintendent should organize and direct the working of the Laboratory.

(ii) He should be responsible to the Council for the management of the Association in Plymouth.

(iii) That he should organize and superintend the collection of specimens for the museum for the students working in the laboratory and for correspondents.

(iv) That he should officiate as librarian.

(v) That he should manage monetary matters at Plymouth.

(vi) That he should control the servants of the Association in Plymouth.

It was then urged that the duties of the superintendent should include daily recording, tabulating and arranging and recording specimens, and he should be recognized by the council as a trusted officer to use his time and to direct his work as seemed fit to him.[63]

The council voted on 27 June, 1888, to replace the position of Resident Superintendent with a director who would also serve as the secretary of the Marine Biological Association and attend its meetings. The position was filled by Gilbert C. Bourne,[64] and Lankester retained his position as honorary secretary.

The reference to Pennington and Bolton in two letters shows that Heape developed a cordial relationship with Dohrn in Naples, and this lasted for many years. Dohrn was owed money by two British businessmen who had agreed to sell microscope slide specimens prepared at the Stazione Zoologica. Heape agreed to try to recover the money and eventually approached the debtors personally. One of them, Arthur Pennington, turned out to be an absconding debtor in receivership and represented by his solicitor. None of those funds were recovered. The other, E. Ward, was prosperous but refused to pay money to Heape unless he had written authorization to collect it. Eventually some money was recovered as well as unsold slides.[65] Heape's departure from Plymouth did not harm his friendship with Dohrn, and both he and his wife exchanged letters with him for the rest of Anton's life. The Dohrns also stayed at the Heapes' home at Chaucer Road, Cambridge, at least once during their visit to England. Their genuine friendship is apparent in a letter written by Heape's wife, Ethel, to Anton just after Christmas 1898:

My dear Professor Dohrn,

Your delightful Christmas present to me stands before me as I write and reminds me very vividly of that beautiful Naples. It is a real pleasure to be remembered like this, and we both wish very much that we could be there to thank you ourselves for thinking of us so kindly. We often talk over the week we all had together and wonder when we shall have another time as nice. We must manage it one day.

I do hope that Madame Dohrn is in better health and able to enjoy Christmas with you all, and that you too are well.

We are very envious just now of some neighbours of ours, Mr. & Mrs. Assherton, who talk of going to Naples in February. Mr. Assherton wishes if possible to work in the zoological station. He dined here one night whilst you were with us but perhaps you may not remember.

My husband is very well and has been shooting a good deal the last two months which he most thoroughly enjoys. Just now of course we are all at home for Christmas and there is great excitement over the Christmas tree. The last few days have been splendidly bright and frosty, but up till then we have had very mild warm unhealthy weather which has done nobody any good.

My husband hopes you received the photograph of the group in the Botanical Gardens which he sent some time ago.

He joins me in very kindest remembrances and in wishing you and Madame Dohrn a very happy Christmas and New Year.

Believe me always very sincerely yours, Ethel Heape[66]

A few years later, as we shall see, Heape and Dohrn exchanged letters over treating the King of Italy's problems in having a son.

Viewed from the perspective of Walter Heape's entire scientific publications, the reports he wrote on the fishing industry, the Plymouth Laboratory and the fauna and flora of Plymouth Sound represent only minor achievements, and he turned away from both marine biology and the politics of institutions. Nevertheless these contributions were not insignificant and demonstrated his ability to make the most of an assignment that required him to launch a new bricks-and-mortar enterprise and execute responsibilities in the midst of conflicting personalities. The laboratory was officially opened at the end of June 1888, but Heape was not on the list of guests, nor was he publicly thanked for his efforts. He had returned to his father's estate in Prestwich to begin a new chapter in life.

4

EMBRYO TRANSFER[1]

AFTER LEAVING his position at the Plymouth laboratory in 1888, Heape returned to the Manchester area to continue private research in his laboratory on his father's estate.[2] Shortly afterwards he began an extensive tour of the East that lasted into 1889 where he visited Egypt, Ceylon, India, Burma and the Straits Settlements (the former British Colonies of Penang, Malacca and Singapore). While visiting Calcutta he became interested in reproduction and development in monkeys, which altered the direction of his career.

When he returned to England, Heape started a research program on rabbits that would have profound implications for reproductive science. He transferred cleaving rabbit embryos from the Fallopian tubes (oviducts) of one animal to the tubes of a surrogate, which he called a uterine foster-mother, and they developed to full-term babies. The experiment was reported in detail:

> On 27 April, 1890, two ova were obtained from an Angora doe rabbit which had been fertilized by an Angora buck thirty-two hours previously; the ova were undergoing segmentation, being divided into four segments.[3]
>
> These ova were immediately transferred to the upper end of the fallopian tube of a Belgian Hare doe rabbit which had been

fertilized three hours before by a buck of the same breed as herself.

It may be well to mention here, I bought this Belgian Hare doe some three months before; the man from whom I bought her bred her, and guaranteed her to be a virgin doe of about seven months old. During the time I had her, until 27th April, she had never been covered by a buck of any breed, being kept *always* isolated from the various bucks in my rabbitry.

In due course this Belgian Hare doe gave birth to six young—four of these resembled herself and her mate, while two of them were undoubted Angoras. The Angora young were characterized by the possession of the long silky hair peculiar to the breed, and were true albinos, like their Angora parents.[4]

Heape noted the behavior of the presumed Angora young as well as their physical appearance to prove the success of the experiment. He emphasized that swaying of the head, a characteristic of all Angora rabbits, was observed in both the parents of the transferred embryos and the presumed Angora offspring. He also noted that there was no sign of Belgian Hare rabbit traits in the presumed Angora young, and that Belgian Hare young showed no likeness to their two foster-brothers (both offspring were males). In this interpretation Heape depended on a genetic argument, whereas today we would use genetic markers. His short paper was presented to the Royal Society of London on November 12, 1890. He repeated the experiment three times in the years 1893, 1896 and 1897,[5] the intervals being due to the award of a Balfour Studentship and a grant from the Royal Society which enabled him to study reproduction in monkeys. The embryo transfers in 1893 and 1896 failed to produce young, and only after a successful transfer in 1897 did Heape feel fully confident in his findings of 1890.

The technique used to recover embryos from the Fallopian tubes was based on protocols in a laboratory course given to Cambridge students by Foster and Balfour in 1883 (see Chapter 2), which Heape adapted for transferring embryos between mothers.

> The Belgian Hare doe is put under anaesthetics and stretched out on her stomach. A longitudinal incision, 2 in. long, is then made through the skin at a place 1.5 to 3.5 in. from the anterior lumbar muscles. A smaller incision is then made through the body-wall just ventral to the lumbar muscles, and the anterior end of the fallopian tube is readily found and pulled out through the opening with the help of a pair of forceps. The foreign ova are then taken out of their maternal fallopian tube on the point of a spear-headed needle, the foster mother's infundibulum is held open with a pair of forceps and the ova placed well within the anterior end of her fallopian tube; after pushing the latter gently back again and washing with some antiseptic solution, the wound is sewn up and dressed with colloidin and cotton-wool.[6]

The success of this technique was due in part to the fact that the embryos were transferred directly from one mother to another without being placed in a foreign environment. In fact the first physiological saline for supporting mammalian cells was not introduced until 1901.[7] In his 1890 paper Heape posited three questions:

> (i) Is it possible to make use of the uterus of one variety of rabbit as a medium for the growth and complete foetal development of fertilized ova of another variety of rabbit?
> (ii) What effect, if any, does a uterine foster-mother have upon her foster-children?

(iii) Does the presence and development of foreign ova in the uterus of a mother affect the offspring of that mother born at the same time?[8]

His results provided answers to each of these questions — yes, none and none, respectively. He concluded:

> The experiment seemed to me to show, as far as a single experiment could show, that a uterine foster-mother has no power of modifying the breed of her foster-children, and that her uterus during gestation and the nourishment she supplies to the embryo is analogous to a bed of soil with its various nutrient constituents.[9]

Although Heape gave no specific reasons for asking these questions, he was certainly aware of contemporary debates about the mechanisms of inheritance. In a lecture given to the Plymouth Institution in 1887[10] he had stated that "natural selection has been the main but not the exclusive means of modification."[11]

The most influential theories about inheritance at the time of his first experiments were Darwin's theory of natural selection (1859) and Lamarck's theory of inheriting acquired characteristics (from 1801).[12] Lamarck's theory was accepted by many naturalists after receiving a great deal of opposition, and even Charles Darwin, Herbert Spencer, and Louis Agassiz never ruled it out. In 1885, the eminent German zoologist August Weismann of the University of Freiburg in Germany had a major influence on the field by promulgating a theory called the "Continuity of the Germ Plasm." He denied the Lamarckian theory that external influences on the body are inherited by the next generation, and stirred an already vigorous and sometimes vitriolic debate among leading biologists.

Heape recognized the relevance of his experiments, although he didn't mention the controversy in any of his publications. In a letter submitting his candidacy for the Balfour Studentship in 1890 he briefly described his first transfer experiment before it was published, and added a telling comment:

> The success of this experiment, the first of its kind I believe, inclines me to believe that a new field of enquiry is thus opened to the student of problems connected with heredity.[13]

Heape was preceded in embryo transfer experiments by George Romanes, a Canadian scientist and son of a Presbyterian missionary who had graduated in physiology from Cambridge and was a friend of Charles Darwin. He hoped to prove whether Lamarckian inheritance can occur by transferring rabbit embryos between Himalayan and Belgian hare breeds, but unfortunately no offspring developed. His efforts didn't quite suffer the fate of so many negative results because they were eventually published, but much later in 1895 and posthumously.[14] Romanes heard about Heape's paper and correctly noted that the other researcher had made no claim that he was testing a theory of inheritance. Shortly before his untimely death in 1894, Romanes concluded that the rabbit was an unsuitable species for this purpose: "inasmuch as rabbits, even when crossed in the ordinary way, never throw intermediate characters."[15] Consequently he dismissed Heape's work as well as his own as irrelevant to the study of heritability. But Heape defended his experiments and rejected Romanes' assertion.[16]

In his second paper on embryo transfer, Heape referred to the mechanism of telegony, a now unfamiliar word introduced by August Weissman in 1893 for a belief that Darwin called "the direct action of the male element on the female form."[17]

Weissman signaled his skepticism in a chapter discussing telegony, entitled "Doubtful phenomena of heredity." It was first described in 1821 in a letter published in the *Proceedings of the Royal Society of London* in which the Earl of Morton described his attempts to domesticate the quagga, a zebra-like animal from South Africa, which became extinct in 1883.[18] He wrote:

> Some years ago, I was desirous of trying the experiment of domesticating the quagga, and endeavoured to procure some individuals of that species. I obtained a male; but being disappointed of a female, I tried to breed from the male quagga and a young chestnut mare of seven-eighths Arabian blood and which had never been bred from: the result was the production of a female hybrid, now five years old, and bearing, both in her form and in her colour, very decided indications of her mixed origin. I subsequently parted with the seven-eighths Arabian mare to Sir Gore Ouseley, who has bred from her by a very fine Arabian horse. I yesterday morning examined the produce, namely a two-year's old filly, and a year-old colt. They have the character of the Arabian breed as decidedly as can be expected, when fifteen-sixteenths of the blood are Arabian; and they are fine specimens of that breed; but both in their colour, and in the hair of their manes, they have a striking resemblance to the quagga.
>
> Their colour is bay, marked more or less like the quagga in a darker tint. Both are distinguished by the dark line along the ridge of the back, the dark stripes across the fore-hand, and the dark bars across the back of the legs.[19]

A belief in telegony became widespread following the description of similar cases in dogs, sheep, goats, cattle and swine.[20] It was also believed to occur in human beings and even included in a textbook of human physiology:

The same influence is observed in the human subject. A woman may have, by a second husband, children who resemble a former husband, and this is particularly well marked in certain instances by the color of the hair and eyes. A white woman who has children by a negro may subsequently bear children to a white man, these children presenting some of the unmistakable peculiarities of the negro race.[21]

In 1893 Weissman argued against the existence of telegony as follows:

Such cases could only be accounted for from our point of view by supposing that spermatozoa had reached the ovary after the first sexual union had occurred, and had penetrated into certain ova which were still immature. The immediate fertilization of the latter is rendered inconceivable by the fact of their immaturity, and the sperm-cell must have remained in the body of the ovum until the maturation of the latter, with the nucleus of which it then united in the process of amphimixis.[22] If this occurred sometime after the first of the offspring were born, it might easily have coincided approximately with the second coitus, from which fertilization would then be apparently due. If the "infection" were proved beyond a doubt, a supplementary of an egg-cell in this manner must be considered possible; we certainly might then reasonably ask why mares, cows, or sheep, should not occasionally become pregnant without being covered a second time. But this has never yet been known to occur, and I incline to Settegast's view that there is no such thing as an "infection" of this kind, and that all the instances which have been recorded and discussed critically by him are based upon a misconception.[23]

Heape was not completely convinced by this argument because four years later in 1897 he wrote:

It follows ... that in case telegony is actually demonstrated, the characteristics of a primary husband which are transmitted to the offspring got by a secondary husband can only be so transmitted through the ovarian ova of the mother.[24]

The existence, or otherwise, of telegony led J. Cossar Ewart, Professor of Natural History at the University of Edinburgh, in 1899 to begin an ambitious series of breeding experiments on inheritance in the horse family. These experiments, which came to be known as the Penycuik Experiments[25] (after Penicuik [*sic*] in MidLothian), attracted considerable attention, including an editorial in *Nature*:

The well-devised breeding experiments now in progress at Penycuik under the direction of Prof. J. Cossar Ewart are, it need scarcely be said, of the highest interest both theoretical and practical. To the general biologist the subject of hybridization is a wide field for the investigation of the laws of heredity, and especially of such subsidiary factors, whether real or only imaginary, as reversion, prepotency, saturation and telegony; while the question of the sterility of hybrids has important bearings on the general theory of evolution. But besides the purely scientific aspects of the problems which are now being attracted by Prof. Ewart, there is also their practical application, which appeals with much more force to the breeder of stock.

It is of course true that the whole history of animals and plants under domestication may be said to provide a body of experiments in these and similar subjects on a very large scale; and it is undoubtedly the case that many of the questions referred to have been already answered, at least provisionally. The experience of many generations of breeders has led to the emergence of certain practical rules which are seldom if ever disregarded by those whose interests are concerned in the rearing of animals with a definite object. But it still remains doubtful how far the widely accepted doctrines of fanciers and other breeders rest upon any firm scientific basis; and it is certainly most desirable that precise experiments should be undertaken with the sole object of arriving at the truth in such matters as prepotency, telegony and the effects of inbreeding. It cannot but be to the advantage of breeders if empiric methods founded on vague conjecture and imperfect generalization can be made to give place to a rational system derived from exact knowledge of facts.[26]

When the results were published in 1902 they produced no evidence for the existence of telegony. It is likely that Heape would have known of these experiments since he and Ewart were members of the Evolution Committee of the Royal Society. Nevertheless, as we shall see in Chapter 11, Heape was convinced that environmental influences can affect the development of ova in the ovary, even influencing the sex ratio. Thus it may not be surprising that he reserved judgment on whether telegony was real. Heape's instinct may have been wiser than we thought, because recent research has provided some molecular and cellular routes that might mediate telegony.[27]

Heape's first embryo transfer experiment is often believed to have been performed in Cambridge since the title page of his paper lists him as a Balfour Student and it was introduced to the Royal Society by Michael Foster of Cambridge. There is a serious possibility, however, that it was done at his home laboratory in Prestwich where he resided from 1888 to 1890.[28] The first transfers were done in April of 1890 and assisted by Dr. Samuel Buckley, a Manchester physician and surgeon.[29] The Balfour Studentship was not awarded until approximately six months later in November, the very month the paper was presented to the Royal Society. If the Manchester area is the correct location, then the production of the first human IVF or test-tube baby about 90 years later by the Cambridge scientist Robert Edwards and Manchester surgeon Patrick Steptoe is an interesting coincidence.

Prior to his experiment in 1890 the transfer of embryos from one mother to another was envisioned only in a myth of the Jain religion in which the new spiritual leader Mahavira was conceived in a woman from an unacceptable caste.[30] The gods ordered the embryo to be exchanged with one from a woman of a desirable caste. Heape's result promoted the old myth to reality.

It may seem surprising that he did not immediately grasp the potential practical value of transferring mammalian embryos. It was an important, even outstanding achievement, not fully recognized at the time, because it provided the chance to experiment with live embryos outside the uterus and opened a new field of mammalian developmental biology. In combination with embryo culture and in vitro fertilization it has led to novel biotechnologies, including genetic engineering in animals,[31] and to the birth of the medical discipline of assisted reproductive technology for treating infertility and preimplantation genetic diagnosis for detecting heritable diseases.[32]

5

MENSTRUAL CYCLE

AFTER HIS RETURN home from India at the end of 1889 Heape had turned his full attention to the study of reproductive cycles. He formulated a plan for research on reproduction and development in monkeys with particular focus on the phenomena of menstruation and ovulation and began to search for funds to support this work.

The external signs of menstruation in monkeys were already well-known to biologists by the end of the 19th century. In 1886, John Bland Sutton at the Middlesex Hospital in London wrote a vivid description of simian menstruation:

> In macaques, menstruation is accompanied by certain unmistakable objective phenomena other than the escape of blood from the uterus, for all the naked or pale-coloured parts of the body, such as the face, neck, ischial regions, etc. become of a lively pink colour; in some cases it is vivid red. The amount of sanguineous fluid discharged from the uterus is very small in amount and soon ceases, but the coincident colouration of the pale parts continues for several days. In warm weather during menstruation the labia, and soft parts in the immediate vicinity, become swollen, as though they were composed of erectile tissue. The baboons present similar objective signs to the macaques, but in an exaggerated degree, so that a menstruating baboon is anything but a comely individual; indeed at times its appearance is so disgusting

that in the Zoological Gardens it is necessary to remove the animal from the cages to rooms not accessible to ordinary visitors.[1]

The physiological changes in the female genital tract that cause the external signs were only poorly understood. Sutton believed that the rhesus monkey and the baboon would be useful animal models for the study of menstruation in the human female.

To support his research, Heape first sought help from the Balfour Memorial Fund, which was established at the University of Cambridge in memory of Francis Balfour with the following objectives:

(i) To endow a Studentship to be called the Balfour Studentship the holder of which shall devote himself to original research in Biology, especially Animal Morphology.
(ii) To further by occasional grants of money original research in the same subject.[2]

In those days the meaning of "animal morphology" was restricted to the comparative study of homologous organs. Heape outlined his plans and motivation for the work in a letter from home to Alfred Newton, Professor of Comparative Anatomy in Cambridge and a manager of the Fund.

6 December, 1889

My dear Professor Newton,

I am very anxious to carry on some work upon monkeys; to investigate the phenomenon of menstruation and ovulation and the early stages of development. I have made arrangements with the Superintendent of the Zoological Gardens at Calcutta to send me (when I apply for them) 50 or 100 adult Macacus rhesus, and if I can get enough money I propose to get these animals over, build a house for their accommodation, and carry on a thorough investigation. The only difficulty is the money—I am quite unable to bear the expense myself and I calculate it will cost me £200. I propose to apply to the Royal Society when the time comes, but I cannot hope they will do more than assist. I hope I may have your support there. Bartlett of the Zoo tells me he is sure that adult M. rhesus if brought into this country in the spring will live comfortably and he sees no reason why they should not breed, but at any rate the menstrual and ovulation phenomena can be worked.

I have been reading the literature of this latter subject for the last few months and am much impressed with the chaotic condition of the minds of medical men and with the immense importance of the subject, and I feel very sanguine that a good understanding of the menstrual phenomenon in monkeys will be of great use to medicine.

With regard to development scarcely anything is known—indeed with the exception of a few papers on isolated specimens of the placenta and on the late development of the skeleton or muscles or [?] development is a blank page.

In order to do any work next year however it is necessary that I should send word to Calcutta not later than January, so that the monkeys can be collected and shipped from Calcutta by the end of March. My immediate objective in writing to you is to ask your opinion with regard to making an application to the managers of the Balfour Fund for a grant to assist me in this work. Sedgwick, with whom I have spoken on the subject, advises me to do this. And I shall be greatly obliged to you if you will tell me whether or not my application would have your approval.

Should I be able to get the promise of a sufficient grant from the Balfour Fund during January, I would at once order the monkeys to be sent and run the risk of getting a grant from the Royal Soc. By this action I should save a year. Will you let me know your opinion, and if it is favourable to my scheme will you tell me how much you think I might apply for from the Balfour Fund?

Yours sincerely, Walter Heape

PS. I was very sorry not to see you when I was in Cambridge a few weeks ago, and still more for the reason which kept you away. I hope you are better.[3]

Newton must have encouraged Heape to import monkeys for he received a grant of £100 from the Balfour Fund and ordered the monkeys from Calcutta. Fifty-five rhesus monkeys were delivered in gang cages, but they were so immature that Heape decided they were useless for his purpose and sold them.[4] Mature monkeys were too expensive to transport because their ferocity necessitated shipping them singly in cages. Heape had underestimated the logistical problems associated with transporting adult monkeys. Nevertheless, had the monkeys been mature enough he would have established the first colony of monkeys in the United Kingdom for scientific purposes.

As mentioned in his letter, Heape also requested of the Royal Society a grant-in-aid for a matching sum of £100 with this brief description:

(i) Investigation of the phenomena of menstruation and ovulation, and of the early stages of development of the monkey; also, if material is available, I propose to study placentation.

(ii) £100

(iii) I have received £100 from the managers of the Balfour fund. There are no results. I have not yet received the necessary animals. I calculate that the cost of this research will be at least £200. It will be necessary to use for the investigation adult monkeys; these are not to be obtained from dealers in England, and I have made arrangements to have them forwarded to me direct from Calcutta.

(iv) No portion of the grant will be used for personal expenses.

(v) No apparatus is required. It will be necessary, however, to build an iron or wood shed or house in which to keep the animals.[5]

The Royal Society awarded him £100 in October 1890. He decided to also seek longer support by submitting his candidature for the Balfour Studentship which was being vacated by William Bateson in 1890 after his three-year tenure. Bateson was a former member of Balfour's laboratory and became a founder of the field of genetics a few years later. Heape submitted his application on 26 September to the Balfour Memorial Fund with an outline of his new research interest:

26 September, 1890

My dear Sir,

In accordance with the instructions contained in the advertisement of the "Balfour Memorial Fund" in "Nature" for 12th June last, I beg to send you my name as that of a candidate for the Balfour Studentship.

I am the author of the following papers: "On the germinal layers and early development of the mole," published in the Proceedings of the Royal Society, 1881. Three papers on "The development of the mole," published in the Quarterly Journal of Microscopical Science, viz. "The formation of the germinal layers and early development of the medullary groove and notochord (1883), "The ovarian ovum" and "Stages E to J" (1886), and two papers in the Journal of the Marine Biological Association, viz. "Preliminary Report of the Fishing Industry of Plymouth" (1887), "Preliminary Report upon the Fauna and Flora of Plymouth Sound" (1888).

I am at present engaged with experiments on the transplanting of ova from one variety of animal to another, and have in one instance successfully transplanted two fertilized ova of an Angora Rabbit into a fertilized Belgian Hare Rabbit (each was covered by a buck of the same breed as herself and the latter gave birth in due course to four young like herself and two Angoras). The success of this experiment, the first of its kind I believe, inclines me to believe that a new field of enquiry is thus opened to the student of problems concerned with heredity.

I am also working at the placentation of mammals and at other problems connected with mammalian development and generation.

Should I be elected to the Studentship I would propose to continue on a more extensive scale my experiments upon the transplantation of ova, and (as in all experiments upon breeding) there would be frequent periods of inactivity I should propose to work also at the embryology and sexual phenomena (e.g. menstruation) of monkeys. In order to obtain material for the latter piece of work it would be advisable for me to spend some months in Calcutta. In 1889 I visited Calcutta and assured myself that material for this work could readily be obtained. In 1890 therefore I imported 55 monkeys and made preparations to keep them here and allow them to breed. When landed however it was found the animals were far too young for my purpose and I was obliged to sell them. It now appears that owing to the fierce temper of adult monkeys the difficulty and expense of transport is increased to a prohibitory degree and that it would be easier, cheaper, and more satisfactory to do the work of collecting material in Calcutta itself.

The foregoing together with a continuation of my work on placentation are the subjects to which I should propose to devote my attention should I be elected Balfour Student.

I am my dear Sir, Faithfully yours, Walter Heape[6]

Out of a field of four candidates Heape was elected Balfour Student on 24 October, and accepted a week later.[7] It was for three years and provided an annual stipend of £200.

With the availability of these funds he immediately left for Calcutta, arriving there in December where he was greatly helped by David Cunningham, Professor of Physiology in the Calcutta Medical College.[8] Cunningham was a highly-respected Edinburgh medical graduate who was active over a range of zoological and botanical subjects and currently the secretary of the Committee of Management at the Calcutta Zoological Gardens. He placed Heape's proposals before his committee, which made a small building available in the Gardens as a laboratory for studying monkeys.

Heape hoped to collect early embryos from two species of monkey – the Hanuman langur (*Semnopithecus entellus*) and the rhesus monkey (*Macacus rhesus*). However, he soon found that his project was easier said than done because all monkeys were divinely associated with the Hindu monkey god, Hanuman, and it was illegal to kill them. With the help of Cunningham, who seemed to know how to avoid controversy, Heape secured his live monkeys without disclosing that they might be killed. They were available for sale in the bazaars, although only immature and therefore useless. The first adult monkeys he obtained were 108 female langurs trapped in the jungle on the banks of the Hugli River, but no embryos were obtained from them. Some had recently given birth, many were suckling infants and the rest were not pregnant.

In February and March he obtained many female rhesus monkeys from the northwest provinces where, although protected, they were a plague in the temples and local people were very willing to capture them for sending away. Of these animals, at least eighty percent carried advanced embryos or had recently given birth. The two earliest conceptuses he observed were comparable to six-week-old human fetuses. These experiences with two species of monkey highlighted the difficulty of collecting embryos in early pregnancy without precise knowledge of the time of conception. He attempted to breed captive langurs, holding an adult pair in one cage and a male with several females in another. The females seemed willing to copulate but the males did not cooperate.

It was fate that cut his work short for, not long after arriving in the country and on a bear hunt in the Himalayas, he suffered an acute attack of rheumatism and fever. His doctor advised him to leave India as soon as possible. He had only been in Calcutta four months. Returning to England in May 1891, he took up residence the following October in Cambridge at St. Mary's, Trumpington,[9] and soon afterwards he married Ethel Ruston of Lincoln. She was the daughter of Joseph Ruston, the self-made industrial magnate and founder of the firm of Ruston & Hornsby Ltd., which manufactured and exported heavy agricultural machinery. Heape's association with the Ruston family was to be important in his work during World War I.

When they married on 7 July, 1891, Heape was 36 and Ethel 23 years old. The Unitarian ceremony took place in Bedford Chapel,[10] St. Giles District, London, attended presumably by members of both families, since Benjamin Heape and Joseph Ruston, fathers of the couple, each signed the marriage certificate. The marriage was conducted by Stopford Augustus Brooke, an eminent member of the Church of England who left the church to become a Unitarian. Bedford Chapel had never been consecrated and so was private property used for Unitarian services by Brooke; it was torn down in 1896.

The Heapes had three children. Brian Ruston was born on 27 June, 1892, Barbara Mary on 11 October, 1896, and Rodney Molyneux on 24 July, 1899. Three years into their marriage Heape signed a 99-year lease for a housing plot in Cambridge on land sold by the Pemberton family for building quality houses. Their house was named *"Heyroun"* on what became number 15 Chaucer Road, and was gated at the Trumpington Road end. They lived there until 1904 among neighbours who were mostly senior members of the colleges and university. After they moved away it became occupied by a succession of owners, and in World War II it was the headquarters of the Cambridge University Air Squadron. Since 1951 it has been occupied and extended by the Medical Research Council as the Cognitive and Brain Science Research Unit.

Despite his short stay in India, Heape did not return empty-handed. He carried home preserved uteri from non-pregnant langurs and rhesus monkeys for studying their menstrual cycles. And while dissecting the fresh specimens he had recorded the numbers of Graafian follicles, discharged follicles, fresh corpora lutea and cicatrices (scar tissue) for each animal. The next months were spent preparing specimens histologically for microscopy and determining the sequence of changes in the uterus during the menstrual cycle.[11] The work was presumably facilitated by the rotary microtome which had been developed in the Balfour laboratory.

A preliminary account of results on langur monkeys was communicated on his behalf to the Royal Society by Michael Foster in 1893,[12] and a much more detailed account was published a year later. Observations of rhesus monkey uteri were not published until 1896-7, again as a brief communication to the Royal Society[13] before a full account appeared.[14] The delay was caused by the different interpretations given earlier by Sutton in 1886, who had concluded:

(i) Macaque monkeys and baboons suffer a periodical loss of blood from the uterus.
(ii) Unlike the human female, there is no shedding of the epithelial lining of the mucous membrane of the uterus and utricular glands.
(iii) The amount of blood which escapes is very small in quantity.[15]

Although Heape's findings were consistent in the rhesus and langur monkeys, he withheld publication of the rhesus data until he felt sure in 1896 that they were correct. The difference between the two observers may well have been due to the fact that Heape had studied wild-caught animals, whereas Sutton had used zoo animals that might have abnormal reproductive function.

The changes Heape recorded in the menstrual cycle of both species were split into four distinct periods and further subdivided into eight stages:

A. Period of Rest
    Stage I. The resting stage
B. Period of Growth
    Stage II. The growth of stroma
    Stage III. The growth of vessels
C. Period of Degeneration
    Stage IV. The breakdown of vessels
    Stage V. The formation of lacunae
    Stage VI. The rupture of lacunae
    Stage VII. The formation of the menstrual clot
D. Period of Recuperation
    Stage VIII. The recuperation stage[16]

Uterine changes during the human menstrual cycle were described in an extensive but heterogeneous literature at the time Heape started working on monkeys. The old descriptions were limited to observations of single specimens that were obtained post-mortem from an accidental death or disease. Consequently, no authors had produced a complete series spanning the entire cycle, and Heape was justified in calling this situation "chaotic" in a letter to Newton. At the end of a preliminary review of the work up to 1894, he wrote:

> ... Thus it is seen there are a great variety of views held by modern investigators of the process of menstruation in the human female; as to the actual phenomena which occur, almost as many views indeed as there are writers on the subject.
>
> The extreme view on the one hand that there is no change in the tissue during menstruation is opposed by the extreme view on the other hand that highly specialized decidual tissue is formed in the mucosa at that time. Again, the statement that not even a portion of the epithelium is lost by denudation is opposed by the

statement that the whole of the epithelium, together with all the underlying mucous membrane, is discarded during menstruation.

The majority of writers appear to hold that a growth of the stroma takes place, and that it is followed by more or less complete denudation of the epithelium and the superficial stroma; that the denudation is preceded by or accompanied by bleeding from the congested capillaries in the superficial mucosa, either by diapedesis or by rupture of the vessels, or by both processes; that more or less degeneration of the tissue of that region occurs, and that the denudation is due either to the extravasation of blood, or to the degeneration of the tissue.

These views are, in a general way, similar to those advanced by me for S. entellus; the details are very variably described, however, and only extended researches can satisfactorily determine which are correct.[17]

It appears to be coincidental that cyclic changes in the human uterus were published at about the same time in two textbooks, although Heape did not see them until after his first paper in 1893. The preceding year Charles Minot of Harvard Medical School published in his textbook *Human Embryology* three stages in the menstrual cycle:

(i) Tumefaction
(ii) Menstruation
(iii) Restoration of the mucosa[18]

He added a period of rest after (iii) and before the cycle is repeated. In a subsequent paper Heape agreed that Minot's classification in women was identical to his own for the rhesus monkey,[19] but he was critical of Minot's terminology because it failed to emphasize features that he regarded as paramount. One of those features was his Stage II in which uterine growth occurs and which Minot's term "tumefaction" does not satisfy.

Moreover, he thought that the term menstruation does not include the degenerative Phase C, but rather believed that degeneration precedes rupture of blood vessels, whereas Minot had adopted an opposite view. Heape wisely understood that a better knowledge of the underlying physiology was necessary for understanding the process at a deeper level.

In the year he published his first paper on langurs, A. Milnes Marshall, Professor of Zoology at Owens College, described a classification of the human menstrual cycle in a chapter on human embryos in his book *Vertebrate Embryology* in which uterine changes were divided into four stages:

(i) The first or constructive stage

(ii) The second or destructive stage

(iii) The stage of repair

(iv) The fourth stage or period of quiescence[20]

How he arrived at this classification may never be known, since he was killed at the age of 41 years while climbing in the Lake District the same year that his book was published.[21]

Milnes Marshall was a student at Cambridge who, after graduating top of the first class division in the Natural Sciences Tripos, left for a research stint at the Zoological Station in Naples. He returned to Cambridge to teach zoology with Balfour before enrolling in medicine at St. Bartholomew's Hospital in London, but appointment to the newly-established chair of zoology at Owens College permanently interrupted those studies. In Manchester he played a major role in transforming the college to Victoria University, which later became the University of Manchester. While at Owens College, Marshall was highly esteemed as a teacher and published several textbooks, including the one recording a remarkably similar classification of the menstrual cycle to Heape's.

It would not be surprising if Heape and Milnes Marshall were acquainted, although no record of their meeting exists. They had similar, non-overlapping careers at Cambridge, both studied at Naples, and Manchester was Heape's home town. Heape declared he invented his classification before he was aware of the other man's book, and Milnes Marshall's duties often kept him away from the research bench so it is unlikely that his description of uterine changes was based on first-hand observations.

The four papers Heape published from 1893 to 1897 are the first extensive and systematic accounts of microscopic changes in a primate uterus. This work soon attracted the attention of clinicians concerned with menstrual problems in women, for shortly after publication of the langur paper he was invited to speak to the Obstetrics Society of London.[22] His work sufficiently interested A.W. Johnstone who had his paper reprinted in the USA.[23] Heape was invited back by the Society for an update of his results in the rhesus monkey.[24] At that meeting he described an examination of two human uteri, but these observations were insufficient to draw firm conclusions about the human menstrual cycle. Not until 1908 was the first extensive histological study of human uterine changes reported by two German pathologists,[25] but Heape had already laid the foundations of our current understanding.[26,27]

During that period of research he was interested in two other areas of reproductive biology. In his final report for the Balfour Studentship he mentioned that he hoped to present studies of the "rut" in animals[28] and ovulation in rabbits;[29] these publications were delayed until respectively 1900 and 1905, though they became of singular importance. There may have been several reasons for the delays. As we shall see, he had become interested in practical aspects of animal breeding and infertility, and was invited by Sir Francis Galton to join the Evolution Committee of the Royal Society. Furthermore, after his tenure of the Balfour Studentship had expired he no longer had a laboratory, although a private income and his wife's wealth relieved him from working for a living. Lastly, he had become a director of the New Elkhorn Silver Mining Company in Leadville, Colorado, which must have absorbed a great deal of time.

6

DEFINING REPRODUCTIVE CYCLES

HEAPE'S WORK on the menstrual cycle naturally led him to study the reproductive cycles in non-primates and how the environment affects rhythmicity. The confusing descriptions of cycle stages led him to propose the alternative terms that are still in standard use today, and the terminology facilitated research towards modern understanding of how hormones control reproduction.

The large variation in frequency of reproductive cycles and seasonality were known for centuries, and prompted much speculation. Lazzaro Spallanzani, Professor of Natural History at the University of Pavia in Italy, had a fair understanding of the differences, for he wrote in 1784:[1]

It is well known that almost all animals, except Man, have a stated season for the propagation of their species. Thus the female cat receives the male in September, January and May. The she-wolf and fox in January; the doe in September and October. The spring and summer are the seasons appointed for the amours of birds, and many species of fishes. The immense tribe of insects have likewise a determinate time for perpetuating their kind; this is the fine part of the year, and particularly in autumn and spring. The last-mentioned class of beings is subject to a variation that is not observed in others. Unusual warmth or cold does not retard or forward the conjunction of birds or quadrupeds; but a late spring delays the amours of insects, and an early one forwards them. Thus it is observed that, in the same country, the insects on mountains are later than in the plains.

Walter Heape's interest in the variety of mammalian reproductive cycles began early in his career while he was working in Balfour's laboratory on preimplantation embryos of domestic rabbits and European moles. It was well-known that while rabbits can breed at any time of the year, moles reproduce strictly between late March and early May.[2] During his time in India in 1890-1891, Heape wondered if the Hanuman langur (*Semnopithecus entellus*) and the rhesus monkey (*Macaca rhesus*) were seasonal breeders or could produce offspring the year round. From the limited information available he tentatively concluded that langurs gave birth twice a year[3] whereas in rhesus monkeys it depended on their location.[4] In the Simla area of the Himalayan foothills, for example, females delivered young in August and September while further south in the northwest plains they were born in March.

A series of lectures given by the obstetrician Alfred Wiltshire entitled "The comparative physiology of menstruation" attracted wide attention in 1883, and were published in the *British Medical Journal* and republished as long editorials in the *Veterinary Journal* and *Annals of Comparative Pathology*.[5] Wiltshire was convinced that studies of reproductive cycles across the animal kingdom, including non-mammalian species, could shed light on the evolution of human reproductive physiology.

Heape's interest in the subject led him to write a paper in 1900 in which he compared the "sexual season" and "prœstrum" of many mammals with the primate menstrual cycle.[6] It was a seminal paper that played an important role in revealing how reproductive patterns are controlled in part by hormones. He wrote:

> The data for a comprehensive account even in mammals does not exist; at the same time there is sufficient material at hand, in my opinion, to permit a foundation being laid, upon which it will be more easy to arrange facts in the future. It is, therefore, not with any idea of finality, but with the purpose of suggesting a whole field of enquiry, and with the hope of assisting therein, that this chapter on the comparative physiology of breeding has been written.[7]

Put another way, Heape was asking if the different kinds of cycles were variations of a common theme.

He based his paper on an extensive survey of species in the literature and face-to-face discussions with breeders and zoo-keepers. It includes data for at least 37 species from ten mammalian orders: Rodentia (e.g. rats), Chiroptera (bats), Insectivora (e.g. shrews), Lagomorpha (e.g. rabbits), Carnivora (e.g. dogs), Proboscida (e.g. elephants), Pinnipedia (e.g. seals) Perissodactyla (e.g. horses), Artiodactyla (e.g. cows) and Primates. In conclusion:

> A sexual season is common to all female mammals; its recurrence may be interfered with in consequence of climatic, individual, or maternal influences, and it may be modified by the influences attending captivity, domestication or civilization.
>
> The modifications brought about by one or other of these various influences is not necessarily the same in different species of the same genus, nor in different individuals of the same species, nor even in the same individual at all times; but whatever differences there may be, they are merely modifications of the same plan.[8]

Long before this paper's publication, reproductive patterns had been described for a number of domestic animals by veterinarians and wild animals in their natural environments or captivity by naturalists and zookeepers, although observations were often anecdotal. The word "œstrum" from the Greek οἶςτρος for frenzy had been in use for over a century to describe the period of sexual excitement when females will accept the male. The *Oxford English Dictionary* records in 1772: "The times in which animals of different species feel the oestrum, by which they are stimulated to the propagation of their respective kinds." However, Heape encountered lots of variety and confusion with the terminology in published works and conversation. The willingness of a female to mate was referred to as "coming in season," and the timing was called brunst, rut, heat, season, brim or oestrum. The word "rut" was applied to the period when stags were able and willing to mate. Heape decided to clear up the muddle by offering some defined terms for standard and unambiguous use.

Up to 1900 the terms breeding season and sexual season were often used interchangeably, but he proposed the meanings should be clearly differentiated, with the former being applied in a general way to embrace the entire reproductive process: "...the whole of that consecutive period during which any male or female mammal is concerned in the production of young, and it is not applicable to any isolated portion of that period."

Thus according to Heape both gestation and nursing are included in the breeding season. He defined the sexual season in males and females more specifically as: "... the particular time or times of the year during which their sexual organs exhibit special activity." By special activity he meant the changes that occur in generative organs and behavior that are necessary for pregnancy. This definition included the sexual season in the

90

breeding season, which begins with activation of the reproductive organs and culminates in female acceptance of a mating male, which he proposed to call œstrus or œstrum: "… the special period of sexual desire of the female; it is during oestrus, and only at that time, the female is willing to receive the male and fruitful coition rendered possible in most if not in all mammals."

He emphasized that he preferred the word "œstrus" to more colloquial expressions, including œstrum, coming on heat and coming in season. Œstrus is, however, but one phase of the sexual season, and he named prooestrus or prooestrum for the prior phase. When females do not mate or fail to conceive their reproductive organs gradually return to a quiescent state and they lose the desire to mate. This closing-down phase he called metoestrus or metoestrum, and leads to the ending of the sexual season with a return to a state of sexual inactivity called anoestrus, which is prolonged in sheep and some other animals. The sequence prooestrus, œstrus, metoestrus and anoestrus represents the œstrous cycle, which occurs repeatedly in most rodents with a short pause between called dioestrus and is akin to anoestrus in species with a single cycle per breeding season, such as wolves. The cycles within a sexual season are called the dioestrous cycles. For example, a mare may experience several dioestrous cycles in a particular season after which she experiences a long anoestrous until the same time the following year.

Thus two types of cycles are recognized in unmated animals, depending on their duration and periodicity. Heape designated the monoestrus type as a single œstrous cycle in a sexual season separated by anoestrous periods (e.g. domestic bitches) and the polyœstrous type exhibiting two or more consecutive œstrous cycles within each sexual season separated by anœstrus (e.g. the mare).

The etymology of oestrus and œstrum has a long history and often confuses students.[9] Although Heape preferred the first over the second, he chose the form œstrum for the derivative words proœstrum, metœstrum, anœstrum and diestrum for reasons never explained. In American English the diphthong "œ" has been dropped in favor of a simple "e", with corresponding differences between the noun form and adjectival forms (œstrus v. estrus, and œstrous v. estrous, respectively).

Heape recognized that environmental factors can affect when the sexual season falls within the calendar year, so that young are scheduled to be born at favorable times of year. He classified these factors under three headings, climatic, individual and maternal, to account for differences in sexual season in the wild, under domestication and in captivity. In monœstrous species these factors may either increase or decrease the duration of the sexual season, while in polyœstrous ones they can increase or decrease the number and duration of cycles within a sexual season. One example of an environmental effect is the earlier onset in sheep grazed on vigorously growing grass, or after feeding them supplements of turnips, cake and corn in the spring. This phenomenon is well-known to breeders, who call it "flushing."

He was puzzled how to fit the primate menstrual cycle into his classification of reproductive cycles. Was menstruation a part of an underlying sexual season? He evidently attached great importance to the question because it is implicitly stated in the title of his 1900 paper, but it was not a new question. Throughout the 19th century there had been a debate whether to equate oestrum or heat in lower mammals with menstruation in women. It was known that vaginal bleeding is not specific to women and found to varying degrees in lower mammals. In some species like the cow the only discharge is mucus stained with blood, and at the opposite end of the spectrum a large amount of blood is shed by bitches in prœstrus. These facts caused the obstetrician Franz Nagele of Heidelberg in 1812 to write that heat and menstruation were homologous phenomena,[10] but this opinion was not held universally. In Berlin, Johannes Müller stated in 1843 that: "... the menstruation of the human female is a phenomenon of a totally different nature, and has no connection with sexual excitement."[11]

Müller was making the point that to compare a behavioral phenomenon (sexual excitement) with a morphological one involving uterine bleeding (menstruation) was akin to likening apples to oranges. The controversy was still unresolved at the time Heape was studying langurs and rhesus monkeys. A paper published in 1892 by E. Retterer caught his attention because it contained a histological description of changes in the uterus of bitches during the œstrous cycle.[12] Heape had classified the uterus of the langur monkey into Stages I through VIII and now concluded from Retterer's paper that the first seven of those stages also occurred in the bitch. Thus he believed vaginal bleeding in bitches during prœstrous was caused by the same process as the discharge in monkeys during menstruation. He repeated the assertion in his classical paper of 1900 as an argument for primate menstruation's being homologous to prœstrous bleeding in lower mammals.

This assumption was held by many investigators for the next 28 years until it was challenged by Carl Hartman in his paper entitled "The homology of menstruation."[13] Hartman had previously reported a slightly blood-stained discharge from the vagina of rhesus monkeys midway between episodes of menstrual bleeding,[14] and noted the same had been reported in women. These observations raised the possibility that it was mid-cycle bleeding and not menses in primates that was homologous to prooestrous bleeding in lower animals. Thus an error held by Heape and many others was finally dispelled.

Heape wondered whether women ever experienced intermittent sexual seasons. Long sections of his 1900 paper were devoted to reviewing the anthropological and biological evidence. He concluded there is suggestive evidence in aboriginal people, and also suggested that with modern civilization and better nutrition women have a sexual season that lasts throughout the year.

The timing of ovulation in the cycle was too important a matter for him to ignore, and had attracted much attention and speculation over the years. In 1845 Félix Archimède Pouchet, Professor of Medicine at the School of Medicine in Rouen, France, presented a theory of spontaneous ovulation and fertilization in mammals and humans in a paper at the French Academy of Science. It was published in a book under the title *"Thèorie positive de l'ovulation spontanée et de la fecundation des mammifères et de l'espèce humaine."*[15] Remarkable for its time, it attracted much interest and was honored by the Academy. Pouchet enunciated five propositions:

(i) That in all classes of Mammalia ova are produced spontaneously in the ovaries.

(ii) That they are expelled spontaneously at regular intervals, independently of coition.

(iii) That in the human female they are expelled at each menstrual period; this period corresponding to the rutting season of animals.

(iv) That the ova are, and can be, fecundated only after their expulsion from the ovary; the various solid membranes, by which they are protected previous to this expulsion, opposing a complete obstacle to the access of the spermatic corpuscles, the actual contact of which is indispensable to the impregnation of the ovum.

(v) That in all probability the part where fecundation usually takes place is the cavity of the uterus or the lower part of the Fallopian tube.

Pouchet's third proposition explicitly stated that ovulation occurred during heat in lower mammals, which was supported by Theador Bischoff who described in 1847 seeing the rupture of Graafian follicles in rabbits with ova released into the Fallopian tube at the beginning of heat.[16] Pouchet's work also confirmed that morphological aspects of ovulation were already well-known in the mid-19th century. It was also known that a transitory structure forms at the site of the discharged Graafian follicle, called the yellow body or the corpus luteum. John C. Dalton submitted a prize-winning essay for a competition by the American Medical Association in 1851 in which he described two types of corpus lutea, one that developed and quickly disappeared if pregnancy was not established and one that persisted and grew if pregnancy occurred.[17] The essay attracted sufficient attention that the University of Buffalo School of Medicine appointed him Professor of Physiology, the first appointment of its kind in the United States.[18]

Heape recorded the number and appearance of Graafian follicles, recently discharged follicles and corpora lutea in monkey ovaries. From those observations he attempted to determine in which of the eight uterine stages of the menstrual cycle ovulation occurred. He concluded:

(i) Ovulation does not necessarily occur during each menstrual period.

(ii) Ovulation is not necessarily brought about by menstruation.

(iii) That the ripening of an ovum in the ovary is a process independent of the process of menstruation.[19]

By 1900 he knew there were exceptions (perhaps many) to the rule that ovulation happens independently of coitus.[20] When he was studying reproduction in rabbits as the Balfour Student in Cambridge, he noted that the discharge of ova occurs about 10 hours after copulation and, therefore, since some spermatozoa ascend to the site of fertilization within only two hours they wait another eight hours before they can penetrate ova. He also observed that if rabbits are prevented from mating while in season, subsequent ovulation may become impaired, but publication of these interesting observations was delayed until 1905. The preceding year Francis H.A. Marshall of Cambridge reported that the ferret is another species in which ovulation only occurs after mating.[21] Their independent accounts are the earliest confirmations of what is now called non-spontaneous ovulation and known to occur widely in mammals.

Heape had a significant impact on young Marshall who adopted the other's terminology for stages of reproductive cycles almost immediately in his three papers describing the œstrous cycles of sheep,[22] ferrets[23] and dogs,[24] and agreed by Herbert Evans at the University of California, Berkeley, and Herbert Cole in their work on the canine cycle of the dog.[25] Marshall frequently acknowledged Heape's perceptive ideas, and dedicated the first edition of his classical text *The Physiology of Reproduction* to him.[26] Commenting on the relationship between the two men, Sir Alan Parkes wrote:

He [Marshall] was preceded in this field by another pioneer, Walter Heape, who was completing his classic studies of the primate uterus and collecting material for his analysis of the œstrous cycle at the time when Marshall was an undergraduate in Cambridge. The two men did not meet until later, but they corresponded freely, and Heape's morphological studies and extensive knowledge of living animals, were of great value to Marshall in his early days.[27]

Heape was deeply curious about the timing of ovulation in the human menstrual cycle for he had found no correlation between menses and ovulation in monkeys. Did it occur between successive menstrual cycles? How was it regulated? As already mentioned in Chapter 5, these fundamental questions were unsolved and information was "chaotic," which he pointed out to Professor Newton when he sought support for his research, because the data were based on few ovarian specimens obtained at autopsy in varying states of preservation.[28] He never found the answer, but indirect evidence in the next few years suggested ovulation did indeed happen at mid-cycle.[29] It was, however, nearly half a century until this was proven by finding embryos at that stage in the reproductive tracts of rhesus monkeys and women.[30,31]

Towards the end of the 19th century there was a general explanation for physiology called "solidism," which had its origins in pathology and claimed that diseases arise through contact between solid structures. This concept brings the nervous system to mind since its branches make cellular contacts with other structures throughout the body, and thus it was thought that it might be regulating the ovary and menstrual cycle through a control center in the spinal cord.[32,33] By the end of the century a revolutionary new idea was taking hold, namely that the nervous system was not solely responsible for controlling body functions but there were chemicals circulating in the blood that played a major role. The new field became known as endocrinology and the first advances were made with the thyroid and adrenal glands, and the alimentary canal. Heape already had an inkling of mammalian reproductive endocrinology before Ernest Starling at University College, London, coined the word "hormone" in 1905.[34] The final paragraph of his 1900 paper contains a prophetic statement:

> I am tempted to suggest the probability that there is present in the blood from time to time what may be called an œstrous toxin, to suggest that its presence is due to the external and internal forces mentioned above, and to relegate to it the power which stimulates the activity of the sexual season, and brings about the actual production of those generative elements which nutrition has enabled the animal to elaborate.

Prior to his work, there were already indications that reproductive functions were controlled by chemical messages borne by the blood stream. Surgical removal of both ovaries caused an immediate cessation of reproductive cyclicity which was reversed by transplanting ovarian tissue to ectopic sites. The final proof that internal secretions were responsible for controlling the œstrous cycle in dog ovaries was provided by Marshall and Jolly in 1905. That year Heape repeated his suggestion that ovulation in rabbits was triggered by an œstrous toxin, although he offered two alternative terms for this physiology, "œstrous ferment" and "gonadin."[35] He was well aware of epoch-making discoveries in reproductive biology at the turn of the century, for he wrote:

> It appears to me that research in this direction would be likely to be rewarded; it would not only be of great theoretical interest, but

may well lead to increase of knowledge regarding some of the causes of sterility, and prove of enormous practical value.

The paper he entitled "The 'sexual season' in mammals and the relation of the 'pro-œstrum' to menstruation" provided the scaffold on which reproductive endocrinology would be built.

7

EXPERIMENTS IN ARTIFICIAL INSEMINATION

IN THE MIDST of work on the primate uterus, Walter Heape received two letters in July 1894 from Sir Francis Galton, a poly-math and expert on heredity, asking for his advice about animal breeding experiments that involved artificial insemination. The letters have not survived but their content can be inferred from Heape's two replies:

1 July, 1894

Dear Sir,

In reply to your note of the 29th [June] I beg to assure you it gives me great pleasure to have the [words missing]—regard to the experiments you are making. I hope you will, as you suggest, send me a short account of what you propose to do, together with any queries which may occur to you.

I am faithfully, Walter Heape[1]

Galton must have replied by return mail, for on 3 July, 1894, Heape enthusiastically replied:

Dear Sir,

I have much to say on the matter of the experiments you suggest, your note of which I duly received this morning and read with very great interest.

I shall be in London tomorrow, and would call on you at 4 P.M. for an hour, if it will be convenient for you to receive me then. May I ask you to send me a telegram on the receipt of this letter, as I leave here early tomorrow morning. If tomorrow Wednesday at 4 is not convenient I could come on Thursday morning about 9.30 or 10, and if neither day suits you I will write on my return here.

I should like to tell you of some experiments I have been engaged in for some months past, upon the mechanisms of ovulation; they bear somewhat closely upon considerations which your proposed experiments will necessitate, and they will I think interest you.

I will of course regard your communication as strictly private.

Very faithfully yours, Walter Heape[2]

The experiments Galton wished to discuss were conceived after he was appointed to the 7th Royal Commission on Horse Breeding in Great Britain. The first Commission was in 1887 in response to the growing concern that the breeding of sound horses was inadequate for the nation's needs. The three million horses in the country in the last decade of the 19th century were immensely important for the British economy besides their use for pleasure.[3] They were needed for moving goods around railway yards, transporting people in horse-drawn omnibuses and hackney cabs, for cavalry brigades and even for exporting horsemeat to Belgium. The 1st Commission had been charged as follows:

Whereas our Royal predecessors and we ourselves have during many years encouraged the breeding of sound horses by the gift, out of the Civil List, of Queen's Plates to be won at race meetings in different parts of Great Britain; and whereas we have reason to believe that our bounty in its present form is not so effective as we could desire and that our object would be more fully attained if the said bounty were bestowed directly for the encouragement of horse breeding; now know ye that we having taken into our consideration, and being heartily desirous to do what in us lies for the furtherance of so important a national object, have authorized and appointed the Duke of Portland [and others] ... to consider and report to us the regulations under which our Royal Bounty may best be expended in prizes to be bestowed by us at the chief agricultural shows in Great Britain, for the purposes of encouraging the breed and maintenance of a race of sound horses, or in such other manner as we may approve.[4]

The Civil List is the name of Queen Victoria's expense account, and the Queen's Plates were monetary prizes for the winners of horse races. By Royal Command the money was raised specifically for improving horse breeding through Royal Commissions, which were appointed annually for several years until after the turn of the century. Galton's appointment in 1894 was a signal recognizing the key importance of equine heredity.

While serving on the 7th Commission, Galton drafted a document entitled "A plea for experiments on the artificial fertilization of Mammalia" which was never published and marked "private for now." The essay was deposited in a Special Collection of Galton's papers at University College, London, and quoted here in full because of the author's influence and its significance for reproductive technology:

It seems reasonable, on the following grounds, that experiments should be made on the possibility of artificially fertilizing Mammalia, beginning with such inexpensive animals as mice and guinea-pigs.

The two facts, that a single spermatozoon suffices to fertilise an ovum when brought to the proper place at the proper season, while the number of them secreted by the male is enormous, show that a vast quantity of material is wasted. A breeder is unable at present to widely introduce in a single generation any fresh strains of exceptional value that chance to make a sudden appearance as a sport, and is therefore hereditarily transmissible. Therefore if artificial fertilization prove to be possible, by using only a minute portion of the available material, a new and valuable power would be placed in the control of breeders. There are two main heads for experimentation—

(1) On methods of preserving spermatozoa in health and life and in fertilising vigour during many days.

(2) On the possibility of fertilising, with fair average success, by mechanically conveying to the mouths of the Fallopian tubes, a minute fraction of the available material.

As regards (1) it is conceivable that some culture fluid should be found more conducive to the vitality of the microbes than that in which they naturally live. They are said to live in milk; therefore other appropriate fluids may exist, possibly all the more suitable if oxygenated, that would admit of their being kept in vigour for some days, and of being easily transported.

As regards (2), the artificial insemination of women, whose husbands have hypospadias, has been tried with success on a considerable scale. Hunter was the first to attempt it, it then became forgotten, but has been introduced both in France and in America during recent years, by making the injection monthly, soon after the cessation of the menses. Particulars may be found in Tarnier, "Art des Accouchements" Paris, 1882, p 176 (see also p. 166 on the vitality of spermatozoa). The apparatus there described might doubtless be further simplified and reduced in size, considering how minute an application is necessary, if directed to the right place. The immense waste of material under the ordinary conditions, is due to the non-fulfillment by nature of this requirement, as may be inferred from the fact that the amount of the material that is discharged by different animals varies roughly with their size although that of the individual spermatozoon is about the same in all, as in the rat, the dog, the man, the horse and the bull. In other words, the number of the microbes that are discharged is proportionate to the area of the walls of the canal which they have to be wastefully dispersed, on the chance of some of them reaching the required spot.

It is scarcely possible to think of the practicality of artificially inseminating domestic animals, without extending in imagination its application to humanity under some other different form of civilization to our own. It is a process which might be effected by female surgeons, in a purely female establishment, even under anaesthetics if thought desirable, and without wholly destroying the Levitical signs proofs of virginity. In short, a maid might bear her first born to the State, wholly unsullied by sexual passion.[5]

Artificial insemination was reported about 100 years before this document was written by Lazarro Spallanzani, Royal Professor of Natural History in the University of Pavia, who successfully artificially inseminated a bitch in 1789.[6] Pierre Rossi at the University of Pisa repeated the experiment a year later,[7] and John Hunter, surgeon to King George III, used the technique to successfully treat an infertile couple by injecting seminal fluid from a man suffering hypospadia into his wife's vagina. The precise date that Hunter treated his patient is unknown, for it was reported indirectly by Everard Home to the Royal Society in 1799 after Hunter died.[8,9] Spallanzani described his experiment as follows:

I chose a bitch spaniel of moderate size which before had whelped. Suspecting, from certain appearances, that she would soon be in heat, I confined her in an apartment, where she continued a long time as will be seen below. For greater security, that she might never be let loose, I fed her myself, and kept the key the whole time. On the thirteenth day she began to show evident signs of being in heat; the external parts of generation were tumid, and a thin stream of blood flowed from them. On the twenty-third day she seemed fit for the admission of the male, and I attempted to fecundate her artificially in the following manner. A young dog of the same breed furnished me, by a spontaneous emission, with nineteen grains of feed [i.e., seed], which were immediately injected into the matrix, by means of a small syringe introduced into the vagina. As the natural heat of the feed in animals of warm blood may be a condition necessary to render fecundation efficacious, I had taken care to give the syringe the degree of heat which man and dogs are found to possess, which is about 30°.[10] Two days after the injection, the bitch went off her heat, and in twenty days her belly appeared swollen, which induced me to set her at liberty on the twenty-sixth. Meanwhile the swelling of the belly increased; and sixty two days after the injection of the feed, the bitch brought forth three lively whelps, two male and one female, resembling in colour and shape not the bitch only, but the dog also from which the feed had been taken. Thus did I succeed in fecundating this quadruped; and I can truly say, that I have never received greater pleasure on any occasion, since I have cultivated experimental philosophy.[11]

Both Spallanzani and Hunter demonstrated artificial insemination nearly 100 years before the details of fertilization were understood; nevertheless they correctly believed that ova needed to be exposed to semen to develop. They shared a common but independent research interest in that they both claimed to have fertilized silk-worm ova after release from female moths by exposing them to semen after which worms developed—in vitro fertilization if you like.[12,13] When they considered viviparous mammals, dog and human, they assumed that they could impregnate ova in vivo by introducing semen into a female without natural coitus. By this route they introduced the technique of artificial insemination; Spallanzani used AID (artificial insemination by donor) and Hunter used AIH (artificial insemination by husband).

Spallanzani's demonstration of artificial insemination in a dog was highly praised by his friend, the influential Swiss biologist Charles Bonnet who, after reading a copy of Spallanzani's dissertations, wrote:

> I congratulate you on your success, and what adds greatly to it is, that it was obtained with less than thirteen grains of semen ... You are now in possession of a sure and easy way of ascertaining what species can procreate together; and the experiments you propose attempting next spring, by putting your voluptuous spaniel in the company of cats and rabbits, promise not so fair as those which you will make, by introducing the semen of this spaniel into the uterus of a doe-rabbit and a she-cat, and on the other hand, by introducing the semen of the male rabbit and cat into the uterus of a bitch. You hold in your hand a precious clue, which will guide you to the most important and unexpected discoveries. I know not whether what you have now discovered may not be one day applied in the human species to purpose we little think of, and of which the consequences will not be trivial.[14]

Later on Spallanzani inseminated two cats with dog semen with no success.[15] He wanted to repeat the experiment with species known to produce mules by natural mating, but was unable to find any patron.

Why was the potential of artificial insemination in basic and clinical research largely ignored in the 19th century when several clinicians had used artificial insemination with some success to treat cases of human infertility?[16] Its general adoption in gynecology was unfortunately impeded by emotional and ethical objections. In 1866, an American gynecologist resident in England, James Marion Sims, published a book entitled *Clinical Notes on Uterine Surgery, with Special Reference to the Management of the Sterile Condition*.[17] It recommended artificial insemination for the treatment of infertility in women, but was poorly received by the medical press.[18] A damning review in the *Medical Times* ended with the statement:

We can express our unfeigned regret that Dr. Marion Sims has thought proper to found an odious practice on such [im]pure assumption. At any rate, if such practices were to be considered the business of the Physician there are a good many of us who would quit Physic for some other calling that would let us keep our sense of decency and self-respect. Better let ancient families become extinct than keep the succession by such means.

In France, another book, written by Jules Gérard, nearly did not get published. It was based on a thesis prepared for the MD degree at the University of Paris under the mentorship of a gynecologist who saw the value of artificial insemination for the treatment of some forms of sterility in women. The examiners refused to accept the thesis and ordered that all copies that had been printed, the proofs and the original manuscript, be destroyed. Fortunately a copy was retrieved as it was about to be used to light a fire and, after Gérard had been awarded an MD with a second thesis, it was eventually published and widely circulated in 1888, attracting much interest.[19]

The story does not end there. The eminent French physiologist Claude Bernard, who as a young man was interested in vaudeville and also wrote a play, albeit unsuccessful, once suggested that a controversial issue could be given widespread attention if it were the subject of a novel. Two novelists, Yveling Rambaud and Dubut de Laforest, were persuaded to write a novel titled "Le Faiseur d'Hommes" in which the value of artificial insemination was strongly praised.[20] Objections to artificial insemination in women came also from another source. In the 1880s, a French amateur anthropologist, Vacher de Lapouge, proposed a doctrine he called "anthroposociology" which involved promoting reproduction in the fit and discouraging it in the unfit by the use of artificial insemination. This eugenic idea was not well received and in 1897 it caused the condemnation of artificial insemination by the Holy See of the Catholic Church.[21]

In the 1880s artificial insemination was used by Sir Everett Millais, the son of Sir John Everett Millais, a distinguished artist and former President of the Royal Academy, to cross two breeds of dog, a physically smaller basset hound and a physically large bloodhound, whose different sizes prevented normal mating. Everett Millais is credited with the introduction of the basset hound from France in 1874 and establishing the breed in the United Kingdom. Eventually, problems arose probably because of inbreeding. Millais wrote:

After inbreeding for nearly twenty years, it was obvious that the English Bassett required fresh blood, primarily because the general mass of hounds were below the average size; secondly, because there was increasing difficulty in breeding and rearing them; thirdly, because barrenness was becoming very prevalent; and fourthly, because when reared they succumbed through constitutional causes to distemper in a most alarming manner.[22]

Millais decided to introduce new blood into the breed by crossing a basset hound with a bloodhound. The first experiment was done in 1884 when a basset bitch was artificially inseminated with spermatozoa from a basset dog.[23] Pups were born dead. The next year three basset bitches were inseminated with spermatozoa from a single basset dog, the semen being split in three parts. A total of 13 live pups were obtained from the three bitches. In 1891 a bloodhound bitch was inseminated by spermatozoa from a basset dog. A single pup was born which had many of the characteristics of the basset. By 1896 19 bitches had been artificially inseminated and 15 became pregnant.

At the time of his meeting with Galton in London, Walter Heape was engaged in studies of the primate uterus. In a change of direction characteristic of his broad research interests, Heape began to plan experiments with artificial insemination using a fluid in which rabbit sperm could be preserved and manipulated. Only five days after their meeting, 31 July, 1894, Heape wrote to Galton saying that pathologists recommended placing the sperm in sterile hydrocoele fluid.[24]

Dear Mr. Galton,

I hasten to send you a line today and will, until I hear from you, write in such a manner as may allow of your sister's reading.

I put some spermatic fluid into sterilized hydrocele fluid on Saturday, left it until Monday in an incubator—the tubes were unfortunately, by error, removed two or three hours before I was able to examine them—I found spermatozoa therein, but they were motionless, and a lively and plentiful crop of bacteria was also present. The latter were doubtless introduced with the spermatic fluid and a plan must be devised to obtain the spermatozoa free from such contamination.

A great proportion of the spermatozoa in the hydrocele fluid had no marked appearance of degeneration, and there seems, so far, no reason why they should not live if proper precautions are taken. I think it will be advisable to gain the assistance of one of the trained bacteriologists in the pathological laboratory here—the experiments will be more reliable and more valuable to you if they are performed by one who is fully conversant with all the methods of that science. If therefore, you are agreeable I will find someone who will undertake this part of the work and we will together report to you.

Please let me have a line before you leave tomorrow. I shall, myself, be much away for the next two months, but see no reason why half a dozen experiments should not be performed in that time.

Very faithfully yours, Walter Heape[25]

The first sentence of this letter is yet another illustration of Victorian prudishness over sexual issues and the care that scientists felt they had to take in their discussions that might reach a lay audience. About 10 weeks later he again wrote to Galton:

... The last experiment Dr. Barlow and I performed was to extract spermatic fluid from the vagina of a doe (killed for the purpose) a few minutes after copulation to place the same in hydrocele fluid and keep it at 37° temperature. The greatest care was taken and every precaution adopted to obtain the spermatic fluid free from septic organisms and the hydrocele fluid was sterilized, but nevertheless about 4 hours afterwards the movement of the spermatozoa had diminished in rapidity at three hours later they were motionless and apparently dead. At the same time there was considerable growth of bacteria in the hydrocele fluid.

Dr. Barlow is quite certain the presence of the bacteria was not due to faulty manipulation, and he does not doubt they were present in the spermatic fluid which was taken from the vagina before it was extracted therefrom. This appears to me exceedingly likely and I do not think any satisfactory experiment in the direction of preserving the spermatic fluid can be performed until it can be obtained by artificial means, viz. by the ejection of it without copulation, into a properly sterilized vessel.

Hitherto I have been unable to effect by artificial means, the ejection of spermatozoa from a rabbit. I fancy it might be managed by introducing a stuffed rabbit into the cage of a buck which has been sufficiently excited by a doe in heat, and by fixing a sterilised tube in the place of the vagina, it might be necessary to blindfold the buck, but I think it might be done and I propose to try it soon as my bucks are in breeding trim. I have tried putting a tube into the vagina of a living doe but have hitherto not succeeded in collecting spermatozoa in it.[26]

Heape continued to experiment with rabbits for another six months but without success, and on 5 May 1895 he admitted defeat:

I have but little to tell you I am sorry to say. We have failed entirely in our efforts to preserve effective spermatozoa for more than a few hours. The spermatozoa has been obtained direct from the vagina of female rabbits a few minutes after copulation, and placed in sterilised hydrocele fluid, but in a very short time bacilli make their appearance and rapidly fill the fluid—the sperm die.

I see no hope of success in this direction. The spermatozoa must be obtained direct from the male in a sterilised condition in order to give it a chance of living. Rabbits are not convenient animals to work with for this purpose; it does not seem to be an easy matter to induce artificially the ejection of sperm from a rabbit. In dogs this is readily done, and I would suggest that some experiments should be made with dogs as soon as artificial fertilisation can be performed with some certainty. At present I have not succeeded in fertilising artificially rabbits. I have injected sperm into the vagina and the sperm has found its way into the uterus, that is not the difficulty we have to contend with, the difficulty is that the injection of spermatozoa alone does not appear to be sufficient to produce ovulation in rabbits. I have now killed a very consider-able number of doe rabbits, and have never found one in which ovulation has taken place without copulation. Electric stimulus of the vulva and vagina, which a doe in heat readily submits to, does not induce ovulation apparently. I am not quite satisfied about this point, and propose to repeat the experiment shortly, upon a doe in which spermatozoa has been injected artificially, but I do not expect the experiment to be attended with any success.[27]

It was Heape's bad luck that the rabbit was a poor model for artificial insemination since it is a non-spontaneous ovulator that requires copulation for the release of an ovum from the ovary. Animals that ovulate spontaneously around or during heat, such as the dog or the mare, would have been much easier to use.

At first, neither man was aware of Everett Millais' success with basset hounds, but when Heape heard of it he wrote to Millais, who responded quickly. Heape wrote to Galton on 11 May:

I have heard from Millais and he tells me he has repeatedly fertilised bitches by injecting spermatozoa into the vagina and without any copulation. He also tells me he has put three bitches in pup from the "single emission of the dog." This seems to me what you want.[28]

Millais was not a scientist so the results of his experiments on artificial insemination were not formally published. But he kept detailed breeding records of his kennel which Galton analyzed to support his theory of ancestral law of inheritance.[29]

Heape wrote to him again on 25 June, 1895, stating that he had heard of artificial insemination being practiced by horse breeders in the United States, but he did not know the source of this information. Galton must have written to Dean Pearson at the School of Veterinary Medicine in the University of Pennsylvania because he replied in a letter Galton showed to Heape. Pearson confirmed that artificial insemination was indeed being used there in horses. Heape also found confirmation in the *Horseman*, a journal published in Chicago, which further stimulated his interest in using artificial insemination in the horse. On 1 December he contacted Galton again:

Many thanks for your note and the two enclosures which I now return. Pearson's letter is certainly very important. He has himself "practiced the system with success." It appears to me that one now requires proof that off-spring produced are not abnormal in any way, that they possess average strength and health and reproduction powers [?].

If this can be shown breeders [will] surely [?] gladly practice the method: but without that assurance I imagine breeders of prize stock will not accept a practice which might so easily get them a bad name…

The high prices paid for covering mares with first class horses ~~makes breeding~~ *(any price being charged from £50 to £400 per mare) would surely make owners of mares anxious to adopt the artificial method if it could be done certainly, provided the offspring produced are satisfactory.*

The best way I can suggest for proving this is to induce the owner of a celebrated mare, which has failed to conceive in the ordinary way, to have her artificially impregnated this next season.

The racing career and the career at stud of a foal so got would be of the greatest interest and importance, and would it appears to me to have more influence upon breeders than any experiment which I can think of.

Will you let me hear what you think of this and whether you are acquainted with the owner of a stud in which a mare might be found to act as a test case? I do not myself know personally any owner of a large stud of first class horses.

Of course a mare may fail to breed one season and may successfully bear a foal the next year, so that the hope of "better luck next time" may make owners difficult to persuade unless they have a mare which has proved to be barren for several seasons.[30]

In the coming months Heape maintained his interest in this subject and wrote a review in 1897 about artificial fertilization in mammals.[31] In discussing breeding, the paper includes a common concern throughout his writings about the use of precisely defined technical terms. Three words that are commonly confused and misused in reproductive biology are impregnate, fertilize and inseminate. Heape insisted that the verb "inseminate" was restricted to the introduction of semen into a female generative organ (vagina or uterus). The verbs fertilize or impregnate should only be used to refer to the penetration of a spermatozoon into an ovum, which occurs at a later stage. He makes an analogy with the verb pollinate, which is the placement of pollen on the stigmata of flowers. His paper included summary protocols of seventeen attempts to artificially inseminate Basset bitches supplied by Millais. A draft was submitted to Galton, who in turn sent it to Sir Michael Foster who commented:

Originality in the strict sense is not the strong point of Heape's paper, but it seemed to me of eminent value as putting into an authoritative form a great quantity of material scattered far and wide, on a very interesting subject; and one of great importance to hybridizing experiments, and of eminent value to horse breeders.

The paper was accepted with acknowledgment to Millais's contribution in a reading by Galton at the Royal Society on February 11, 1897.

Soon afterwards Heape published another paper on artificial insemination in mares.[32] He may only have had cursory practical experience in the subject when he supervised in the spring of 1896 the artificial insemination of a thoroughbred mare belonging to Lord Roseberry, a former chairman of a commission on horse breeding by the House of Lords that preceded the Royal Commission. He used the common practice of first covering a mare with a stallion, recovering the semen in a syringe from the vagina, and then injecting it into the uterus via the cervix. Later on he learned that James Boyd, a working horse breeder from Koroit in Victoria, Australia, had success, which he described in a personal communication:

On November 30th, 1895, I took two mares, both showing to the horse; No. 1 a brown mare, and No. 2 a chestnut. I plugged the mouth of the womb of No. 1 with a piece of sponge to prevent the semen passing in during service, and placed in the vagina of No. 2 the syringe., before described, to heat it to blood-heat ready for use. I then served No. 1 with the horse; as soon as she was served I took the syringe direct from the vagina of No. 2 and charged it with the semen in the vagina of No. 1. I then took the charged syringe from the vagina of No. 1 and placed it as soon as possible in the vagina of No. 2, inserted the tube of the syringe carefully into the mouth of the womb, and discharged it. I once again charged and discharged the syringe, and then turned the mares out ...

On November 6th, 1896, 342 days or eleven calendar months and six days from the date of service, the brown mare No. 1

served by the horse foaled a bay or brown colt; on November 14th, 1896, 350 days or eleven calendar months and fourteen days from the date of service the chestnut mare No. 2, served by the syringe only, foaled a bay or brown filly.

The meticulously described experiment showed that the practice of covering the mare with the donor stallion first was unnecessary. Heape regarded Boyd's contribution as particularly important:

> *I think that everyone will agree that the straightforward account given by Mr. Boyd is of very great importance and worthy of the closest attention. He has, in the most independent way, shown the truth of the contention that artificial insemination is both possible and of great value under certain circumstances.*

He recognized that a single semen sample from a genetically valuable male animal, such as a bull with genes promoting high-quality milk, could be used to inseminate several females. However, we do not know if he recognized the immense economic value of applying the method to the domestic animal industry. Adoption of artificial insemination in the United Kingdom was slow and met considerable resistance for fear that it could adversely affect the development of the offspring. Besides, it offended Victorian sensibilities, even when used on animals, and moral objections to artificial insemination in women played a role in discouraging adoption in animal production. Sir John Hammond, who was responsible for promoting artificial insemination of cattle in the UK, recalled a meeting he had with a committee of the Church Council which had raised objections to legislation laid before the British Parliament, where he made counter arguments:

I am not going to argue human, I am going to argue cattle, which we want it for. Humans are not my line, but do you know what happens now with cattle? In lots of villages throughout the country, there is a long village street and a man at one end keeps a bull and a man at the other end keeps some cows. When a cow comes on heat the owner leads it along the village street to the bull at the other end. Everyone knows what is happening and all the small boys come and watch. That is what happens now. Under my conditions, the owner would phone up, a car would appear, and a man with a little black bag would do the insemination before any boy in the village knew about it. Which is best for morals? That settled them! There was no opposition.[33]

Il'ya Ivanov of St. Petersburg had recognized the benefits of artificial insemination around the time Heape wrote his two papers, although he seems to have been unaware of the Russian's work. In 1898 Ivanov began systematically studying artificial insemination in mares and the possibility of creating inter-specific crosses, such as between a donkey and zebra. Since his early papers were in Russian they did not immediately become widely known in Western Europe until 1907 when a long review in French appeared.[34] World War I and the Russian Revolution delayed applications until 1923 to 1928 when the number of artificially inseminated mares increased from about 1,000 to 70,000 per year.[35] Thus it was in Russia as a result of Ivanov's pioneering work that Galton and Heape's forecast of the potential usefulness of the method was first realized on a large scale. It is now used all over the world as an assisted reproduction technique for treating human patients and breeding domestic animals and captive wild animals in zoos.

8

EVOLUTION COMMITTEE OF THE ROYAL SOCIETY

WALTER HEAPE was appointed by the Royal Society in January 1897 to a committee that had been founded about three years earlier and later became known as the Evolution Committee. Its remit was being expanded and several new members were added for political reasons. Heape was invited by the chairman, Sir Francis Galton, who must have been impressed by his interest in artificial insemination. His participation would lead him to write a book on the politics of animal breeding, which has been regarded among his most valuable contributions.[1]

Galton was the driving force behind the committee because, like so many other scientists, he was inspired by the theory of natural selection originated by his cousin Charles Darwin and the naturalist Alfred Wallace.[2] According to the theory, individuals whose phenotypes enable them to live long enough to reproduce successfully are the "fittest" and determine the future course of evolution. By 1865, Galton proposed that research on human evolution needed a multitude of exact measurements on as many characteristics of the body as possible, and over at least two generations. With this in mind he set up an Anthropometric Laboratory, which was initially located at the International

Health Exhibition in 1884 at the gardens of the Royal Horticultural Society in South Kensington. He recruited volunteers at the exhibition and by the time it closed the following year he had collected data from 9,337 individuals.[3] For statistical analysis he applied the normal distribution and developed a set of descriptive methods many of which are still in routine use, including the correlation coefficient. He published results in an influential book entitled *Natural Inheritance* (1889),[4] which was the first application of mathematics in biology and marked the birth of biometry.

Raphael Weldon,[5] the Jodrell Professor of Zoology at University College, London, along with Galton, was a proponent of small changes directing the course of evolution.[6] They used his statistical methods to analyze differences between individual shrimp in Plymouth Sound, and later studied a population of shore crabs in the Sound and another in the Bay of Naples.[7] Concluding their work in 1892, Weldon wrote:

> It cannot be too strongly urged that before we can properly estimate the changes at present going on in a race or species we must know accurately: (a) the percentage of animals which exhibit a given amount of abnormality [i.e., variation from the mean] with regard to a particular character; (b) the degree of abnormality of other organs which accompanies a given abnormality of one; (c) the difference between the death rate percent in animals of different degrees of abnormality with regard to a particular character; (d) the abnormality of offspring in terms of the abnormality of parents, and vice versa. These are all questions of arithmetic, and when we know the numerical answers to these questions for a number of species we shall know the direction and the rate of change in these species at the present day—a knowledge which is the only legitimate basis for speculations as to their past history and future fate.[8]

Their collaboration and shared enthusiasm for applied mathematics in biology drew the two men into a closer working relationship.

At an informal meeting in the Saville Club in London on 9 December, 1893, they met with Raphael Meldola, a professor of organic chemistry in the City and a distinguished entomologist. They agreed to jointly propose to the Royal Society the formation of a committee to study biological variation, and this was approved by its council on 18 January, 1894. It was named the Committee for the Purpose of Conducting Statistical Enquiries into the Measurable Characteristics of Plants and Animals, and its major objective was to expand the statistical studies they had started.[9] Galton was its chairman and Weldon the secretary. At the first meeting Raphael Meldola, Francis Darwin (botanist and third son of Charles), Sir Donald Macalister (mathematician and physician) and Sir Edward Poulton (evolutionary biologist) were elected to the membership. Karl Pearson (mathematician and statistician) joined in 1896. Galton received a grant of £50 in 1893-4 on behalf of the committee from the Donation Fund of the Royal Society, presumably to support further study of Weldon's database.[10] The committee published its first report in the name of all its members, and there followed immediately an essay in which Weldon forcefully argued that natural selection operates through the preferential selection of small deviations rather than by large jumps.[11]

The research came under vigorous attack from William Bateson despite his friendship with Weldon from their undergraduate days together at St. Johns College, Cambridge, and working in Balfour's laboratory. Bateson would not accept that natural selection only worked through small variations and argued that evolution involved selection of larger discontinuous jumps known as "sports." He published his views in the book *Materials for the Study of Evolution*.[12] Weldon countered with a critical review of the book in *Nature*,[13] which naturally riled Bateson, who reacted in a series of arrogant letters attacking not only Weldon but other influential members of the committee.

Galton was likely to be sympathetic to both mechanisms of natural selection. He could ally with Bateson in believing an important role for "sports," but he was also attracted to the importance of small variations between individuals promoted by Weldon. He consequently found himself in the middle of an unsavory dispute and tried to quell the controversy diplomatically by enlarging membership of the committee to include less mathematically inclined biologists. The new members elected on January 14, 1897, were Frederick Godman (entomologist and ornithologist), Maxwell Masters (botanist and taxonomist), Osbert Salvin (ornithologist and Strickland Curator in Cambridge), E. Ray Lankester and William Bateson.[14] Bateson had to be persuaded to join and his invitation required Weldon's agreement, who reluctantly agreed. Four additional members were elected on February 11, 1897: William Thiselton-Dyer (Director of Kew Gardens), James Ewart (University of Edinburgh), E.J. Lowe (zoologist), and F.E. Beddard (zoologist and taxonomist).[15] The new members changed the balance of the committee from statistically sophisticated scientists to distinguished biologists who were less enthusiastic about their methods.

Galton had another objective in mind when he enlarged the committee. He wanted to follow up a suggestion made by Alfred Wallace in 1891 to create an institution including a farm for experimentally investigating the process of evolution. Wallace continued to urge Galton and funding was found for starting a farm at Down House, Darwin's longtime residence in Kent, where selective animal and plant breeding could be carried out. Galton had already sounded Heape out about the role he might play in promoting research on selective animal breeding if he was elected to the committee. Heape replied on 16 December, 1896:

Dear Mr. Galton,

In reply to your note I shall be very happy to serve on the committee.

With regard to a scheme of experiments to be carried out by persons in the country who might be willing to help, I cannot help feeling that any experiments should be very carefully considered before being adopted, and for this reason that the practical man before whom they will be placed will be disposed to criticise severely any scheme on such a subject submitted to him by scientific men, and it is most important the practical man should feel that the scientific man on this occasion has at heart practical needs.

I would suggest that a member of the committee should be authorised to confer with certain practical breeders such as Lord Walsingham,[16] who will know what the practical man wants and what he can carry out, and then report to the committee the result. I should very much like to come over and consult you about the whole of this matter which I have much at heart. Should I find you at home and disengaged on Saturday or Monday next, would it be convenient for you to see me at 11 o'clock or after on either of these days.

Yours faithfully, Walter Heape[17]

They met on the Saturday. On 5 January of the following year Heape wrote to him at length with detailed proposals for research on animal breeding. He emphasized the manner of interviews required for encouraging farmers and breeders to cooperate; he also stressed the need to restrict questions to practical matters, such as infertility, and to inquire into all farm animals, including sheep as well as horses. He wrote again, rather more fully this time:

Dear Mr. Galton,

I am very sorry I shall be unable to attend the meeting on 14th, I have a long standing engagement in Lincoln on that day.

With regard to the suggestion that I should be made a secretary of the committee, I feel that so long as the aims of the committee are within my ken I shall be very glad to do the work, but that my position as secretary must depend on that and I don't know what the aims of the committee properly are.

For instance, I would gladly act as secretary on matters concerned with breeding but could not undertake botanical questions involving special botanical knowledge.

With regard to conferring with breeders, may I suggest that my power to do this I shall not be confined to horse-breeders. We shall not find many practical men willing to help and returns will be small for several years I suspect. It would be well I think to interest breeders of all stock wherever possible. Besides would it not be a waste of time and energy to visit a horse-breeder and neglect his next door neighbor because he may breed sheep.

With regard to possible investigations for breeders to undertake. It will undoubtedly be well to be in a position to suggest investigations to them, we may find some breeders willing to undertake one problem and others another. The main points we have to bear in mind at first seem to me 1) to propose investigations which they can see are of practical importance to them as breeders, 2) to propose schemes which they can carry out satisfactorily without expending money, and 3) to bear in mind that they are very busy men who do not recognize yet the importance of scientific aid, and who will probably regard any time spent on such matters as wasted. If such men are judiciously handled, I think they __may__ give us great help and may themselves benefit thereby, but it must take time to bring this about I should be very careful not to frighten them __at first__.

Among the topics you suggest I do not recognise any which I think will interest breeders generally except infertility—its annual variation they would, I think, be willing to record, the causes of it they would certainly gladly know, the degree of infertility of inbred stock some would probably be found to record, but the prevalence of malformation they would be quite unable to investigate since they fatten infertile stock and sell it to the butcher. Exceptionally intelligent breeders may be found who will express opinions and record cases of

124

Heredity, Prepotency and Telegony, Variation, Fraternal and Sports and their stability, but I fear the value of such evidence will not be great and think these and similar problems can only be satisfactorily attempted in a suitable scientific form.

Investigations on infertility may I think bring to the fore various other questions of importance such as questions concerning "Heat", the influence of certain pastures (food), meteorological influences, the effect of different stock on pastures and so forth.

With regard to the rules of breeding, I quite agree with you it would be very interesting and important to discover the rules followed by different breeders and how they work. I hope some schemes can be framed for that end.

I do not know what publications breeders read and write in, beyond the Field, Land and Water, The Farm Journal (I think it is), Stonehenge or the Horse & Dog, various dog papers like the Fancier's Gazette, the Dog Owner's Annual and so forth.

I am not surprised to hear that Millais lecture amazed you. He is a bold experimenter, but his ideas regarding epiblastic and mesoblastic prepotency, the fertilising of immature ovarian ova by means of spermatozoa of a previous sire etc. etc. are well—comical…

Yours faithfully, Walter Heape[18]

Heape summarized these points in a short statement as to the role he could play if he was appointed to the Evolution Committee:

With regard to my suggestion it is that I should be appointed to act with you for the purpose of conferring with breeders:

(a) As to problems which they are desirous of having solved, and

(b) As to a scheme or schemas for recording data bearing upon those problems which they will be willing to supply.

Besides this I agree with you it will be very desirable to be prepared with a series of problems the importance of solving which should be urged upon breeders as opportunity offers and their aid obtained whenever possible.[19]

Not being a Fellow of the Royal Society, Heape could only be elected an associate member of the committee on 14 January, 1897. After Galton had read his shortened statement on how animal breeding research should proceed, he appointed Heape to be the secretary of a sub-committee including himself for implementing the plan.

But Heape was unreceptive to Galton's second objective of establishing an institution and experimental farm at Down House. He explained his reasons in a letter to Francis Galton on 11 February, shortly after joining the committee:

Dear Mr. Galton,

I do not know what view the Committee is likely to take of the position of affairs as they now stand, and I should like to put before you the following in favour of a waiting policy.

My view is that in order to conduct such experiments as are necessary for the solution of problems on breeding (heredity etc.) a permanent establishment is necessary, and the requisite income for carrying on such establishment assured.

The value of such experiments may be expected to show itself in about 50 years after they have been initiated, and the importance of a permanent establishment will be apparent. One cannot expect annual subscribers to maintain their interest in an institution or in experiments which, as far as they are likely to see, can produce no results of importance.

In the same way it would hamper, very greatly, the institution if the continuance of experiments should be dependent upon the raising of sufficient money each year.

It appears to me therefore that a sufficient endowment is essential to the scheme, and I should personally greatly regret the establishment of an experimental station on however a small a scale unless it was endowed with sufficient income, and unless it occupied land and owned that land on which the experiments were conducted.

I think the failure of any such scheme for want of funds would have the effect of seriously hampering any subsequent efforts to obtain money for a like purpose; and for these reasons I am strongly of the opinion that it will be wise not to attempt to begin work on a temporary basis, but to concentrate our energies on the establishment of a permanent institution and to wait until the requisite capital sum can be obtained for that purpose.

In the meantime I think valuable work can be done by collecting information from breeders and societies and in endeavouring to obtain their cooperation in the solution of problems they are interested in, and in the work the committee is desirous of eventually undertaking.

Yours faithfully, Walter Heape[20]

The idea of creating a research institution on animal breeding at Darwin's old home did not get off the ground because other committee members objected too.

As we will see in the next chapter, Heape quickly got to work on the new project and within two years had sufficient material to publish two papers,[21,22] which was fortunate since the Evolution Committee became increasingly dysfunctional. Galton's political manipulation displeased some of the original members. At least Thiselton-Dyer, and perhaps others, was unhappy with expanding their original objectives and at the next meeting on February 11 he offered the proposal that the committee should confine its work for the present time to "variation, its amount and transmission." After the motion was lost, Michael Foster was more successful in suggesting that "the committee does not propose to carry on investigations by itself as a body, but by all means in its power to assist and generally supervise investigations of which it approves, and for which adequate investigations can be found."

He then moved that "a sub-committee be appointed to consider and report on the enquiries which should be undertaken by the committee in accordance with the foregoing resolution." This motion was passed with Galton and Heape along with five new members voting in favor: Messrs. Bateson,

Darwin, Masters, Meldola and Weldon.[23] It was resolved at their next meeting on the 26th February to request their title be revised to Evolution (Animal and Plants) Committee to Promote Accurate Investigations of Variation, Heredity, Selection, and other Phenomena Relating to Evolution.[24] Three more members were added: Sir W. Turner, Dr. T. R. Frazer and Professor I. B. Balfour, and they were asked to form a sub-committee to investigate the possibility of extending their remit to Scotland.

William Bateson was empowered to draft a circular to express the expanded purpose of the committee:

EVOLUTION COMMITTEE OF THE ROYAL SOCIETY

This Committee has been appointed by the Council of the Royal Society to promote accurate investigations of Variation, Heredity, Selection, and other phenomena relating to the Evolution of Plants and Animals.

Those who are engaged either in breeding the various races of domestic animals, or in scientific horticulture, have exceptionally good opportunities of making observations on the above subjects. In the course of their business attention is necessarily directed to the effects of various systems of breeding, to crosses between different species or varieties, to the transmission of parental characters, to the origin of new varieties, and to other facts of a similar nature. Breeders and horticulturalists are, in fact, continuously engaged in experiments on a large scale, which, if they were recorded in detail, would have a high scientific value.

The importance of such records as these is now generally admitted, and has been especially exemplified by the use Darwin was able to make of them in his writings, particularly in his "Animals and Plants under Domestication."

Though publications connected with the farm and garden frequently contain notices of striking phenomena witnessed in the propagation of animals and plants, such accounts are, for the most part, imperfect. If they were systematically made and more precisely described, and if greater precautions were taken to exclude the possibility of error, the records thus obtained would constitute a valuable body of trustworthy evidence.

Those who are professionally engaged in breeding and horticulture have, as a rule, little leisure for observing or recording their results with more detail than is necessary for their own purposes; but it is suggested that this Committee might facilitate the additional work that they desire to see performed, in various ways appropriate to particular cases, either by making arrangements for the maintenance of full and continuous records, or for the preservation, measurement, drawing and photographing of specimens in such a way that their essential features shall be permanently recorded.

The Committee is assured that in suitable cases this could be done without interference with the directly practical side of the operations, and they are convinced that, by co-operation between breeders and horticulturists on the one side, and naturalists on the other, numerous valuable opportunities for observation could be utilized which are now lost.

To bring about such co-operation is one of the primary objects of the Committee. The manner in which it could be best effected must necessarily be the subject of special arrangement in each case.[25]

Bateson's draft incorporated many of the ideas put forward by Heape. The statistician Pearson, however, doubted the value of the newly constituted committee. He warned Galton that if it extended into an "omnium gatherum" of various schools of biological thought, it would achieve nothing further for statistical inquiries into the measurable characters of plants and animals. Galton wrote to Pearson the day after the extended subcommittee was appointed to justify it and seek his cooperation:

My dear Professor K. Pearson,

You will not, I am sure, doubt that I fully share the view that the future of biology lies mainly in the exact treatment of homogeneous statistical material. The first thing is to get it. Now the Sub-Committee seems to me better adapted than perhaps any other collection of men that could be named, to do this. They represent between them the departments of mammals, birds, fishes and insects. They know the conditions of rearing and the existing workers, and they have the confidence of the latter. I have already a considerable list of suggested experiments such as would be statistically serviceable. The details of each would be of course a serious problem, so as to be arranged that neither sterility nor disease shall interfere with it, and, again, such that will lead to no ambiguous results. After Tuesday's meeting of the Committee it will be more easy than it is now to anticipate, but at present I am in high hopes that we shall ultimately succeed in the really important task of controlling in a useful sense, a vast amount of existing work that is wasted for want of scientific sympathy, criticism and encouragement. It must always be borne in mind that we are dealing with human workers, who have their own ideas which must be respected and humoured, if we are to gain their cordial co-operation. We have, to speak rather grandly, statesmanship problems to deal with. I trust we shall often have occasion to consult with you as to the best of alternative plans. Just now, we must busy ourselves in finding out lines of least resistance in pushing forward our nascent work.

Very faithfully yours, Francis Galton[26]

This letter too contains many of the views expressed by Heape in his letter to Galton when he accepted the invitation to join the committee.

Unfortunately Galton's hopes were not to last. The changes led to a lack of cohesion of the membership instead of quelling the conflict between Weldon and Bateson. At a meeting on 25 January, 1900, Galton, Weldon, Dyer, Meldola and Pearson resigned, and Bateson was elected the new secretary.[27] Much later, in a letter dated 6 July, 1906, Galton explained his disappointment:

My dear Karl Pearson,

… The work of the Committee was a great disappointment to me. For one thing, I had hoped that it would be sufficiently authoritative, or rather that its weight would suffice to weld numerous bodies that have gardens or menageries into common action, to allow some plots or cages, etc. for research. The Clifton Zool. were prepared to do this, but Thiselton-Dyer said that even he could not depend on the gardeners at Kew to carry out any experiment accurately, so the plan fell through. I knew that the Zool. were untrustworthy helpers—I mean the keepers.

The Cttee talked more than worked, and Z. [Bateson] was very boring, writing very long letters to me and always adverse to compromise. V. [?], who he brought in as an Associate, was to my mind, distinctly objectionable in using the name of the Cttee when he had received no sanction to do so. On the whole, the Cttee seemed to be doing so little and working with so much friction that I did not care to be longer connected with it, so I resigned. Weldon did so too, guided by much the same motives …

Ever yours, Francis Galton[28]

Foster wondered if the Evolution Committee should continue to exist after these resignations and asked Bateson to justify its continuance. Bateson talked to Heape, who reacted strongly and wrote back to Bateson on 1 February:

Dear Bateson,

I have been thinking of our conversation about the Evolution Committee and Foster's request for a letter. It seems to me that the course we are asked to take is a most unusual one. We are in point of fact appointed to serve for 12 months, and in spite of the fact we are requested to show cause why we should exist. I do not hesitate to say that were I in your place I should refuse to reply to the question unless it was made officially.

Yours ever, Walter Heape[29]

Bateson replied diplomatically to Foster:

We all very generally regret Galton withdrawing his name from the Committee, but I am not alone in feeling that so long as he acted as Chairman progress was almost impossible. The loss of the other members does not affect us in any way. I have no doubt that Goldman who has generally attended our meetings will be willing to become Chairman.

Two days later, Heape approved of Bateson's response.[30] The Committee was not dissolved and continued to exist until 1909 with Frederick Goldman in the chair and Bateson as secretary. Most of its support was given to Bateson and his colleagues for studying Mendelian genetics and discontinuous variation, for which they collectively produced five reports.[31] Further support for the animal breeding research initiated by Heape was not forthcoming.

This period was the dawn of modern genetics when Hugo de Vries in Holland, Carl Correns in Germany and Eric Tschermak in Austria independently discovered an unknown paper by the monk Gregor Mendel.[32] When Bateson read de Vries's account of Mendel's experiments he immediately grasped its significance and became a leading disciple, suggesting that the new subject should be called genetics. After his resignation, Weldon continued to challenge the Mendelian explanation for inheritance,[33] prompting a vitriolic response from Bateson at the end of the preface to the book *Mendel's Principles of Heredity*:

Mr. Galton suggested that the new scientific firm (the journal Biometrika) should have a mathematician and a biologist as partners, and—soundest advice—a logician retained as consultant. Biologist surely must one partner be, but it will never do to have him sleeping. In many well-regulated occupations there are persons known as "knockers-up" whose thankless task is to rouse others from their slumber, and tell them work-time is come around again. That part I am venturing to play this morning, and if I have knocked a trifle loud, it is because there is need.[34]

Heape approved of Bateson's promotion of Mendelian genetics, since in a letter to Bateson in 1902 he wrote:

Dear Bateson,

Many thanks to you for your "Report" and for the Book. I congratulate you, they are big strides in the right direction. As for your preface, well I take it, it is a declaration of war! And I am with you to the best of my abilities.

In the role of "knocker-up" I am not quite sure you would receive unstinted praise or continuous support from clients, but as a knocker-down I venture to think you will have a lot of backers and amongst them is—

Yours ever, Walter Heape[35]

Heape recognized the potential value of Mendelism to the breeding industry, which he declared in his book *The Breeding Industry: Its Value to the Country and its Needs* (1906).[36]

Although Galton's original aims were never achieved, the disputes that led to the fracture of the Evolution Committee fostered the maturation of two new disciplines, genetics, pioneered by Bateson, and biometrics, pioneered by Pearson and Weldon. Heape remained a member of the committee until it was finally dissolved, presumably hoping there would be support for animal breeding experiments, but he received no further grants.[37]

9

ANIMAL BREEDING

HEAPE WASTED no time after his appointment to a sub-committee with Francis Galton to demonstrate how the Evolution Committee could support research on animal breeding. He pursued these new responsibilities with such energy and enthusiasm that it soon led to their squabbling in an exchange of letters. The details in each letter and in Galton's personal notes reveal much about the character and professionalism of the two men.

One of the first things Heape considered was the study of sheep breeding in the United Kingdom, and on 27 March, 1897, he informed Galton that he would shortly visit a breeder in Essex to work out a protocol to study barrenness.[1] Afterwards he wanted the Royal Agricultural Society to print it for sending out to ask selected flock-masters for their assistance. By 26 May he was reporting back to Galton:

An enquiry regarding barrenness in ewes has been set on foot. The Roy. Agricult. Soc. has undertaken to print and circulate a schedule of questions and in the course of the next six months I hope to receive some replies. I then propose to visit such of my correspondents who show interest and intelligence, and when that is done, to report to you. With regard to the sum of money at the disposal of the Committee, the only use I should have for the money would be to supply funds for travelling expenses.[2]

A copy of the proposed cover letter to the flock-masters signed by the secretary of the Royal Agricultural Society, Sir Ernest Clarke, was also sent to Galton in June:

> *Dear Sir,*
>
> *The co-operation of the Royal Agricultural Society has been sought by a Committee of the Royal Society in an enquiry now being made upon the question of sterility in animals, and it is proposed as a first step, to make an investigation as to the causes and extent of barrenness amongst sheep.*
>
> *The collection of the necessary information on this point has been entrusted by the Royal Society to Mr. Walter Heape, M.A., of Heyroun, Chaucer Road, Cambridge, and the Royal Agricultural Society will be obliged if you will favour Mr. Heape with the results of your own experience on such of the matters referred to in the accompanying Schedule as are within your knowledge.*
>
> *Duplicate forms are enclosed in the hope that you may be willing to hand them to other flock masters in your district, whose experience will be likely to be of value for the purposes of the investigation.*
>
> *Thanking you in anticipation for any information with which you may favour Mr. Heape (to whom the schedule should be returned, and any further correspondence addressed).*
>
> *I am, yours faithfully, Ernest Clarke*

Galton was displeased because he was not consulted about the circular and, more seriously, he disagreed with some of the content. He drafted a strongly worded letter to Heape, but did not send it because it could have harmed the cordial relationship between them. Instead he wrote:

> *Dear Mr. Heape,*
>
> *Late last night I received copies of the circular about to be distributed which as you ~~mention~~ say in the accompanying letter ~~you had~~ was drawn up after conference with several practical breeders & with Mr. Ernest Clarke. So far as the body of the circular is concerned, ~~I have no doubt that it is quite~~ it*

seems to have been carefully considered and appropriate & I quite agree to it with pleasure.

But as regards the ~~first page~~ preamble, it is quite another matter. You are there represented as ~~having been~~ entrusted by "The Royal Society" to collect certain data. ~~which~~ This status you assuredly do not possess, neither did the Evolution Cttee so far transgress their own powers as to ~~give it to you on their own responsibility~~ bestow it with the certainty of deserving and the probability of incurring grave censure from the Council for doing so.

~~All they did was~~ They did no more than to appoint a Sub-Cttee consisting of yourself and myself, to collect the data, with the understanding that you should be the working part and that I should be chiefly responsible for seeing that the action of the Sub-Cttee harmonised with the general wishes of the Cttee.

In the present case, you have however acted entirely on [by yourself] your own responsibility without ~~giving me any information whatever as to what you have been doing in the matter, with~~ consulting with me in any way. The result is that I must disavow all share in the responsibility and leave you to get out of the extremely awkward irregularity as you best can.

The circular must not go forth ~~in its present state~~ with the objectionable words uncorrected. Neither do I think the earlier part of the preamble, correct.

I have altered both in the enclosed copy.

I am sure that the Cttee as a whole, will disavow your action. You would do well if in any doubt to consult with a Cambridge member of our Cttee who is a member of the R. Soc. Council, as Mr. F. Darwin or prof. M. Foster showing them at the same time this letter & my correction to the circular.

Pray let me hear in reply with as little delay as possible.

Faithfully yours, ~~Francis Galton~~[3]

When Heape visited Galton two days later a heated argument took place, followed by an exchange of letters in which both strong-willed men appear to have overreacted. Galton's notes summarize his memory of the meeting:

First he asked to see his own letter, wh. I showed him. He did not appreciate the degree of irregularity. He had been to the R. Agr. S. on his way, and told me that the circulars were not printed off and there was plenty of time to alter. Also that he had only glanced at the copies for a few minutes before sending them me. He had much family trouble (a father-in-law's illness & death). He also spoke of intending to send me a proof 3 weeks ago, but was not sure that he did. Altogether the explanation seemed wanting in frankness, precision and good taste. Then he said that even if he had acted as I had supposed he did not think my letter was justified. I at once insisted that it was & that if there were any chance of such a proceeding hereafter, I could not content to serve with him on the Sub-Cttee. He was evidently very angry & contained himself with difficulty saying he would consider whether or no he would continue to act. He left the corrected paper with me as I had said the time had been insufficient for me to study it ... [words missing] phrases would meet this small but important objection, & that I should have liked to consult Weldon who as Sec ought to know what was going on. The next day was Jubilee & the day after I returned the corrections with notes of explanation posted on the side of them, such as Mr. Clarke cd see.[4]

Upset by Galton's complaints, Heape brooded over the interview for several days until he wrote again on 29 June:

With reference to our conversation some days ago, I understand you to say that the schedule of sterility in sheep had evidently been hatching for some time, that you knew nothing about it, and the whole proceeding was very irregular and that you were bound to add that if it occurred again you would feel obliged to resign the chairmanship of the committee.

I gather from these remarks that you feel I have, for some reason or another, attempted to do what I had no right to attempt. If I have misunderstood you I beg you to correct me. I am anxious clearly to understand what it is you complain of, and I do not understand now.[5]

Galton replied the following day with a sheet of explanatory notes about his objections:

Dear Mr. Heape,

Your letter ~~received this morning~~ dated yesterday does not rightly construe my attitude, which was this. I had received from you 3 copies of a luxuriously printed ~~on good paper~~ circular that did not bear the word "for correction" or proof ~~or any equivalent to it but which were clearly~~ and therefore was apparently intended for immediate circulation, a view that seemed was confirmed by your accompanying letter from which it appeared that the content of the circular had been discussed between yourself & Mr. Clarke for some time.

~~In Mr. Clarke's letter were the unfortunate statements that I have already pointed out which you made no remark whatever about in the accompanying letter to me. Everything therefore concurred to show that you had by yourself, in connection with Mr. Clarke sent the letter to press, and were about to circulate it without having let me, as a joint member of the sub-ettee with yourself know anything on the matter.~~

Your verbal explanation was that ~~I had drawn a false conclusion, that~~ the circular was really a draft open to correction revision, and again that you had sent the 3 copies to me without properly reading them. I thought the explanation was made in a way rather deficient in assurance and clearness, still I frankly accepted it and was withdrawing my remarks when you ~~Of course I withdrew my objections, but you immediately reopened~~ put the matter in a new aspect by saying that even if you had ~~done~~ acted as I supposed, ~~it did not in your opinion~~ you did not see the great irregularity or that it would have justified my writing ~~to you~~ as I ~~had done~~ did. ~~That you did not.~~ I protested strongly against that view & added that if there was any likelihood of action in the sense that I deprecated, I could not continue to serve with you on the sub-committee.

Yours faithfully. Francis Galton[6]

The attached notes were as follows:

The sentence conveys the idea that the inquiry of the Cttee is limited to the one specified investigation. This inference should be avoided because sterility in domestic animals (however ~~excellent~~ good a subject for a beginning) is hardly a typical and central instance of their province of inquiry. On the contrary it is one that may seem to many, as to myself, to be very close to ~~the~~ its limits.

Many alternative phrases would meet this small but important objection,
"... now being made upon questions of great ~~interest~~ important to breeders of
stock, and it is proposed ..."

Mr. Heape is not entrusted by the Royal Society to collect information.
The ~~statement in the draft letter~~ sentence as it stands puts him in an altogether
false position & would give rise to serious protests from many quarters and
disavowals, ~~and would place the Cttee and most particularly myself as a joint~~
~~member of this Sub-Cttee into serious difficulties with the Council and the~~
~~Society that they would have to take steps of disavowal.~~ The substitute of the
word "them" (i.e. the Cttee) for the phrase "Royal Society" would remove the
difficulty.[7]

Heape still wanted to have the last word since he wrote
again to Galton on 4 July claiming that the whole affair was a
misunderstanding on his part:

Dear Mr. Galton,

I have been away from home and unable until now to reply to your letter
of June 30. I am glad to learn from it that you frankly accepted my explana-
tion and that you were prepared to withdraw your remarks; I certainly did not
understand you were prepared to do so, for, after I had given you the
explanation, you said that if it occurred <u>again</u> you would be obliged to resign
the chairmanship of the committee. I think perhaps the explanation of the
whole matter may probably be found in the fact that I failed to understand at
our interview that you supposed I had designedly attempted to do what I had
no right to attempt.

This is not the case. I had no intention whatsoever of issuing the circular
without submitting it to you; if I had done so I should have done wrong, but as
it was not so (I thought I had clearly expressed as much, and do not know in
what way the explanation was deficient in assurance and clearness), I did not
understand why you made the remark quoted above and felt you were not
justified in making it.

There is another point in your letter which requires mention, namely that
I put a new aspect upon the matter by saying that even if I had acted as
supposed I did not see the great irregularity, or that it would have justified you

in writing as you did. I have not a clear remembrance of making the remark nor of what led up to it, though I do not doubt you have quoted me correctly; I would merely point out that the remark referred to my supposed action, and, as I have already pointed out, I did not at the time fully understand what you supposed I had done.

If, as I gather from your letter you rightly interpreted my remark as upholding the view that I was justified in issuing the circular without first submitting it to you, then I was undoubtedly wrong in making it; I can only say that I find it hard to believe the remark was made in such connection for I do not uphold that view.

With regard to the circular itself I see by your "Notes in explanation", which accompany the corrected copy, that you think the enquiry is one which lies very close to the limits of the province of enquiry of the committee of the Royal Society. I discussed with you the advisability of making this enquiry some time ago, in fact it was one of the first propositions I made, and I understood you fully agreed with me, if however you have changed your views I am quite willing to withdraw the schedule altogether.

Yours faithfully, Walter Heape[8]

Fortunately Galton and Heape agreed to set their differences aside so the work could continue. Galton's changes were made to the circular, which was signed by Ernest Clarke on 12 July for circulation to breeders.

Clarke's circular must have generated favorable responses from breeders because a motion thanking him for assistance with the project was passed at a meeting of the Evolution Committee on 16 November. At that meeting Heape submitted the following proposal:

The Subcommittee appointed for the purpose of conferring with breeders make application for the sum of £50 to assist in providing travelling expenses necessary in order that personal visits should be made to breeders in order to consult with them regarding problems to be investigated and the best methods of carrying out such investigations, for small gratuities to herdsmen, and for clerical assistance from time to time.[9]

The application was granted and work proceeded with alacrity for, at a meeting of the committee only seven months later on 24 June 1898, Heape reported progress with an outline of a forthcoming paper. He was then granted another £50. The following year, he published a paper which summarized the database that had been collected with some descriptive statistics, and explaining the purpose of the study:

> ... for the purpose of finding out the amount of abortion and barrenness which flockmasters on the average experience, and at the same time of discovering the relative liability to loss from these causes in different breeds of sheep, and their relative fertility.[10]

On 20 April, 1899, a communication was given before the Royal Society entitled "Note on the fertility of different breeds of sheep, with remarks on the prevalence of abortion and barrenness therein."[11] It was not introduced by Galton but by Weldon as secretary of the Evolution Committee.

The project had begun with a questionnaire sent by Sir Ernest Clarke to sheep breeders requesting feedback to a list of questions, including the ages of their animals, size of breeding flocks, proportions of rams and ewes, incidence of barrenness, food supplements at specific times of year, physical condition during the breeding season, and methods of management. The breeders were also asked for their opinions in writing or at interview about the factors commonly supposed to affect fertility, abortion and barrenness in ewes.

Heape recognized the risk of bias if he chose the breeders to be questioned so he let Ernest Clarke make the selection. Of 413 responders, 397 provided useful information for a total of 122,673 animals and 18 pure breeds during the years 1896-7. There were sufficient numbers for separate analysis of eight breeds—Suffolk, Kent, Southdown, Hampshire, Oxford Down, Dorset Horn, Shropshire and Lincoln—and data from the remaining breeds were pooled. Heape was worried that breeders often provided incomplete information because stillbirths and perinatal deaths were not always recorded. Hence the estimated fertility of ewes based on the ratio of the total of lambs born to the number of ewes that delivered was unreliable, and instead the ratio of twins to ewes that delivered was used.

When analyzed statistically the frequencies of ewes that aborted or failed to conceive were fairly constant within breeds but varied between them. Variations in fertility were sufficiently marked to be characteristic of the breed: Suffolks and Hampshires seldom aborted or were barren whereas Lincolns suffered heavily from both causes. The analyses further suggested that five factors of decreasing order of importance affected the fertility of ewes: physical condition at the time of mating, flushing before mating and during pregnancy, district where sheep were raised, season when mating occurred, and age. The practice of "flushing" advances breeding condition by feeding ewes with additional food, such as turnips, oats, and maize. Heape was particularly impressed with the benefits of boosting nutrition. For experienced breeders these findings were unsurprising, but Heape's analysis placed the subject on a quantitative and therefore more reliable basis, which was an objective of the Evolution Committee and prompted Francis Marshall a few years later to study the relationship between nutrition and fertility in sheep.

It was probably the first planned survey of a farm animal aimed at revealing the key factors affecting fertility. At the time, many statisticians still believed that surveys were unreliable and could not replace the census methods that required complete enumerations. The usual way of recording fertility in domestic animals was to use data from breed stud or flock books, and only in the last decade of the 19th century was attention turning to designing surveys in which representative sampling was introduced to minimize selection bias, a procedure introduced by the Norwegian statistician Anders Kaier.[12] Perhaps Heape and Clarke took advice from Pearson or other statisticians, but unfortunately Heape does not describe in his paper how Clarke selected breeders for the study.

This work attracted attention from Francis Marshall who was becoming well known for his pioneering work on the physiology of the sexual cycle of sheep. He applied Heape's methods for surveying ovine fertility with the help of the Highland and Agricultural Society of Scotland and obtained very similar results.[13] Marshall summarized Heape's contributions in detail in the first edition of his book *The Physiology of Reproduction* (1910)[14] and dedicated it to Heape (later editions are still important reference sources in the field).

Although Heape's work was funded through the Evolution Committee's program, its place seems marginal at first sight to the stated goals of the committee. It did, however, provide background knowledge for understanding the genetics and regulation of reproduction, and his list of key factors affecting the inheritance of fertility was confirmed by studies of data from the *American Flockbook* for the Southdown breed.[15]

On 15 December, 1904, ten Fellows including three who were also members of the Evolution Committee (Frederick Godman, William Bateman and James Ewart) honored Heape by nominating him a Fellow of the Royal Society of London. Others supporting his candidature were Alfred Newton, W. Weldon,

Joseph Lister (Secretary of the Royal Society) and Sir William Herdman (marine biologist). Not everyone is elected in the year of their nomination, and Heape had to wait until 1907 to join the chosen list.

He entered the field of public policy in 1906 when he wrote a book entitled *The Breeding Industry: Its Value to the Country and its Needs*.[16] It seems to have been written in haste, more like a first draft and in a contentious style. Nevertheless, it succeeded in drawing attention to the Cinderella status of the breeding industry in British agriculture at the beginning of the 20th century.

Between 1875 and 1900 the farming industry suffered a severe depression. Visitors to the English countryside before the depression would have seen productive fields of grain crops, but the scene had changed by the end of the century. Instead of the golden wheat of August, many fields were fallow where farms were abandoned and looked derelict. The depression arose from the competition of cheaper foodstuffs from overseas, especially wheat and meat from the United States of America.[17] Heape wrote in his book that despite this turndown Britain still had a valuable asset in its many breeds of livestock, and they could be improved by applying science to animal breeding. From a detailed analysis of data from several sources he estimated that about £450,000,000 was invested in livestock in the country, apart from the value attached to housing, equipment and husbandry for farm animals. He proposed the industry needed support from research grants administered by the Ministry of Agriculture, a radical idea at the time. A similar economic analysis was done ten years later for the American animal production industry by Raymond Pearl, an eminent biometrician and demographer who had studied under Karl Pearson and worked on this problem early in his career at the Maine

Agricultural Experimental Station in Orono. His results agreed so closely with those of Heape nearly a decade before that he ended his paper with a verbatim quotation from Heape's book on the breeding industry:

> We have here an industry of enormous importance to the country, and one which merits far more attention than has ever yet been accorded to it; an industry to which, it must be remembered, "Science has never yet been applied."[18]

In the year that Heape's book was published, a prominent plant breeder at Cambridge and student of Mendelism, H. R. Biffin, lent support to his belief that science could benefit animal breeding, particularly through genetics.[19]

Over a long period highly desirable breeds of domestic animals had emerged by selective breeding on British farms, but the choice of desirable characteristics, such as lean meat and milk, was more of an art than science. Only occasionally were more scientific and quantitative methods used, such as breeding thoroughbred horses for performance on the racecourse. By 1910 there were 17 distinct British breeds and varieties of horses, 13 of beef cattle, 7 of dairy cattle, 34 of sheep and 8 of swine produced from unsupervised breeding practices over many, many years.[19] Wealthy breeders owned most of the valuable stock while most farmers could only afford animals of inferior constitution. Several of the finest breeds were in great demand in the United States, Argentina, Australia and New Zealand. The United States imported large numbers of pedigreed bulls in the late 19th century at the time the Great Plains were settled. The most popular was the Hereford, and 4,000 were imported between 1889 and 1894. The activity of American buyers in Herefordshire was feverish:

The early 1880s became known as the "Yankee Boom" in Herefordshire as American buyers and their agents trawled the top breeding farms and bid recklessly at sales.[20]

Heape was concerned about the loss of so many valuable pedigreed animals, which were exported in numbers so great that some breeds were at risk of dying out in their country of origin. He argued for scientific applications wherever possible for conserving, improving and producing livestock of all types. There is still a market for exporting prime genetic stock, and two techniques that Heape helped pioneer — artificial insemination and embryo transfer — have replaced the inhumane conditions in which animals were at one time transported.

He noted that by the end of the 19th century the British population was consuming more milk products and foresaw a large expansion of the dairy industry, for which he advocated scientific methods for breeding cows yielding higher volumes of milk of better quality. This vision was eventually realized through the adoption of artificial insemination of cattle, which was started by Arthur Walton and John Hammond in Cambridge in the 1930s.

Agricultural science had really meant agricultural chemistry since most research was on the chemical and physical properties of soils and their enrichment with fertilizers. That work began at the now famous Rothamsted Experimental Station, which was founded in 1843 by the entrepreneurial scientist John Lawes whose factory was the first to manufacture fertilizer. He set up experimental plots on his estate to compare different types of fertilizer on crop yields, but it took about 60 years until Rothamsted received state support and meantime had to rely on funds from non-governmental sources and help from the Royal Agricultural Society.[21]

Little planned research was done on animal breeding because it was considered peripheral to agricultural science, though it had benefitted marginally from basic research on animal physiology. Most research projects were private enterprises. For example, James Cossar Ewart of the University of Edinburgh started to study reproduction in horses and sheep from 1895 on his own experimental farm at Penycuik, Midlothian, supported by money from Lord Carmichael of Stirling. It was at this time that Ewart was working on telegony (see Chapter 4). Another example is Heape's work on sheep breeding funded by the Royal Society through the Evolution Committee. While working at the University of Edinburgh, Francis Marshall managed his research from 1900 with support from several sources: sheep were studied on Ewart's farm, ferrets through an endowment by Lord Carmichael at the Department of Physiology, and dogs by grants from the Government Grants Committee of the Royal Society, the Moray Fund of the University of Edinburgh and the Carnegie Trust for the Universities of Scotland.[22] Ewart, Schäfer and Marshall submitted a joint application to the Royal Society of Edinburgh on 7 March, 1904, with letters of support from Bateson and Heape[23] to establish a biological research institute in Edinburgh, but it was unsuccessful. In October, 1910, Heape wrote a pessimistic letter to Ewart about the difficulty of raising money from private sources:

> For the appeal, it is very difficult to get money. I have tried it over and over again with very poor success—but your work should appeal to big breeders with lots of money and I think you ought to get all you want from them.
>
> I will do anything I can for you and with pleasure, but I am afraid you should not count on anything. All the same, one does come across men who will give freely, they have not shown themselves desperately keen to help me, but they might help you, and if so I'll do my best for you to be sure.[24]

A major change of policy was taking place at that time. At the instigation of the Chancellor of the Exchequer, Lloyd George, an Act was passed by the British Parliament in 1909 for providing financial support for research that promised to help economic development in the country, and particularly the languishing agriculture industry. Seven very general areas were named, including re-afforestation, livestock improvement, marketing cooperation for farm products, experimental farms, and equipment for agricultural instruction. The Act established a Development Commission to oversee the projects,[25] and on 27 April, 1910, a list of Commissioners' names was announced in Parliament, among them was Alfred Daniel Hall, then director of the Rothamsted Experimental Station. Hall's appointment was important because it enabled a highly experienced and well regarded agricultural scientist to influence the decisions of non-scientific commissioners.[26] The funds were administered using the following formula: (1) No money was provided for existing commitments, (2) Capital expenditure was matched pound for pound by recipient institutions, (3) Institutions were to be expanded and new ones established close to or part of an agricultural college or university, and provide security of employment and thus careers for scientific specialists, and (4) Scholarships were to be awarded to attract talented young men into agricultural research.

The commissioners planned for twelve research areas, mostly crop-related. Support for animal breeding through the formation of two research institutes was delayed, but in the meantime a small grant was awarded in 1911 for improving light horse breeding. An advisory committee for animal breeding was formed in 1912,[27] and in 1913 Edinburgh University and the East of Scotland College of Agriculture collaborated to form a joint committee on animal breeding that submitted a successful proposal to the Development Commission. With funds from the University, the Board of Agriculture and the Commission, a Department for Research in Animal Breeding was established,[28] but it did not become active until after World War I when Francis Crewe was appointed as director and, later on, the first incumbent of the Buchanan Chair of Animal Genetics. His department was the forerunner of the Institute of Animal Genetics in 1930 which became an internationally recognized center of excellence for animal genetics. But Edinburgh was the only location where the Commission facilitated formation of an animal breeding research center. This relatively low level of support contrasted noticeably with the much greater support for animal nutrition that was funded immediately at Cambridge and subsequently at the University of Aberdeen. Perhaps the commissioners thought that work on animal nutrition would yield benefits more quickly than animal breeding, as soil research had for growing crops.

The impact of Heape's book *The Breeding Industry* on government funding of animal breeding is hard to measure, but it received two reviews. It is not surprising that Marshall's was positive,[29] and the *Saturday Review* was on the whole sympathetic to Heape's criticisms of current practices, though it doubted that his arguments would have much sway over funding policy:

> ... it will be long before Mr. Heape or anyone else persuades our politicians that to invest boldly on the advancement of agricultural knowledge would result in a good deal of saving elsewhere in the near future. How many votes would such a policy be worth, even among the farmers themselves?[30]

The Development Commission began to provide more support from 1911, but not until twenty years later was a large-scale commitment made by the founding of the Agricultural Research Council.[31] Marshall and Hammond wrote a review in 1946, entitled "The science of animal breeding in Britain" in which they summarized the life's work of five pioneers in animal breeding, namely Francis Galton, Cossar Ewart, William Bateson, F.A.E. Crew and Walter Heape.[32] Heape's contribution was summarized years later in 1954 by Harvey:

> He was, indeed, a doubly prophetic figure. He both foretold many things that came to pass and foreshadowed the growing part which science in its various manifestations was to play in the agricultural system of the twentieth century.[33]

10

BUSINESS REVISITED: THE NEW ELKHORN MINING COMPANY

WALTER HEAPE returned to the world of business when he was elected a director of the New Elkhorn Mining Company on 4 May, 1898. Along with several family members, he had invested in the mine in Leadville, Colorado, a center of large scale mining operations in the late 19th century. In its heyday the town enjoyed enough prosperity to sport its own opera house and invite celebrities such as Oscar Wilde to entertain its citizens.[1] Heape's management role in the company required him to return to the United States after a long interval since his visits on behalf of marine biology and the fishing industry. Later on when the company fell into serious financial difficulties in 1901, he became chairman of the Board and was struggling to save it.

Between 1860 and 1901 at least 518 joint-stock companies were registered in Britain to exploit the mineral wealth of the American West, apart from the Pacific Coast.[2] The Elkhorn Mining Company Ltd. (Montana, U.S.A.) was registered on 4 February, 1890, "for the purpose of acquiring and working the Elkhorn Silver Mines situated in Jefferson County, Montana."[3] It had a capital value of 200,000 shares at £1 each,[4] and by 23 April of the same year 175,007 shares had been purchased by investors, including Heape and his in-laws in the Ruston family.[5] The Board was typical of most British companies of the time, composed of "respectable" men who were members of parliament, military officers and gentlemen, preferably with a title and retired.[6,7]

The Elkhorn mine was very productive for the first six years and contributed significantly to the settlement and betterment of the State of Montana.[8] Ore mined with a value of £652,987 was returning 150 percent to shareholders on their investment, but despite this profitability the directors were warned that the mine had only a few more years of productive life before it would be exhausted, and that they should seek a backup property.[9]

In November, 1895, the directors and their chairman, the Hon. A.G. Brand, MP, were informed by their brokers of other properties becoming available in Leadville, Colorado. As was the custom in those days, they were advertised through an American promoter, Francis N. Collins of New York City who had a large option on them. After receiving strong recommendations, the directors decided to acquire the properties which were geologically characterized as Fitzhugh lode[10] and Kennebec lode[11] from the leased claims in Leadville's California Mining District. There were also about 50 acres of patented lodes available nearby, known as the Ovens Donnelly Group of United States Patented Lodes, representing seven claims which the company bought outright as freehold property. The leased Fitzhugh Mine was located on the east side of Fryer Hill just south of Evans Gulch, and the freehold land was northeast of it on the other side of the gulch. In the previous 15 years the yields of silver-lead ore from adjacent properties in the district had been huge, equivalent to £40 million.[12]

To make the purchase, the Board of Directors liquidated the old company and re-registered it as the New Elkhorn Mining

Company Ltd. on 3 December, 1895.[13,14] The authorized capital was £300,000 in shares of £1 of which 87,500 were in preferred shares and 212,500 in ordinary shares. The preferred shareholders were to take all the profits until remittances reached 100% in all, after which the shares were to rank equally. The preferred shares carried two votes per share compared with only one for ordinary shares until the 100% threshold payment had been reached on preferred shares. On 14 April, 1896, Walter owned 1,000 preferred shares, his father-in-law Joseph Ruston owned 5,000, his brother-in-law Joseph S. Ruston 200 preferred and 8 ordinary shares, and sister-in-law Mary Ruston 25 preferred shares.[15] Thus Walter's family had considerable interest in the new company.

The company took possession of the Leadville properties on 1 January, 1896, with Frank Robbins appointed as its resident agent to direct local operations.[16] During the first three months of operation 1,559 tons of dry ore were extracted from the Fitzhugh mine, which the smelters bought at $40,206. Further exploratory drifts or tunnels connecting shafts were dug, and a new shaft called the Plummer shaft was started on 8 April, 1896.[17,18] The latest machinery was installed for these excavations and by June the shaft had reached a depth of 224 feet. This propitious start would soon come to an end, however, owing to labour disputes that year and two natural disasters—a flood in 1896 and a severe snow storm two years later.

Labour troubles arose from the low wages paid to miners. On 23 May, 1896, representatives of a newly formed union of miners met with mine owners and managers, including Robbins. They asked for an increase from $2.50 to $3.00 per hour, and when the proposal was rejected the union called a strike on 19 June. Almost immediately, the managers drafted an agreement for concerted resistance to the unions' demands. Violence during the prolonged strike led to the calling out of the Colorado militia and enforcement of martial law. When the strike ended after nine months it had failed to achieve its aim.[19]

Flooding was always a major problem at Leadville and continual pumping of water added to operational costs. Where pumping was halted to save money during the strike the mines flooded and filled with sand. This happened at the Fitzhugh Mine, which was still flooded two years later,[20] causing the company to lose a critical source of revenue. Work continued on the Plummer shaft in the freehold properties because it involved higher paid men who were not on strike. By 1 January, 1897, it had reached a depth of 302 feet.

Unfortunately, the continuing financial losses were so serious that on 1 November the company stopped operations and only retained the local agent and watchmen. At the second annual meeting of shareholders in London on 4 May, 1898, Mr. A.F. Wuensch gave an expert report on the prospects for the mines:

> ... taken as a whole the New Elkhorn property at Leadville today presents the position of being a promising prospect property in a very good district; a property that is sufficiently equipped for all practical needs and upon which the greater amount of money required to prove up its value has already been expended. In fact the territory should, in a very short time and with little more expense, be made to disclose paying bodies of ore or their non-existence satisfactorily demonstrated and the venture abandoned.[21]

Afterwards, an article in the *Anglo-Colorado Mining & Milling Gazette* reviewed the state of the New Elkhorn Mining Company as "A Costly Colorado Venture" and concluded that the mines were a questionable investment.[22] When Heape was unanimously voted to a seat on the Board, J.W. Hart, whom he replaced, gave a warm endorsement:

> ... I believe it to be in the best interests of the company that Mr. Heape should be elected on this board. He represents a very large interest, and having regard to the state of my health and other considerations, I think it desirable that I should make way and resign in favour of Mr. Heape. I, therefore, beg to propose that he be elected a director of this company.

However, the chairman warned:

> I can assure you that it is no bed of roses to be a director of a company such as this, which is not earning a profit, but giving a great deal of trouble.

These were the circumstances that Heape found himself in when he joined the Board, but why did he agree to be nominated? He was busy writing papers on reproductive cycles and animal breeding as well as serving on the Evolution Committee.

The larger shareholders must have been alarmed when they were consulted over the advisability of suspending mining operations the previous November. Adjusting for inflation, the shares owned by the entire Ruston family were worth the equivalent of £680,000 in 2012.[23] After Joseph Ruston's death in June 1897 it seems likely that Walter became the guardian of the Ruston investments, and his interest in the company grew accordingly.

Leadville was hit by successive monster snow storms in 1898 that shut the town down from November to May.[24] One hundred and eighty seven inches of snow fell in the first three months of 1898, the most prolonged storm in the district's history, rendering many mines in the Leadville area inoperative for months.

The original Elkhorn Mine in Montana was finally sold early in 1900 and its manager, Mr. Walter Kelley, was transferred to Leadville where he began a detailed inspection to determine whether mining operations should be resumed. His report to the Board on 12 August, 1900, advised against restarting because he estimated it would cost the company £168,000. His reasons were:

(1) The contact [meeting of two different bodies of rock] was without value where cut by the Plummer shaft, and the drill holes were barren of result.

(2) No good mines have been developed in the vicinity of the freehold or east of the leaseholds.

(3) There was little unexplored ground remaining in the Fitzhugh upper contact.

(4) The lower contact developed in the Kennebec was small and low in grade.

(5) The faulting [fracture in the earth's crust with displacement] had resulted in the loss of a large amount of ore on the upper contact, and the extent of the undisturbed ground remaining was largely conjectural.[25]

Heape questioned the recommendation and convinced enough directors that he should consult Kelley in Leadville to achieve five objectives:

(a) A close analysis, together with Mr. Kelley, of the substance of that gentleman's recent report to us, an examination of the evidence he has placed before us, and a criticism of the deductions he has drawn therefrom.

(b) The further collection of evidence bearing upon the actual or possible value of our property, derived from resident financiers, land-owners, mining engineers, mine managers, and underground foremen.

(c) The cost and the best plan to be adopted in exploring the property in case it was decided to do so.

(d) The value of the property and the best means of selling it in case it was decided to abandon it.

(e) The possibilities of leasing the property, or other means of dealing with it, in case it was decided to hold the property and not to work it ourselves.[26]

Heape was putting into practice his belief in the usefulness of personally talking to people on the ground to solve problems, as he had in earlier studies of animal breeding and the fishing industry. He sailed from Liverpool to New York on 15 September, 1900, and returned on 24 November. The transatlantic crossings were on the *Luciana* westbound and the *Umbria* eastbound, two of the most luxurious and fastest passenger ships of the Cunard Line. After reaching New York he had a long train journey via Chicago and Denver, ending with a final stretch on a narrow-gauge railway to Leadville at an elevation of about 10,000 feet. The journey was time-consuming and must have been exhausting.

He presented a detailed report of his month-long visit to the directors after returning to London.[27] He concluded:

(1) So far as the leasehold land is concerned, it seems very doubtful whether there is sufficient probability of finding ore of sufficient value or in sufficient quantity to induce us to undertake further work there.

(2) So far as our freehold land is concerned, we have nothing more than a property of prospective value; there is no actual evidence of the existence of pay ore deposits on that property, and nothing under any circumstances can demonstrate its value except through exploration.

(3) To sell it now is undoubtedly to sacrifice it, and to lease it under satisfactory conditions seems impossible.

(4) But the evidence I have put before you appears to me sufficiently indicative of the possibilities of finding pay ore there; that, taking into consideration the facts of our having a shaft and machinery in a condition fit for immediate work, and a cash balance of over £17,000, which while it is most unsatisfactory for the purpose of distribution, will suffice to enable us to make a very fairly thorough examination of the property, I am of the opinion we should risk this money and undertake the necessary work to prove the value of our property.[28]

The conflicting recommendations of Kelley and Heape split the Board so that at the 4th annual general meeting on 22 December the Chairman, the Hon. A.G. Brand, moved:

That in the opinion of this meeting the necessary steps are taken with a view to placing the company into liquidation.

Brand was opposed to Heape's views from the beginning and thought the visit to Leadville unnecessary. Referring to Heape's report he commented:

I should like to say with regard to Mr. Heape's report that the Board is indebted to him for the great care and industry he has shown in drawing up that report; but I cannot help saying this, that I would much rather have a mining engineer's report than one from a gentleman, however able, who has not been brought up to that line of business.

Heape then read an amendment he intended to move:

That it is the opinion of this meeting that the further development of the Leadville property be prosecuted with the funds of the company available for that purpose.

Heape responded to Brand by explaining:

I went out to Leadville not as a mining expert in any sense, but to find out the opinion of the men there apart from our representative, Mr. Kelley, who is not familiar with the Leadville deposits. I found that the experts of Leadville are not agreed—are opposed, I should say—to Mr. Kelley's report.

Then followed a detailed technical summary of his report with a cautionary note:

The shareholders had paid a large sum for a property they had practically never explored. They had erected machinery but had not explored the ground to any great extent. They had touched two or three contacts but had not drifted along any of them. In other words, they had spent a large sum for working a mine, but had done nothing to prove whether or not they had a mine. Of course, mining in Leadville was a gamble, and no one could tell where to find ore. In order to find it they must seek for it. That there were indications of the probable existence of ore bodies was the belief of miners familiar with the conditions prevailing in the Leadville district. The evidence they had was sufficient to satisfy them their property was of good prospective value. No one could guarantee they would find silver there, but the chances of doing so made it worth their while looking for it.

Heape concluded:

It comes to this, you run the risk of losing an amount of cash which, if the company liquidates, will yield you—the Chairman says 4s—but I should say 3s in the £ [i.e. 15% of the original

161

investment]; so far as I am personally concerned, and I hold 1,000 shares in this company, it is a risk I will willingly run. I am not content for the sake of 3s in the £ to sacrifice a property of such prospective value as this appears to me to be, and I am not willing to sell that property now at a ridiculously low figure, probably one-fifteenth or one-twentieth of what it has cost you, with the prospect of seeing someone else get my money out of it. I beg to propose the amendment I have already read.

The amendment was seconded by R.S. MacLaren and passed by a vote of 12 to 8, thus saving the mines from liquidation. The decision of the directors to continue exploring the mine attracted several notices in the press, although it is odd that the *Denver Times* attributed the decision to Kelley and not Heape.[29] Perhaps the reporter confused Walter Kelley with Walter Heape. Following the adoption of Heape's amendment the chairman resigned and MacLaren assumed the role according to a legal document signed on February 1901 when Kelley was appointed as mine agent.[30] MacLaren was, however, soon replaced by Heape.

One of the first actions of the new Board was the appointment of Major Bohn as a consultant engineer to assist Kelley because he had deep experience of the geology in the Leadville area. By April 1901 there were new plans for the Plummer shaft. A pump to deliver 1,000 gallons of water per minute would be installed, drifts would be extended at 340 and 455 feet to explore for ore, and one of the most elaborate rigs ever seen at Leadville was ordered.[31] By July work was well underway.[32] Water was pumped from the mine at a rate of 720,000 gallons per day and the search for ore radiated in several directions from the main shaft, but no profitable ore was ever found. The directors in London were discouraged and asked Heape to revisit Leadville. He sailed again for the USA on 19 October and returned from

Leadville on 8 December, reporting his findings at the next annual general meeting after his return:

> ... and, on my arrival in Leadville, found that ... a streak of ore had been found which promised better than we had yet seen ... Major Bohn, who inspected the mine in my presence, told me that such indications of ore that we had he would consider sufficient to justify a belief in the near approximation of an ore body in any other part of the camp, and amply sufficient to encourage further development of our property ... Since November 20 moreover, further work has been done; and when I left Leadville ... the indications were still more favourable.[33]

A letter from Walter Kelley was also read at the meeting:

> *If the Company was in possession of sufficient funds, he would unhesitatingly urge a continuance of the work, believing that the present development may be considered favourable.*

A decision about the future of the company was not made at that meeting because the directors were not sure of the best course, but in closing the meeting Heape declared:

> I will undertake that your directors shall declare their policy on or before Feb. 28—in all probability sooner; but I put that as a limit.

An Extraordinary General Meeting was called on 28 January, 1902, when it was decided that the news from Leadville was sufficiently favorable to justify raising more money to continue to search for ore. After a debate about how the money should be raised it was decided to offer the shareholders the option to subscribe £15,000 without delay to continue exploring for new seams. Towards the end of February 1902, however, the subscriptions were insufficient and the Board had no alternative but to close the mine down.[34] All company assets were sold, with the exception of the freehold property.

But the collapse of the company under Heape's leadership was not used to bring shame on him. Rather he was praised by fellow directors for his dogged efforts and at the 5th Annual General Meeting in 1901 W. Lindsay conveyed compliments on behalf of the other directors:

> I need hardly tell the shareholders that under the circumstances they could not have a better chairman than Mr. Walter Heape. He has taken the trouble to go again to Leadville, and he is as well acquainted with the mine as anyone can possibly be. He has a large personal interest and a strong fiduciary interest in this concern, and, therefore, he is marked out as the best man, under the present circumstances, to be Chairman, and in hoping that I shall have the opportunity of proposing him as Chairman hereafter, I beg now to propose that he be re-elected a Director of the Company.[35]

And J.G. Smith who seconded his nomination added:

> I beg to second the proposition. As a considerable holder of priority shares, I feel that my interest in the company is safeguarded while Mr. Heape is in the lead.

The London Stock Exchange Year Book listed the company chairman as Walter Heape until 1912 and that it was wound up in 1913. On 18 February, 1918, a civil suit was filed by Lake County with the District Court of the Fifth Judicial District of Colorado for serving on the defunct company, but since there was no response the freehold property passed by default to the plaintiff.[36]

Heape should not be blamed for the decision of the company to unknowingly buy a lemon, even if its failure looked inevitable in hindsight. Brand, the first chairman, wanted to liquidate the company much earlier and salvage at least a small part of the original investment. Heape and his supporters felt that holding on was a risk worth taking for a relatively small further investment to make a more thorough exploration of the freehold property, which had only been explored superficially. Unfortunately, insufficient high quality ore was found by the time the available money was spent.

Heape must have spent a great deal of time on this business venture, which probably interfered with his biological research. There was a gap in his scientific publications from 1900 when he became actively involved in running the company until 1905. During those years he did little scientific work in Cambridge, although he maintained a relationship with Trinity College. In 1904 he sold *Heyroun*, the house he built in Cambridge, and moved to the coastal town of Southwold,[37] Suffolk in East Anglia where he lived comfortably, maintaining a household with a cook and at least one maid, like many upper class families.[38,39]

11

SEX DETERMINATION

THE DISSOLUTION of the New Elkhorn Mining Company must have freed up a lot of time for Walter Heape to return to scientific work. Sex determination attracted his attention because of the potential economic value of a bias to females in dairy cattle, for example, and the opposite bias in human societies which was originally for practical reasons of survival and persists today for cultural motives.[1,2]

Since the process of sex determination is not uniform throughout the animal kingdom, the state of knowledge was puzzling and confusing in Heape's day, with Hippocrates' authority still swaying belief.[3] The ancient error that male offspring arise from the right ovary and females from the left ovary was eventually swept aside by experimental removal of one ovary from mice and rats, which had no effect on the sex ratio at birth.[4] There was also the strange occurrence of hermaphrodites in many invertebrate and plant species in which individuals possess both male and female organs. When a chicken loses its only ovary it may become a "crowing hen" with wattles like a rooster, which was a superstitious object in the Middle Ages that was often burned alive.[5] The whole subject was so obscure that Thomas Hunt Morgan of Columbia University and founder of Drosophila genetics wrote in 1906:

> There are few biological questions that appeal more directly to the human race than whether the sex of the child can be determined by the external conditions under which the parents live, or whether the conditions are internal and, therefore, beyond the power of control. This problem has been examined by the statistician, argued by philosophers, discussed by naturalists and exploited by the quack. Theories of sex determination have flourished like weeds, and, while perennial, are apt to be like their prototypes, short-lived. The history of these theories is, nevertheless, full of interest and not without significance.[6]

Jane Maienschein of Arizona State University, a leading historian of science, has suggested that currently accepted theories of sex determination emerged from interactions between three different areas that developed independently.[7] The first was supported by the so-called "externalists" who believed that the sex of an individual was determined by factors external to embryos, such as nutrition and temperature. The second was endorsed by the "internalists" who thought that the development of a male or female was determined by factors in the egg, which at that time were called "epigenetic" (which has a more nuanced meaning today). The internalists were split into two groups according to whether the key factors were located in the cytoplasm or nucleus. A third area was supported by internalists who were a new breed of biologists — geneticists — who argued for sex determination by the chromosomes. It is now common knowledge that a boy develops when a male-determining sperm fertilizes an egg, and a girl when the sperm has a female-determining factor: the ova have a passive role in the process. These facts were not finally established until 1921 when

Theophilus Painter at the University of Texas showed that sperm determine the sex of babies according to whether they carry a Y-chromosome or an X-chromosome.[8]

Heape accepted the genetic interpretation with reservations. Perhaps he was influenced by his association with Bateson on the Evolution Committee because in his first paper on the subject in 1907, he wrote:

> The most recent writers on the subject claim that the sex of the generative products is governed by the laws of heredity, and so far as I understand the effects of extraneous influences on the sex of the progeny is wholly denied by them.[9]

He endorsed the view that sex is irrevocably decided at the moment of fertilization:

> ... the ovum and the spermatozoon are themselves sexual, that the latest moment at which the sex of the offspring can be determined is the time of fertilization, and that no influence exerted subsequently can alter that sex.[10]

Thus he was still an externalist insofar as he reserved the possibility that the sex of offspring may be influenced by external factors such as nutrition and temperature before fertilization. Furthermore, he thought that ova can be either male- or female-determining, and that environmental factors could operate through gametes of either sex.

These were not eccentric views at the time, and were shared by a number of distinguished biologists. The hypothetical existence of two forms of ova emerged in 1902 from the observation of Clarence McClung[11] at the University of Kansas that a small chromosome was involved, then called an accessory chromosome. The importance of this suggestion was immediately recognized by Bateson in Cambridge and William Castle at Harvard. Bateson and his assistant Rebecca Saunders[12] thought there were male- and female-determining spermatozoa *and* ova, and Castle[13] went further in suggesting that a male-determining sperm can only fertilize a female-determining ovum, and a female-determining sperm can only fertilize a male-determining ovum. These ideas sound very confusing beside the clarity of current understanding.

Three years after McClung's pioneering study the role of chromosomes in sex determination became better understood, largely owing to the work of two American entomologists.[14] One of them was Nettie Stevens,[15] a young researcher at Bryn Mawr College in Pennsylvania, whose studies of chromosomes in mealworm beetle larvae (*Tenebrio molitor*)[16] led her to conclude:

> Since the somatic cells of the female contain 20 large chromosomes, while those of the male contain 19 large ones and one small one, this seems to be a clear case of sex determination, not by an accessory chromosome, but by a definite difference in the character of the elements of a pair of chromosomes of the spermatocytes of the first order, the spermatozoa which contain the small chromosome determining the male sex, while those that contain 10 chromosomes of equal size determine the female sex.

The other study was done independently and almost simultaneously by that doyen of cell biology, Edmund Wilson,[17] who first heard of Stevens' work when he received her paper for review. Wilson strongly recommended publication and referred to her results in a footnote to his own paper on the idiochromosomes in Hemiptera, a large order of insects known as true bugs.

Heape was probably told about both studies by his friend Bateson at the Evolution Committee. He also knew about the work of Leonard Doncaster[18] at King's College, London, on sex determination in sawflies in which unfertilized ova develop parthenogenetically into females in some species while in others they become males. He would have been familiar with the poultry breeding experiments of Bateson and Reginald Punnett in Cambridge from which they concluded that the ovum was sometimes responsible for sex determination.[19] Heape wrote:

> Thus it may be that for certain species of animals, or for certain individuals, the sex of the embryo is derived from the ovum while for others it is derived from the sperm, and that is as far as present evidence permits us to go.[20]

Hence Heape strongly adhered to Castle's original scheme which predicted that both members of a mating pair have two types of sex-determining gametes to allow for selective fertilization.[21] This raised the question of whether two types of ova can be identified morphologically.

There was a flurry of debate among geneticists in 1907 when a paper by Achille Russo, the Professor of Zoology and Anatomy at the University of Catania in Sicily, claimed that the proportion of female rabbits in a litter could be increased by an injection of lecithin.[22] He claimed that two types of ova exist, both male and female, the difference being decided by the greater abundance of fatty deposits in the female ovum. Russo challenged the genetic theory of sex determination by promoting the older explanation that it is affected by environmental factors. Punnett and Bateson,[23] and later Castle,[24] criticized the Russo paper for using highly selected observations that favored his hypothesis. Fortuitously, Heape had saved a set of serial sections of rabbit ovaries from his studies of ovulation and allowed Bateson and Punnett to examine them. They concluded that the ova claimed by Russo to potentially be male-determining were degenerate, and called for further studies. Heape made a thorough examination of his sections which led him to conclude, somewhat reluctantly:

> ... it is with great regret that I am obliged to conclude that he [Russo] has not proved what, at first sight, seemed to be such a clear exposition of the correctness of my own belief.[25]

Russo's attempt to replace a genetic explanation for sex determination with an externalist theory was soundly rejected by Punnett, who failed to confirm the effects of lecithin in Russo's experiments.[26]

During the early years of the 20th century the widely held view that the sex ratio was determined by external factors gradually lost favor, starting in 1902 when Bateson and Saunders suggested that it obeyed Mendel's laws. By the time of Heape's first paper on the subject in 1907, Wilson[27] was influentially advocating the genetic explanation.[28] There were still some researchers, including Punnett,[29] who found it difficult to understand how the proportions of males and females could obey Mendel's laws.

Two biometricians, David Heron[30] and Frederick Woods,[31] published back-to-back papers in *Biometrika*, a journal launched by Karl Pearson and Walter Weldon after they resigned from the Evolution Committee. Heron had analyzed data from 348 families supplied by Pearson and 2,197 from the large Quaker Whitney family of Connecticut and its affiliations, as well as 1,000 thoroughbred horses from *The General Studbook*. He found no significant correlations between the sex ratio of successive generations in humans and horses, concluding that Mendel's laws cannot predict the sex ratio. He maintained that deviations from equality were due to the effects of only the environment, nutrition and behavior. Woods reached a similar conclusion from different methods. Heape tended to agree with them, conceding that both environment and genetics play a role:

(1) That through the medium of nutrition supplied to the ovary, either by the quantity or by the quality of that nutrition, either by its direct effect upon the ovarian ova or by its indirect effect, a variation in the proportion of the sexes of the ova produced, and therefore of the young born, is effected in all animals in which the ripening of the ovarian ova is subject to selective action.
(2) That when no selective action occurs in the ovary the proportion of the sexes of ovarian ova produced is governed by laws of heredity.[32]

Heape's belief that there are two types of ova whose proportions can be affected by external factors such as nutrition led him to try to control the sex of babies in women. In a letter to his old friend Anton Dohrn on 14 September 1903, he wrote:

... some 16 cases have been brought under my notice during recent years and my treatment has been attended with somewhat remarkable success. Since a child must be either male or female a large number of cases is necessary to actually demonstrate the efficacy of any particular treatment and I cannot claim that my cases exclusively prove the efficacy of the treatment I have adopted, at the same time I would add that in every case in which my treatment has been carried out the child born was of the sex foretold.[33]

His treatments appear to have been tailor-made for each case, but the vague way they are described to Dohrn makes them of limited interest.

He wrote to Dohrn because in 1903 Victor Emmanuel III, King of Italy, and his wife Elena had no heir. The king was married in 1896 and inherited the throne in 1900 after his father was assassinated. They had a daughter in 1901 and another in

1902, but neither child was eligible for the throne. Heape may have heard about the concern over the succession when Victor and Elena made a state visit to England. He asked Dohrn to inform the king about his treatment for controlling the sex of babies and offer practical help. Dohrn's reply has disappeared, but from a subsequent letter Heape wrote to him it is clear that he firmly declined the offer a month later.[34] Their correspondence is reproduced in the Appendix.

Heape believed that the variability between ova, which he assumed was caused by external influences, could be understood by studying the ratio of male and females at birth, which he did in dogs and humans. Since mammals are viviparous there are two sex ratios: (1) the primary sex ratio at fertilization, and (2) the secondary sex ratio at birth. The conventional assumption is that equal numbers of male- and female-determining spermatozoa are formed in the testes and have an equal chance of fertilizing ova. Consequently, any variation in the secondary sex ratio is due to differential survival of the sexes during gestation. But Heape believed that two types of sex determining ova existed, concluding that variations in the ratio at birth were due at least in part to differences in mortality of male- and female-determining gametes of either sex. In that case the primary sex ratio would not be determined entirely by the probability laws of heredity, and other external factors, such as nutrition, would be involved.

He started these studies in dogs,[32] following the work of Charles Darwin who in his book *The Descent of Man* reported that for greyhounds 110 males were born for every 100 bitches (52.3% males) between 1857 and 1868.[35] The data were obtained from records of 6,878 births in *The Field* sporting magazine. Heape believed the excess of males was biased from breeders failing to record all births for three reasons: (1) if litters were large, breeders often reduced them to reduce competition between suckling pups, (2) weak members of litters were culled, and (3) dead pups were not recorded. He also noted that Darwin's results might not apply to other breeds, and thus a re-examination of the subject with elimination of these sources of error was needed.

Heape obtained data from three sources: (1) records of 17,838 pups from the *Greyhound Stud Book* for 1888-1892, (2) 19,150 pups from *The Stock Keeper Kennel Records* for 1889-1891, and (3) 1,793 pups from Breeders' Schedule Returns. He recognized, however, that the first two sources had the same defects as Darwin's study, but the third source, although a small sample, was considered more reliable because it included all pups born and was based on records made at the time of birth. Heape used (3) as a gold standard for checking the reliability of the other two sources. A huge effort was required to tabulate and analyze all these data in the age before computers. They revealed a preponderance of males, particularly in large breeds like greyhounds and collies (about 118 male dogs born per 100 bitches, or 54%), which was slightly lower in small breeds, like terriers (about 114 male dogs born per 100 bitches, or 53%). He gained little support for his theory about environment influences from these studies, and was clutching at straws when he reported seasonal differences:

> The conclusion is drawn that conception during August to November is especially favourable to the production of dog pups among Greyhounds under the conditions of breeding now practiced, and this result is attributed to a selective action on the ova produced at this time.[32]

His next project was on the secondary sex ratio in humans in which he recognized that external factors would have only slight effects, if any, and require large, carefully compiled databases. He obtained birth and stillbirth records of 135,881 whites and 41,823 non-whites, which had been compiled for 1904-1906 by Carlos Finlay, the chief sanitary officer of Cuba.[36] They were broken down into months, provinces and marital state. He had great fortitude and conviction to spend a huge amount of time analyzing records by hand and summarizing them in 64 tables. The sex ratios of white and non-white populations were 107.14 males per 100 females (51.7%) and 100.7 males per 100 females (50.2%), respectively. Since a similar result had been reported elsewhere, he concluded that racial variation is determined by hereditary factors. He also noticed that birth rates were lowest in January-February and September-October, followed by a fertility spike in the autumn and spring when the proportion of females rose. He claimed that seasonal variations had no obvious genetic explanation, but rather that increased metabolism may have boosted fertility and the probability of ovulating female-determining ova.

Unfortunately, all these efforts were misdirected because of his dogged acceptance of Castle's belief in genetically regulated male- and female-determining ova. This assumption had encouraged him to explore external factors affecting these putative types of ova, and hence the sex ratio at birth. His mistake is excusable for it was not apparent for another decade that ova only carry an X-chromosome and never a Y-chromosome. Nevertheless, it is surprising that Heape paid so little attention to the possibility that differential fetal loss in utero affected the secondary sex ratio. Much later it was suggested that the higher ratio of dogs to bitches at birth could be a result of dominant X-linked lethal mutations in some breeds, causing higher prenatal mortality of female fetuses.[37]

Another of his missteps was in believing that the large numbers of degenerating ova in rabbit ovaries tended to be of one sex, which he argued were more susceptible to stress. This argument helped him to suspect that nutrition could skew the sex ratio. He was in fact observing the important natural phenomenon we now know as atresia (ovarian follicle death) which accounts for the loss of large numbers of ova throughout the lifetime. The notion of cell death as a natural phenomenon was unthinkable until an influential review in 1951 by A. Glücksmann[38] at the Strangeways Research Laboratory in Cambridge.

12

SEX ANTAGONISM AND HUMAN REPRODUCTION

HEAPE PUBLISHED a strange book in 1913. Titled *Sex Antagonism*, it dealt with two apparently unrelated subjects, namely totemism and exogamy in primitive and modern societies, which emerged from his intense discussions after 1909 with Sir James Frazer, a Fellow at Trinity College, and the debate over feminism.

Frazer, the author of the famous anthropology book *The Golden Bough*, was strongly influenced by Sir Edward Tyler at Oxford, and together they are regarded as founding figures of social anthropology, including the study of mythology and religion.[1] Neither of them did much field work, but collected information from ethnologists and explorers and missionaries returning home from the expanding territories of the British Empire. This mode of research earned them the nickname "armchair anthropologists."

Heape's interest in human reproduction grew out of his research on menstrual cycles in monkeys from his first visit to India,[2] and several years later he wrote a paper in which he discussed whether women have a comparable season of sexual receptivity. He gathered statistics in native people for the monthly number of births reported by several anthropologists.

His tentative conclusion for primitive and ancestral human societies was that "sexual and reproductive functions were stimulated at definite times of the year," whereas he knew that modern women reproduce with only slight variations throughout the year:

> It would seem highly probable, therefore, that the reproductive power of man has increased with civilization, precisely as it may be increased in the lower animals by domestication; that the regular supply of good food, together with all the other stimulating factors available and exercised in modern civilized communities, has resulted in such great activity of the generative organs, and so great an increase in the supply of reproductive elements, that conception in the healthy human female may be said to be possible almost at any time during the reproductive period.[3]

His interest in anthropology was reawakened when Frazer was finishing his four-volume work *Totemism and Exogamy*[4] in 1909. They exchanged letters of which only Heape's survive, but several passages from their correspondence were incorporated in Frazer's books.

Frazer defined totemism as "an intimate relation which is supposed to exist between a group of kindred people on the one side and a species of natural or artificial objects on the other, which objects are called the totems of the human group."[5] For example, kangaroos, butterflies, and some other animals were totems for pregnant women in Australian aboriginal societies. He consulted Heape about maternal impressions and birth marks which were common myths he thought might help explain how a specific totem was chosen by primitive people. Heape replied with two examples of fancies expressed by modern women:

It does happen occasionally that a pregnant mother foretells the occurrence of a blemish on her unborn child in consequence of some experience she has while pregnant. The following is a case of this kind—Captain W. told me that while in China his wife was sleeping lightly in bed one hot night without bed-clothes and with her nightdress open and her chest exposed. A lizard fell from the roof onto her chest between the breasts; she woke with a start and saw the animal running away. She foretold that her child would be marked on the chest and Captain W. assures me that when the child was born there was a mark of the lizard's long body; four outstretched legs and tail, on the child's chest precisely the corresponding position to that upon which the lizard fell on his wife's chest. He added that the mark was a red mark and that it persisted, though for how long it persisted I don't know.

As an example of the effort to account for a blemish which existed upon a child's body the following may serve: Mrs. H. told me that when her sister—who is many years younger than herself—was born, she had marked in clear outline on the back of her neck, in red, a raspberry. This mark still persists and the lady is about 30 years of age. It was "explained" by the mother as due to the fact she eat [sic] very largely of raspberries during pregnancy. As a matter of fact I am assured that she did so, that she had an extraordinary longing for the fruit and eat them continuously for many weeks; they were rich people and she was provided with the fruit as long as it was possible to eat them.[6]

Heape also pointed out that maternal impressions are widely accepted phenomena by animal breeders:

... Breeders of horses too, when breeding for pure colour, will not allow their pregnant mares to mix with white faced horses or even to allow a white faced horse to run in the next field where it can be seen over the fence. They assert that if they do so they run great risk of getting foals with white faces, or otherwise badly marked. I may quote, as a further modern example of this firmly established view, the well-known breeder of black polled cattle who would not have any white or coloured article on his farm but who had all his fences, gates, etc. all painted black. The influence of surroundings in this respect is of course a very ancient belief, it existed in the time of Jacob.

Moreover, the ancient Greeks placed handsome statues in the rooms of pregnant women in hope (if not expectation) that they would deliver a more beautiful baby. Heape continued:

> *So far as I can see if there is such a thing of transference of mental impressions from mother to ovum in the ovary or from mother to embryo in the uterus, it is brought about by means of some force or agency of which we know nothing. I think we may say that most scientific men are inclined to deny that such transference really occurs. Personally I am not prepared to deny it, but if it is true I cannot explain how it is done.*[7]

Frazer suspected that maternal impressions were myths, but argued that frequent repetition of them provides evidence supporting the view that similar fancies in primitive people practicing totemism could determine a child's totem. From a vast amount of information Frazer proposed a theory to explain the origin of totemism, suggesting that primitive people believed that pregnancy begins when a spirit totem enters a woman's womb.

> We conclude, then, that the ultimate source of totemism is a savage ignorance of the physical process by which men and animals reproduce their kind; in particular it is an ignorance of the part played by the male in the generation of offspring.[8]

Anthropologists believed that exogamy originated after totemism. Frazer defined it as: "a common, indeed general, rule that members of a totemic clan may not marry each other but are bound to seek their wives and husbands in another clan."[9] He consulted Heape about the effects of breeding domestic animals from their close relatives, which he believed would help to explain the origin of exogamy. On 17 December, 1909, Heape wrote:

From what you tell me of exogamy in its simplest form, i.e. insofar as it provides against the marriage of brother and sister and the marriage of cousins (concubitants and others), it is so closely in accord with the experience of breeders of animals that, failing a clear social reason for the law, it might be fairly assumed to have its origin in accordance with known biological phenomena. I cannot claim to be considered capable of expressing a final opinion on the subject, but I think I may say that, so far as breeders know, inbreeding of brother and sister, father and daughter, grandfather and grand-daughter, and cousins, is essential for the rapid fixing of a type and is the best method, if not the only method, of producing the ancestor of a new and definite variety (see "Evolution of British Cattle"). At the same time indefinite inbreeding ("in and inbreeding") is found to be associated with deterioration … Thus the practice of exogamy is in accordance with the experience of breeders.[10]

Heape also noted that infertility is a common result of inbreeding, and Frazer, after reviewing a large amount of other evidence, concluded:

Thus exogamy, especially in the form in which it is practiced by the lowest of existing savages, the aborigines of Australia, presents a curious analogy to a system of scientific breeding. That the exogamous system of these primitive people was artificial, and that it was deliberately devised by them for the purpose which it actually serves, namely the prevention of the marriage of near kin, seems quite certain; on no other reasonable hypothesis can we explain its complex arrangements, so perfectly adapted to the wants and the ideas of the natives …

What idea these primitive sages and lawgivers, if we may call them so, had in their minds when they laid down the fundamental lines of the institution we cannot say with certainty; all that we know of savages leads us to suppose that it must have been what we should now call superstition, some crude notion of natural causation which to us might seem transparently false, though to them it doubtless seemed obviously true. Yet egregiously wrong as they were in theory, they appear to have been fundamentally right in practice. What they abhorred was really evil; what they preferred was really good. Perhaps we may call their curious system an unconscious mimicry of science.[11]

Heape thought Frazer's conclusions about the origin of totemism and exogamy were totally wrong, and conflicted with what he called "natural biological laws" that ought to apply to every aspect of fertility. He insisted that some reproductive behaviors were the result of instincts evolving by natural selection and that cognition came into play later as the brain developed. He distinguished between the sexes two kinds of instinctive behavior—male sexual desire and the impulse for maternal care in females. Totemism and exogamy had evolved from these ancient drives:

> If I am correct, just as exogamy is a practical effort to satisfy a male sexual impulse, so totemism arose from a desire designated to satisfy a maternal impulse. These two divergent impulses are at the root of sex antagonism; they exert their influence on all the laws which govern sex relations in all social communities, and are never divorced from the minds and from the actions of all normal healthy men and women.[12]

Heape's book barely conceals his exasperation with Frazer for failing to apply common sense to what aboriginals could have known about reproduction. He doubted claims made by Frazer and his informants that aboriginal women did not associate intercourse with pregnancy, which those anthropologists had used to support their views about totemism. Wearing his biological hat, he argued that anthropologists had ignored the natural sexual instincts because even those women would recognize early signs of pregnancy, and men too understood the connection.

Heape was agitated at that time by the rising tide of feminism in the UK since it originated in the mid-19th century. Its most publicly conspicuous expression was the suffragette movement which sought the right of women to vote, one that had been denied by the *Reform Act* of 1832. The Woman's Social and Political Union was formally constituted by 1906 and from then until the outbreak of the Great War there were violent demonstrations such as the stoning of police, trashing of letter boxes and arson. But in addition to suffrage the feminist movement sought the more profound goal of releasing women's role in society from the definition of their biology. Since this challenged Heape's "natural laws" it is not surprising that he was strongly opposed to the movement, and declared his attitude unequivocally in the last chapter of *Sex Antagonism*. He feared the male population would find the unfolding societal changes so objectionable that they would cause unrest and war between the sexes.

Heape believed there are "natural laws" defining motherhood as the purpose of women in life, and he introduced the idea that they risked losing their fertility if they did not bear children, behavior he regarded as a "luxury" and harmful to the nation.[13] He also charged that unmarried women, "spinsters, a dissatisfied and, we may assume, an unsatisfied class of women," were the majority of the suffragists, who may become deranged for lack of sexual activity and try to legislate against motherhood if they gained the vote.[14] Besides these rather extreme arguments he feared suffragist literature was promoting "anti-male prejudice." Perhaps he had read in *The Suffragette*,[15] edited by the leader of the movement Christabel Pankhurst:

The men of the country and the dishonest and reactionary government they have put in office must bear the whole blame ... for the attacks upon the letter-boxes, because by rejecting every quiet and lawful appeal for the vote, they have driven women to methods of revolution.

He prescribed a sedate lifestyle, even free from athletics, so that adolescent girls could prepare themselves for marriage and motherhood. A demure nature would inhibit development of the secondary male characteristics that encouraged militant activism. The different characteristics of men and women were firmly determined by natural selection and attempts to narrow them could have harmful consequences. Thus he suggested that the underlying cause of antagonism between the sexes was the failure to recognize distinct biological roles of men and women and their value in stabilizing society. They were shaped by natural laws of reproduction that had evolved long before cultural factors:

> It seems clear that woman's usefulness, her value to society, and therefore her power and her happiness depend, not on her likeness to, but on her dissimilarity from man. By training her recessive male qualities she can never attain to more than a secondary position in the social body; but by cultivating her dominant female qualities, by increasing their value, she will gain power which no man can usurp and will attain that position as a true compliment of man which is essential for the permanence and the vigor of the race.[16]

Sex Antagonism attracted considerable attention, although most of it is hard to understand in the absence of familiarity with Frazer's totemism and exogamy. It continued to draw notice more than a decade later and, surprisingly, its ideas were discussed by cultural critics as recently as 1988.[17] Its content and often outspoken style generated a range of responses, both favorable and unfavorable and in both professional and general interest journals. Reviews in the two leading medical journals, *The Lancet*[18] and *British Medical Journal*,[19] commended the author for stressing the unique physiological and behavioral characteristics of men and women, which had not received due attention in medical practice. One of the reviewers described the chapter on maternal impressions as "anecdotal" and "devoid of any real scientific value," and J. P. Lichtenberger[20] of the American Academy of Political and Social Sciences criticized Heape for exaggerating sex differences, although he recommended the book for serious students of social science. A published note in *The Atheneum*[21] endorsed the book's conclusions, and while the *Saturday Review*[22] approved its title and arguments about totemism and exogamy, it found it had oversimplified the relationship between the sexes, which were depicted from a "strict breeder's point of view."

Sex Antagonism was dismissed by A.B. Wolfe[23] of the University of Texas in a few words: "Such a book, neglecting all economic, psychological, and ethical values, deserves slight attention." The *New York Times*[24] praised it for bravely raising the subject, but rejected the notion that only biological factors determine sex antagonism, because economic and social factors were equally important. The review began: "We tremble to think of the treatment Walter Heape and his recent 'Sex Antagonism' will receive at the hands of the suffragist contingent."

There was, however, surprisingly little comment from that direction. In her thoughtful essay "Modern feminism and sex antagonism," Ethel Coloquhoun[25] embraced the idea that natural laws contribute to differences between men and women. She was a feminist opposed to the suffragettes whose militancy she thought unhelpful to the cause. Other women were sympathetic to her attitude, including many belonging to the Women's National Anti-Suffrage League which was formed in 1908 by fifteen peeresses and Gertrude Bell, the eminent Middle East traveler and authority who became its secretary.

Heape's views on feminism attracted as much attention as his discussion of Frazer's theories, and despite the passage of time they are still not forgotten while Frazer's totemism has faded to obscurity. As for the militant suffragists, Heape's fears that society would collapse and become dystopic have not, of course, been borne out by history. English women won a limited franchise in 1918, and ten years later they gained full voting rights from the age of 21 years.

When Ava Pauling, wife of Nobelist Linus Pauling, read the book in 1927 it prompted her to jot down some perceptive remarks:

> Heape certainly leaves much to be desired in his boasted "biologic ability" e.g. his statement that "sexual desire" is the only motive in the male and "maternity" the only one in the female in coition. However ... I'm inclined towards his idea of the origin of exogamy being more ancient than that of totemism and that it arose as a natural result of man's inherently wandering nature and not from a horror of incest.[26]

In a wide review of culture and literature, *No Man's Land* (1988) singled out *Sex Antagonism* along with contemporary works by Ford Madox Ford, T.S. Eliot and D.H. Lawrence, all of which recognized and depicted a new antagonism between men and women. The volume editors wrote that fervent women of the pre-war era stood for a social upheaval "whose implications Walter Heape has analyzed and protested."[27]

An obsession with sex antagonism reflected his very conservative views about women's roles. He embraced the pervasive anxiety that more relaxed mores, contraception and women's emancipation were dangerously lowering the nation's fertility. It was a notion he often expressed at hearings of the Commission of Inquiry into the Declining Birth-Rate of the National Council of Public Morals, stating that "if you prevent animals from breeding, they degenerate."[28] His conservatism was voiced for laypeople in *Preparation for Marriage* (1914),[29] part of a series entitled *Questions of Sex*. We might wonder if he took practical steps towards helping couples to conceive, but we only have a hint in a postscript to Frazer: "I have just read this letter over and I would add that my experience of men and women, who come to me for treatment …"[30] As far as we know he never opened an infertility practice, or if he was occasionally consulted it is likely he would have prescribed dietary changes.

We might throw up our hands at the author's views and write him off as an extremist. But he was not so regarded in his own day because sexist attitudes were widely held by Victorian men. After the outbreak of war in 1914 his interest switched to weapon development and he withdrew from public discussions of sex antagonism for the rest of his life.

WORLD WAR I: THE HEAPE AND GRYLLS CINEMATOGRAPHIC MACHINE

A CHANCE conversation just before World War I between Heape and an official for a company producing large armaments led to the design of a high-speed camera that could photograph shells penetrating armor plating.[1,2] Together with the engineer Horace Grylls, he submitted a proposal to the Ordnance Board at the Royal Artillery Barracks in Woolwich on 27 November, 1914.[3] They appeared before the Board on 21 December, which forwarded it to the Admiralty with a recommendation to make a prototype instrument. Thomas Cooke and Sons Ltd., a preeminent manufacturer of scientific instruments, was commissioned to undertake the work at their Buckingham Works in York[4] where the company had switched almost entirely to making munitions for the war effort during 1915-1918.

The instrument came to be known as the Heape and Grylls high-speed cinematographic machine. It could take sequential photographs on regular film at rates of 500 to 5,000 frames per second, greatly exceeding the speed of all other instruments at that time.[5] Another unique feature was its ability to take stereo-scopic pairs of images. It consisted of three main parts:

(1) A film drum on which are wound two separate strips of cinema film side by side.

(2) A pair of lens wheels each carrying 40 lenses, mounted on shafts geared to the film drum in such a way that the image cast by each lens, in turn, on the film at the optical axis moves precisely at the same speed as the film on the drum.

(3) A shutter to make it possible to start taking a series of photographs and to stop taking them.[6]

The machine's success depended on its ability to synchronize movement of the film and the lenses so that every image remained sharp and exactly in position on the film strip. The high rate of images required very intense illumination which was achieved by focusing two searchlights fitted with arc-lamp electrodes.

When sufficient progress had been made they submitted a formal application entitled "Apparatus for obtaining photo-graphic records" to the British Patent Office on 17 January, 1916:

The invention has for its object to obtain photographic records of phenomena the duration of which is a very small interval of time, or which takes place at a very high speed.

As specific examples it may be mentioned that by means of this invention photographic records of a kinematographic nature can be obtained of the bursting of projectiles, impact of projectiles on armour-plate, effect of explosion, as well as all kindred as well as many other classes of phenomena, which records can after-wards be examined directly, or projected on to a screen, to ascertain what took place in the time during which the operations were in progress.

It is obvious that for such records to be of real assistance, the rate at which they must be taken should be of the order of thousands per second, while each separate record should be clearly defined.[7]

It was approved a year later on 15 January, 1917, but because of military interests in wartime it was immediately classified as secret under section 30 of the *Patents and Designs Act* of 1907.[8] Further improvements made by Heape and Grylls for the manufacture and orientation of the electrodes resulted in four more patent applications between 5 February, 1917, and 27 March, 1918,[9] all of which were approved but none had to be classified.

Engineering problems so delayed the project that it was not ready for field testing with ordnance until after the war.[10] The late Eric Cussans, who joined Thomas Cooke in 1918, as an apprentice recalled one trial in which the machine recorded the fracture of a glass globe struck by a hammer.[11] An Admiralty report in July, 1920, revealed that the camera was due to be transferred in a few months from York to Shoeburyness, the Royal Navy Proving Grounds on the north shore of the River Thames estuary. It outlines the machine's applications and limitations:

The whole outfit is expected to weigh about six tons, so that the machine, in its present form, is in no sense a mobile one, though further improvement will probably remedy this disability ... Some of the uses to which the machine will be put are:

(a) The investigation of the motion of projectiles in flight.

(b) The determining of the velocity of fragments of bursting shells.

(c) The acceleration of the projectile in the bore of a gun. The investigation of the effect of whip and jump on a gun firing.

(d) Velocities of recoil, from the point of view of gun mounting design.

(e) The performance of armour.[12]

The primary patent was released from its classified status on 18 October, 1920, but general publication was delayed until 10 February of the following year. Meanwhile, an application was filed and later approved on 1 April, 1924, by the American patent office under the title "Apparatus for obtaining photographic records."[13]

The camera was in place at Shoeburyness sometime in 1921, but preliminary trials uncovered minor defects[14] and it arrived without a technician who knew how to operate it. This seems to have been a common problem with new equipment; the superintendent complained in a memorandum that resident technicians frequently neglected their regular duties to attend the machine.[15] Getting it in working order must have been slow since there was no reference to the camera in gunnery reports for 1922.[16]

It attracted wide attention when Heape described the machine at a Royal Society conversazione on 16 May, 1923. He showed a series of photographs taken at 2,500 per second of the disintegration of a glass bulb after being struck by a hammer, and the deformation of a rubber ball hitting a steel plate after being shot from a gun. The demonstration caused a sensation and was reported in many journals and newspapers. The films were so popular that they were shown again at another conversazione on 20 June, and many other reports followed in the press,[17] some of them colourful, like the headline "Former Rochdale Gentleman's Wonderful Machine" in the *Rochdale Observer*.[18]

Although Heape was primarily responsible for the idea, the project would never have been realized without a competent, collaborating engineer. He may have been embarrassed to receive most of the credit and publicity for in a letter to *Nature* he wrote generously on Horace's behalf:

> The lion's share of credit for the successful completion of the design of the camera, however, is due to my friend Mr. Horace B. Grylls, who became partner with me in the adventure in 1914.[19]

A few months later on 2-3 January, 1924, the machine was described by Grylls at a joint meeting of the Physical and Optics Societies at Imperial College, London, but records of its use in ballistics research are sparse and incomplete.

There are photographs taken from a film shown by Sir Robert Hadfield in a lecture at the University of Birmingham on 30 October, 1923, and again later to the Oxford University Junior Scientific Club showing a 15-inch shell from a large naval gun at Shoeburyness striking an armor-plate with an energy equivalent to 60,000 foot-tons.[20] The photographs were taken by a camera within 50 feet of the target and believed to be the first of their kind. Hadfield was a British metallurgist famous for his development of stainless steel and head of a large company that manufactured steel and munitions. He was also an influential advisor to the Admiralty on armor-plating and armor-piercing shells, which was a major issue after British naval guns performed poorly at the Battle of Jutland in 1916. A senior German officer testified at hearings after the war:

> Of all the British heavy-calibre hits sustained by our ships at Jutland, not a single armour-piercing shell penetrated any vital parts.[21]

A series of photographic reproductions were published in 1925 in the popular journal *The Graphic*[22] showing the effects of a heavy gun discharging—billowing smoke, flying fragments, a hole in the armor-plate and the shell emerging from the other side.

For its time, the machine was a remarkable piece of recording equipment that was able to take stereographic photographs at far greater frame rates than ever before, but its cumbersome size rendered it hard to transport between projects. It became obsolete when more portable electronic cameras were developed,[23] but it nevertheless proved the value of high speed cinematography for scientific and engineering problems. The fate of the original machine is unknown: probably it was dismantled as too large for a museum to accommodate.

There is one piece of evidence to indicate that Heape may have been involved in improving the efficiency of other weapons during World War I; according to a letter in the British Archives:

> *I am also to inform you that the Controller has just been advised by the Department concerned, under date 26.7.18, that one elevating gear, of the type invented by Walter Heape, for the 240 mm Trench Mortar, will be sent to Section Technique de l'Artillerie, 1, Place St., Thomas d'Aquia, in the course of a few days. This is in compliance with the request contained in your letter No. 28760A dated the 24th June, 1918.*[24]

14

REPRODUCTIVE BEHAVIOR AND ECOLOGY

SOON AFTER the Great War, Heape launched an ambitious project which was unfinished at the time of his death in 1929. The main object was "… to stimulate a wider research in … the comparative physiology of the reproductive system." It originated from his recognition that the gonads have two major and independent functions, namely the generative function that produces gametes from the germ line and the growth function which regulates many somatic tissues in the body. He regarded gamete production as critical for the preservation of species, and growth control as essential for preserving the individual. Ever a stickler for precise definitions, Heape argued that the areas embraced by the two functions should be given separate labels: the "physiology of reproduction" restricted to the production of gametes, and the "physiology of the reproductive organs" concerned the growth of somatic tissues. Put in modern terms, he wanted to separate the developmental from the endocrine/ neurological aspects of reproduction.

About 18 months before his death, Heape realized that it was unlikely that he would be able to complete a book on this subject, although a draft was nearing completion. He asked Francis Marshall at Cambridge to edit and oversee its publication, which his friend declined until later on when Heape's youngest son, Rodney, persuaded him "to carry out the revision of the manuscript, arrange publication, and to see the work through the press."[1] The book was published posthumously in 1931 with a preface by Marshall.

The book, *Emigration, Migration and Nomadism*, is an enquiry into the ultimate and proximal causes of those three behavioral drives and their relationship to nutrition, climate and breeding cycles. As in his earlier work on the fauna of Plymouth Sound and the breeding cycles of mammals, Heape had embarked on an encyclopedic survey of the published literature and gathered unpublished observations on the movements of vertebrates (including mammals, birds, reptiles, amphibians and fish) and invertebrates (insects). The book is not an easy read, as John Baker of Oxford University remarked in the opening of his review in *Nature*:

> Dr. F.H.A. Marshall has edited and prefaced this posthumous work by the distinguished authority on the sexual cycle, Walter Heape. Few books cast a wider net for readers than this. The physiologist, the natural historian, the ecologist, the anthropologist, even the alienist, is concerned with the subjects treated. Yet how many of these, except the physiologist, will get past the first chapter? And how many physiologists will read the rest?[2]

Nevertheless, Baker considered the book useful, as did a reviewer in the *Spectator*:

> But it is idle to attempt to summarize in a paragraph the argument of this most important and stimulating essay on some of biology's most difficult problems. We must leave it with this bare announcement, with the proviso that the book claims the notice of anyone with the slightest love for natural history.[3]

Many of his examples of animal emigration, migration and nomadism were already well-known in whales, terns, salmon, monarch butterflies and locusts, but he classified them as scrupulously as always. The area he called the "home territory" was a circumscribed and strongly defended area often associated with a nest for eggs, parturition, and rearing young. The "neutral territory" was a much larger territory in which food was hunted for without the enforcement of territorial rights.

To Heape, the word migration meant "that class of movement which impels migrants to return to the [home and hunting] regions from which they migrated," and he sub-classified three types: alimentary, gametic and climatic. Alimental migration occurred for the sake of self-preservation when there was a temporary shortage of food in the home and neutral territories. Gametic migration involved temporary movement to an area outside those territories where nesting or parturition occurred in a more favorable environment. Climatic migration was a temporary movement beyond those territories to avoid adverse climatic conditions.

He defined emigration as "movements which entail change of environment, but which do not involve return to the original home and hunting territories." It was ultimately caused by hostile factors such as rainfall, temperature, predation and overpopulation, although the proximal causes may be drought and starvation, or persecution and war in humans.

By nomadism he meant roaming over a definite area or territory, or even an unbounded territory.

He paid special attention to two mammals in which spectacular emigration occurs. One chapter was devoted to the lemming, an arctic rodent, and a large part of another chapter to the springbok, an antelope in southwest Africa.[4] The lemming is a familiar animal after featuring in Walt Disney's *White*

Wilderness (1958), but the movie promulgated the mistaken belief that lemmings commit suicide on reaching the sea at the end of emigration. The springbok is less well-known because of declining numbers from hunting, enclosure of its habitat for farming and a pandemic of rinderpest.

Heape collected most of his data for Norwegian lemmings from studies by the highly respected naturalist Robert Collett, Director at the Zoological Museum in Oslo. Irruptions of lemmings occur irregularly, sometimes over more than one breeding season, when the home territory becomes rapidly overpopulated. Collett[5] reported 31 so-called "lemming years" between 1739 and 1894 when the food supply in the home territory was exhausted and the animals were forced to emigrate to avoid starvation.[6] The behavioral change was so intense and focused that they tried to cross every physical barrier, including large rivers and fjords, in search of greener pastures. Many of them drown or perish from physical exhaustion, contrary to the old myth of mass suicide. Heape commented on lemming years:

> At this rate of increase I calculate that, allowing five litters with an average of eight young per litter, and deducting 25 percent for death of young from disease and enemies, a pair will produce fifteen pairs for next year's breeding. That is to say, a large colony of 5,000 pairs may be expected to leave 75,000 pairs capable of breeding the following season. This is, of course, a very rapid rate of increase, but is nothing like rapid enough to provide the many millions which emigrate in a lemming year. For this reason it is, I think, certain that, under the influence of some undetermined factor, their reproductive activity gradually increases more and more year after year for several years, until the climax is reached either in the year of exodus or the year before, persists for three, four or more years, and finally dies down again.

Far more is now known about the population dynamics of lemmings than when he had to admit the physiological trigger for emigration was an "undetermined factor."[7] His calculations assumed that they only breed in the summer months, but there is new evidence that this continues through the winter under snow cover as long as there is plenty of moss and lichens to eat. Lemming populations expand quickly because females mature no later than four weeks of age, pregnancy lasts only 19 days, and females mate almost immediately afterwards at a postpartum oestrus. Thus, after a favorable winter a large population can emerge in springtime which can explode under favorable summer conditions to even greater numbers than Heape estimated. But if their vegetable diet becomes depleted as the season progresses a lemming year may result.[8]

Heape was also impressed by the huge herds of springbok, or "trek-bokke," in South Africa whose occasional movements resembled "lemming years."[9] His information was obtained from travelers who had encountered them since the 18th century, although the numbers of animals reported in some irruptions may have been exaggerated.[10] William Scully was one of the sources he acknowledged because he described a trek-bokke in his novel *Between Sun and Sand*.[11] Scully was a distinguished South African author-naturalist and sometime civil commissioner for Namaqualand and special magistrate for the northern border of Cape Colony south of the Orange River. He was thoroughly familiar with the topography, natural history and Boers of the region, and drew from first-hand observations for his novel.

Herds of springbok did enormous damage during emigration to grazing lands for nomadic farmers. On one occasion Scully issued 100 stand of arms to the local Boers to help control the herds, but the trek-bokke became rare after the turn of the

20th century.[12] The spread of farming and associated fencing and an increase in hunting by farmers and sportsmen was an important cause. It has also been suggested that a viral pandemic, rinderpest, that affects artiodactyls (cloven-footed animals) killed a huge percentage of springboks in 1896-8,[13] but this is disputed.

Shortly before parturition, the ewes emigrated west from their home territory in the desert to mountainous regions where rain promoted more luxuriant plant growth for their young. If they returned with their lambs to the home territory this was true gametic migration, whereas emigration was rare, irreversible and always preceded by a population explosion which their home and neutral territories could not support. The behavior of starving animals was like lemmings because they ignored every obstacle in their desperate trek for food. Heape thought their behavior bordered on hysteria, judging from Scully's description:

> The springboks as a rule live without drinking. Sometimes, however—perhaps once in ten years—they develop a raging thirst, and rush madly forward until they find water. It is not many years ago since millions of them crossed the mountain range and made for the sea. They dashed into the waves, drank the salt water and died. Their bodies lay in one continuous pile along the shore for over thirty miles, and the stench drove the Trek-Boers who were camped near the coast far inland.

Heape suggested that irruptions of springboks always followed a rapid increase in fertility, of which the cause(s) were unknown, although it was the severe shortages of food and/ or water that prompted the behavioral change. Skinner confirmed the exponential increase in numbers prior to emigration:

Ewes can conceive as early as five months of age, and following a gestation period of 172 days, have a post-partum oestrus as soon as the uterus has involuted (some 10 days post-partum). As they are opportunistic breeders and do not have a restricted breeding season, a lambing crop of 200% per annum (assuming no mortality) is theoretically possible despite the absence of multiple births. It is theoretically possible for springbok ewes to breed 6.5 times in three years, and the populations as such will more than treble.[14]

Heape worked in exciting times when endocrinology was emerging and several new hormones were discovered. By 1905 he accepted the idea that reproductive functions were controlled by chemical signals, which he called "ferments" although later replacing it with the more appropriate word "gonadins." Oestrogens and progesterone in the ovary and the gonadotrophins in the anterior pituitary gland were discovered shortly before his death, but he seems to have been unaware of these breakthroughs. Alan S. Parkes reviewed progress in great detail in *The Internal Secretions of the Ovary*,[15] but that book was not published until the year Heape died.

The nutritional role of vitamins was also under scrutiny.[16] He had a long interest in the effects of nutrition on fertility, so it was natural to be attracted to a 1925 paper by Herbert Evans and George Burr entitled "The anti-sterility vitamin fat soluble E,"[17] which was first described two years earlier in a short note by Evans and Katherine Scott Bishop.[18] Heape regarded this discovery as such a major advance that he added comments at the end of *Emigration, Migration and Nomadism,* highlighting their conclusion that vitamin E deficiency had different effects in males and females. In males it caused complete destruction of the seminiferous tubules and germ cells, while females were unaffected until fetal death and absorption in pregnancy.

The final decade of Heape's life was a period that saw the birth of animal ecology, largely through the influence of 27-year-old Charles Elton's seminal book *Animal Ecology*.[19] Elton became a faculty member at Oxford, was elected to both the Royal Society of London and the American Academy of Arts and Sciences, and is honored as the grandfather of this vital subject. It is a pity that Heape was only superficially aware of progress in ecology and endocrinology because they provided answers to the physiological mechanisms he had sought for so long.

While reproductive biologists paid scant attention to Heape's book, ecologists were more receptive. Elton commented in the 1935 edition of *Animal Ecology* that "valuable facts about migration of animals are contained in the book by Walter Heape."[20] Another reviewer suggested it could help geologists explain the distribution of fossil remains, and George Myers, a distinguished ichthyologist at Stanford University, mentioned it warmly in 1949:

> Heape's book is perhaps the most important single work on the movements of animal populations. Although few of his ideas were totally new, his critical study for the first time brought order into the migrational phases of ecology, and clearly distinguished the several distinctive types of population movements which most writers had previously uncritically lumped under "migration."[21]

It has stood the test of time. In a 1993 account of the movement of springboks by Skinner,[22] Heape's book was described as "a thorough study of migration," and ecologists continue to quote from it.[23,24] It was conceived as comparative natural history, which to some ears sounds old-fashioned, but it encompasses a field with a wealth of data that are still valuable in this information age.

15

FINAL WORD

DURING THE Great War, Heape and his wife lived for a time at "King's House" in Bicester, Oxfordshire, and then in King's Bench Walk in the Temple district of the City of London. Their move from the quiet Suffolk coastline may have been prompted partly by German zeppelin bombing attacks.

After the war they were residing at "Manor Lodge" in Tunbridge Wells, Kent, perhaps for the benefits of its famous spa. It was there that Walter died from unknown causes on September 10, 1929, at age 74 and three years after Ethel. He was buried in the local cemetery three days later. An obituary was published in the London *Times* on September 11, 1929, and afterwards in *Nature* by Heape's old friend Francis Marshall who acknowledged the man's decency and contributions to science, for he "had a strong enthusiasm for his subject and was ever ready to help and encourage others."[1]

Gallery

BENJAMIN HEAPE (1817-1899.)
From a photograph.

1. Benjamin Heape, father of Walter Heape. He made his fortune in Australia. Permission of Cambridge University. *Records of the Family of Heape, of Heape, Staley, Saddleworth, and Rochdale from circa 1170 to 1905.* (Rochdale: Aldine Press, United Kingdom, 1905)

MARY (HEAP) HEAPE (1826-1900.)
From a photograph.

2. Mary Heape, née Heap, mother of Walter Heape. Permission of Cambridge University. *Records of the Family of Heape, of Heape, Staley, Saddleworth, and Rochdale from circa 1170 to 1905.* (Rochdale: Aldine Press, United Kingdom, 1905)

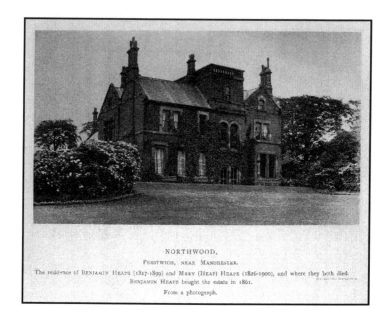

NORTHWOOD,

PRESTWICH, NEAR MANCHESTER.

The residence of BENJAMIN HEAPE (1817-1899) and MARY (HEAP) HEAPE (1825-1900), and where they both died.

BENJAMIN HEAPE bought the estate in 1861.

From a photograph.

3. "*Northwood*," Sedgley Park, near Manchester. Walter Heape grew up here and returned as an adult to conduct scientific experiments. Permission of Cambridge University. *Records of the Family of Heape, of Heape, Staley, Saddleworth, and Rochdale from circa 1170 to 1905.* (Rochdale: Aldine Press, United Kingdom, 1905)

4. *View of Manchester from Kersal Moor*, painted by William Wyld, 1852. The haze of smoke from the many chimney stacks is visible. Royal Collection Trust. Copyright ©, Her Majesty Queen Elizabeth II, 2016

5. Arthur Gamgee, Brackenbury Professor of Physiology at Manchester University. Walter Heape was an assistant in his laboratory. From *The Remarkable Gamgees*, by Ruth D'Arcy Thompson (Edinburgh: Ramsay Head Press, 1974)

6. Francis Maitland Balfour. Professor of Animal Morphology at Trinity College, Cambridge. Influential mentor of the young Walter Heape. Permission of Department of Zoology, Cambridge University

7. Skeleton of an elephant shot by Walter Heape in South Africa and presented to the University Museum of Zoology, Cambridge (author in foreground)

8. The Great Court, Trinity College, Cambridge at about the time Heape was a Balfour Student. By permission of The Master and Fellows of Trinity College, Cambridge

9. Ethel Ruston Heape, wife of Walter Heape. The couple would have three children and be married for thirty-five years. Courtesy of Steven Heape

10. Anton Dohrn. Respected figure in marine biology and Founder - Director of the Naples Stazione Zoologica. His advice to Walter Heape on establishing the laboratory at Plymouth created a lifelong friendship. Copyright © Stazione Zoologica Anton Dohrn di Napoli, Archivo Storico La.121.40

11. Sir (Edwin) Ray Lankester, by Charles George Beresford, NPGx19879. Distinguished biologist who became Director of the Natural History Department of the British Museum. Lankester hired Walter Heape for the Marine Biological Laboratory, eventually falling out with him. Copyright © National Portrait Gallery, London

THE PLYMOUTH LABORATORY

12. The Plymouth Marine Laboratory. Walter Heape became the first superintendent to oversee the building's construction. From the cover of the Journal of the Marine Biological Association Vol. 1 (N.S.), 1889-1890. Permission of National Marine Biological Laboratory

13. *"Heyroun,"* on Chaucer Road in Cambridge. This house was built for Walter Heape and his family soon after their marriage. Courtesy of the Director of the MRC Cognition and Brain Sciences Unit, Cambridge

14. Sir Francis Galton, by Eveleen Myers, NPGx19814. With this eminent scholar Walter Heape conducted experiments in artificial insemination in the rabbit. Galton invited Heape to join the Evolution Committee of the Royal Society of London. Copyright © National Portrait Gallery, London

15. Sir James Frazer, by Walter Stoneman, NPGx21923. Widely known "armchair anthropologist" and author of *The Golden Bough*. His interest in reproduction led to correspondence with Walter Heape. Copyright © National Portrait Gallery, London

16. The *Coral* underway. Courtesy of Steven Heape

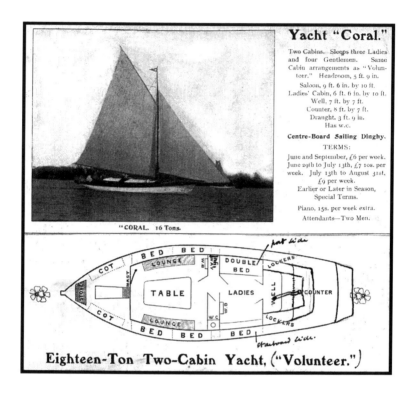

17. The yacht *Coral*, used by Heape for sailing on the Fens. Courtesy of Steven Heape

18. Walter and Ethel Heape with an unidentified companion on board the *Coral*. Courtesy of Steven Heape

19. The Heape and Grylls Cinematographic Machine, from W. H. Cornell, J Sci Instr 4, 82 (1926). Copyright © IOP Publishing. Reproduced with permission, all rights reserved

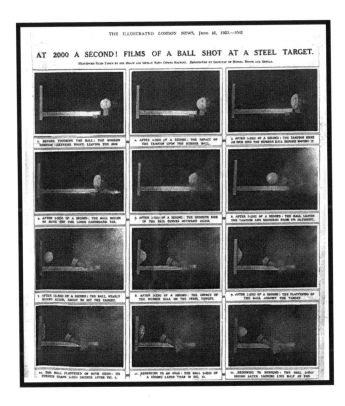

20. Photograph taken by the Heape and Grylls Cinematographic Machine. Images of this type were shown twice at a conversazione of the Royal Society of London in 1923 and published in popular magazines. Copyright © London Illustrated News

Appendix

Heape's correspondence with Anton Dohrn about treating the king and queen of Italy was written from home at *Heyroun* in Cambridge.

7 January, 1900

My dear Dohrn,

... I am worrying along at oestrus, menstruation, breeding, and sterility and so forth. The results do not come out so freely as I could wish, but at any rate the ground is getting cleared gradually ...

Yours sincerely, Walter Heape

14 September, 1903

My dear Dohrn

I want you to tell me, what do you think of the enclosed? In your opinion is the proposition I made one which is likely to interest the King? If so who do you think would be willing to put it before him and how do you advise such a man should be approached? I shall be greatly obliged to you for your opinion and for any help you may be able to give me.

It is long since I have heard from you, when you write back tell us how you are. We are all well and my wife sends you her kindest remembrances and tells me to ask you when we may again expect to see you here! All is well we hope with you and Mrs. Dohrn.

Our greetings to you. Yours sincerely, Walter Heape

PS. I want to get an heir for the King and I think I can do it!

14 September, 1903

My dear Dohrn,

After many years of work and experience I am disposed to think I may, under the circumstances, be of some service to His Majesty the King of Italy.

As you know I have been a student of biology since 1879, and have spent most of my time in original research, while during the last 15 years I have specially investigated matters concerned with the generative system of mammals. During this latter period I have also paid attention to the production of sex and to the means whereby the sex of offspring may be influenced. When I was in the midst of this work the subject was unfortunately brought into disrepute by one who presumed to publish generalisations on very insufficient data and on that account my opportunities for experiment were greatly curtailed; in spite of this however some 16 cases have been brought under my notice during recent years and my treatment has been attended with somewhat remarkable success.

Since a child must be either male or female a large number of cases is necessary to actually demonstrate the efficacy of any particular treatment and I cannot claim that my cases exclusively prove the efficacy of the treatment I have adopted, at the same time I would add that in every case in which my treatment has been carried out the child born was of the sex foretold. Two of these cases, since they bear more than usually conclusive evidence of the result being due to the treatment are of special interest and may be quoted here.

(1) The case of a mother with one son; she was treated with the object of producing a daughter and she bore a daughter, while two years later she was again treated, this time to satisfy her desire for a son, and she bore a son.

(2) The case of a mother who had a son, she was treated with the object of producing a daughter and she bore a daughter; the interest of this case lies in the fact that neither she herself nor any of her near relatives of the same generation had born a daughter, although they had produced eight sons.

In other cases mothers with two or more daughters and no sons, after treatment bore sons. The success of these cases is I think remarkable, and though I do not of course claim that the system I adopt is infallible, in my opinion, under the circumstances when it is urgently desired to bear a child of a particular sex, it is worthy of trial.

My system is not one which need cause any anxiety as regards the health of the patient. The mother alone is treated, it is necessary to begin the treatment some weeks before conception takes place, and it is necessary also that insemination should take place at a desired time. My experience undoubtedly demonstrates that each case must be treated on its own merits, and that the powers of assimilation of each individual, and the facility which each one possesses in a different degree for storing up nutriment and transmitting it to the embryo are factors of the first consequence.

The treatment is largely one of diet, but not entirely so, climate and its effects on exertion and on the stimulation of secretory powers bears a part, while the drugs, if any, which I may advise from time to time, are of the simplest nature, a tonic, a liver stimulant, or a purge.

This is my story, and, if you think if may possibly interest His Majesty, will you advise me what course you think it would be best to take with the object of placing myself at his disposal for such a purpose.

Believe me, yours sincerely, Walter Heape

30 September, 1903

My dear Dohrn,

Thank you for your letter. You treat my communication with the honesty I expected from you! Of course I don't expect you to put your name to anything you don't understand and approve of. There is no secret about my methods; my letter was a statement of my case to see what you thought of it as of possible value in certain cases; if, after reading this, you feel disposed to place the matter before His Imperial Majesty the Czar, "well and good."

I will tell you details of my treatment, but before doing that let me make a few comments on what you write, for, I think there are good reasons why a Royal personage should allow herself to be treated!

(1) So far as the lower animals are concerned, I have tried certain of them with the result that, I find interference with their natural food at the

breeding time is apt to prevent them from breeding altogether. The dietary of the lower animals is naturally very restricted, and their powers of adaptability to digest and assimilate strange foods is also very limited. Human beings, on the other hand, are not only more able to accommodate themselves to such changes but their symptoms under treatment are readily diagnosed, and they can <u>tell</u> you how they feel. This is no small advantage, as any veterinary surgeon will admit, and in my opinion, on this account, one experiment on a woman is worth fifty experiments on the lower animals!

(2) As for poor people it is difficult to get cases from this class

A. Because they are ignorant and superstitious and fear to meddle with what they call "the course of nature."

B. Because they don't really care very much which sex their child turns out to be, and,

C. Because they find great difficulty in providing themselves with the requisite foods, on account of the cost, and difficulty in following the treatment because of their daily duties.

For middle class people, the first two reasons hold also, and further, their indifference to the sex of their offspring is increased because they are rich enough to provide for girls as well as boys, and "heirs" are not of any great importance to them.

While for the aristocrats, they are almost as difficult to approach as Kings, and there are but few in this country who are not already provided with "heirs", which is all they care about.

(3) On the other hand, I would suggest, that, to none of these classes of people is an heir of such immense importance as he is to a King! and, therefore, providing there is no danger in the experiment, there is the greatest of all reasons why a Queen who needs a boy should make the experiment.

Do I make myself clear? And do you not agree with me?

It is of primary importance to state, as I have already done, that it is an experiment, the inquiry is not yet beyond that stage, nor can it possibly get beyond that stage for many years. But, I have had considerable success, and, as there is no danger in making the experiment, I claim that it is worthwhile to make it, where an heir is of imperative importance.

Now, with regard to my treatment, it is influenced very largely by the habit of body, the powers of digestion and assimilation, the tendency to the formation of acidity in the blood, by the vigour, the recuperative power, even the temperament, of each individual. I have not found it possible to lay down a definite rule, indeed I have never treated any two patients absolutely similarly, but yet, so far, I have made no mistake!

My first process is designed to break through the ordinary habit of body, and I find that is readily done by putting the patient on a strict diet, and, if possible, changing her usual place of abode, i.e., the climate she is most accustomed to. Thus, for 2 to 3 weeks, she would avoid all red meats and animal soups, live on vegetable soups, small quantities of fish and chicken, as much milk, cream, bread, butter, and starchy foods of all kinds as she is disposed to take, with jams, and fruits and other vegetables. During this time she is weighed and measured (round the hips) every week, and her diet modified in accordance with these results and with regard to her health.

Then, for the next 2 or 3 weeks, an opposite dietary is followed, of meat, meat soups, fish, eggs, protein biscuits, [?], dry toast, green vegetables, salads and so forth; milk and starchy foods being avoided. In the same way cafe´ au lait and chocolate is alternated with cafe´ noir and cocoa without milk; wine, with water, etc.

The strictness of the diet depends upon the variation in weight and measurement. With little trouble the weight can be altered from 5 to 10 percent and the measurement from 3 to 5 inches, on either side of the mean weight and measurement, according to the patient's physique. The alternation of diet would probably have to be repeated at shorter intervals and the result would be, what I call, a state of "unstable equilibrium", in which state the patient may be played upon with ease, and her reserve of nutriment increased or decreased as required.

There are various matters to be watched, such as acidity, the patient's vitality, the condition of her digestion and so forth, but I need not go into all such matters. I think the patient's physician would note what was necessary and treat her as his experience of her normal habit required.

In the case of a Royal patient I should of course require that everything done should be done with the knowledge of her physician, on the understanding that, while he would be free to give what drugs he found needful, he would not administer drugs of any kind without informing me of the fact and of the nature of them.

The time taken for this preliminary preparation depends upon the patient's powers of adaptation and the speed with which she reacts to treatment. It has taken one 3 months, on the other hand 6 weeks has been sufficient. This preliminary preparation is done before conception takes place, with the object of influencing: 1) the nature and amount of nutriment supplied to the ova in the ovary, and 2) the reserve of nutriment which every woman (and every mammal) stores up for the use of the prospective foetus.

Having gained a condition which appears to me satisfactory in accordance with the sex of the child required, the husband is advised. Then, for 2 to 3 months after conception a definite diet, founded on one or other of the above schemes, is continued, the strictness being gradually reduced until, at the end of the third month at the latest, complete liberty of diet is accorded, and I have no further work to do.

The above schemes of diet are the foundations of the lines upon which I work, but every individual requires modifications of them, more of one food, less of another; the proportions for each individual can only be determined by experience of her capacities and needs, and by experiment.

I think this is all. It is not much to look at! But you would be surprised, as I have been, to find what an extraordinary difference can rapidly be induced by these simple means. That this variation in habit of body affects the ovary, as well as every other organ in the body, there can be no doubt, and the success of the scheme depends on the completeness of the change produced and the diagnosis of the time when conception should take place; my work on menstruation, on ovulation, and my observations on the nutrition of the ovarian ovum, gives me the clue to this.

If you want to know more, ask me and I will tell you. If it is enough, you have carte blanche to use it as you think well. I regret to say, it is essential the physician, with whom I should have to work, should speak English! I could not trust myself to be sufficiently accurate in any other language.

Yours sincerely, Walter Heape

APPENDIX

30 September, 1903

My dear Dohrn,

I have not mentioned in the enclosed letter, which treatment is favourable to boys and which for girls. As a rule I find the protein diet favours the production of boys, the starch of girls; but this is not unreservedly so. A woman who naturally lives largely on meat may still produce an excess of females, and in such cases my rule in its extreme strictness does not apply. It is more nearly a general truth to say, that, a reduced supply of available nutriment, of a definite kind, favours the productions of boys; but here again this is not absolutely correct, for the mother with a comparatively small amount of reserve nutriment may transmit more to her foetus than another woman with a much larger reserve store.

Thus, not only does digestion, the power of assimilation and the power of storing up nutriment affect the question, but the mother's power to transmit nutriment to the embryo is of vital importance.

Some women, with good digestions and good assimilating powers, are capable of storing up very large reserves of nutriment, but they do not necessarily transmit this in an equally generous fashion to the embryo, they are not good mothers. On the other hand women who never retain nutriment in large quantities for themselves, may be excellent mothers, in as much as, when pregnant, they may eat largely, assimilate readily, and pass on nearly the whole of this food material at once to the foetus. These and other qualities comprise the "habit of body", of which I speak in my letter and needs such close attention.

Thus it is not one simple quality which determines my treatment, and my treatment is not itself a rigid one; the qualities and capacities of the patient herself are important factors. If you will think of this I believe you will not fail to see it must be so, and it is, in my opinion, the neglect of the individual or personal equation which has hitherto been the chief stumbling block to a solution of the problem.

It appeared to me in writing the enclosed letter that these details were not essential, and that it was possible they would rather confuse than simplify the account I have given, at the same time, if you require to make use of this letter you have also carte blanche to do so.

Yours sincerely, Walter Heape

31 October, 1903

My dear Dohrn,

I received your letter this morning and reply at once to assure you of my thanks for what you could <u>not</u> do!

It is very kind of you to write me so fully of the circumstances of the case, and you must believe I clearly understand what you tell me. Understand also please, that I will surely regard your letter as strictly confidential.

Even I, who am so specially interested in this particular matter, recognise that it is of very much less importance than the science as a whole, and of very much less importance than the welfare of the Zoological station! And you must know that I would not ask you to prejudice the influence you use so well and so judiciously, nor to hamper in any way the opportunities you may have to forward the interests of science, for so small a matter as my experiments on sex!

As for the disappointment! Why! I have had many disappointments in my life and expect many more! But one disappointment I do not expect, and that is the loss of your friendship! For that I have some pride, and that I would be greatly disappointed to lose! And so, with this sentiment of my regard for you, I would close this matter, and sign myself ...

Yours sincerely, Walter Heape

Bibliography of Walter Heape

1. Heape W. On the germinal layers and early development of the mole. Proc Roy Soc B Biol Sc 33:190, 1881.

2. Heape W. The development of the mole (*Talpa europa*). The formation of the germinal layers, and early development of the medullary groove and notochord. Quart J Micr Sci 23:412, 1883.

3. Heape W. The development of the mole (*Talpa europa*), the ovarian ovum, and segmentation of the ovum. Quart J Micr Sci 26:157, 1886a.

4. Heape W. The development of the mole (*Talpa europa*). Stages E to J. Quart J Micr Sci 27:123, 1886b.

5. Heape W. Notes on the fishing industry of Plymouth. J Marine Biol Assn 1:45, 1887.

6. Heape W. Description of the Laboratory of the Marine Biological Association at Plymouth. J Marine Biol Assn 1:96, 1887.

7. Heape W. Preliminary report upon the fauna and flora of Plymouth Sound. J Marine Biol Assn 1:153, 1887.

8. Heape W. Recent proposed modifications of the Darwinian Theory. J Plymouth Institute 9:389, 1887 (Abstract).

9. Heape W. Preliminary note of the transplantation and growth of mammalian ova within a uterine foster-mother. Proc Roy Soc B Biol Sc 48:457, 1890.

10. Heape W. The menstruation of *Semnopithecus entellus*. Phil Trans Roy Soc B Biol Sc 54:169, 1893.

11. Heape W. The menstruation of *Semnopithecus entellus*. Phil Trans Roy Soc B Biol Sc 185:411, 1894.

12. Heape W. The menstruation of *Semnopithecus entellus*. Trans Obstet Soc 36:213, 1894.

13. Heape W. The menstruation and ovulation of *Macacus rhesus*. Proc Roy Soc B Biol Sc 60:202, 1896.

14. Heape W. The menstruation and ovulation of *Macacus rhesus*, with observations on the changes undergone by the discharged follicle. Part II. Phil Trans Roy Soc B Biol Sc 188:135, 1897.

15. Heape W. The artificial insemination of mammals and subsequent possible fertilization or impregnation of their ova. Proc Roy Soc B Biol Sc 61:52, 1897.

16. Heape W. Further note on the transplantation and growth of mammalian ova within a uterine foster-mother. Proc Roy Soc B Biol Sc 62:178, 1897.

17. Heape W. On the menstruation of monkeys and the human female. Trans Obstet Soc 40:161, 1898.

18. Heape W. On menstruation and ovulation in monkeys and the human female. Brit Med J 21 (1982):1868, 1898.

19. Heape W. On the artificial insemination of mares. Veterinarian 71:202, 1898.

20. Heape W. Note on the fertility of different breeds of sheep, with remarks on the prevalence of abortion and barrenness therein. Proc Roy Soc B Biol Sc 65:99, 1899.

21. Heape W. Abortion, barrenness and fertility in sheep. J Roy Agric Soc Ser III:10, 1899.

22. Heape W. The "sexual season" of mammals and the relation of the "pro-oestrum" to menstruation. Quart J Micr Sci 44:1, 1900.

23. Heape W. Ovulation and degeneration of ova in the rabbit. Proc Roy Soc B Biol Sc 76:260, 1905.

24. Heape W. The source of the stimulus which causes the development of the mammary gland and the stimulation of milk. J Physiol 34:1, 1906.

25. Heape W. *The Breeding Industry. Its Value to the Country, and its Needs.* Cambridge University Press, Cambridge, 1906.

26. Heape W. Notes on the proportion of the sexes in dogs. Proc Camb Phil Soc 14:121, 1907.

27. Heape W. Notes of the influence of extraneous forces upon the proportion of sexes produced by canaries. Proc Camb Phil Soc 14:201, 1907.

28. Heape W. Note on Russo's attempt to show differentiation of sex in the ovarian ova of the rabbit. Proc Camb Phil Soc 14:609, 1908.

29. Heape W. The proportion of the sexes produced by whites and coloured peoples in Cuba. Proc Roy Soc B Biol Sc 81:32, 1909.

30. Heape W. The proportion of the sexes produced by whites and coloured peoples in Cuba. Phil. Trans B Biol Sc 200:271, 1909.

31. Heape W. Note on the so-called musculature of *"Taenia elliptica."* Parasitology 3:217, 1910.

32. Heape W. *Sex Antagonism.* Constable, London, 1913.

33. Heape W. *Preparation for Marriage.* Cassell, London, 1914.

34. Heape W. *Emigration, Migration and Nomadism.* Heffer, Cambridge, 1931 [posthumous].

Editorial contributions

Foster's and Balfour's *Elements of Embryology.* 2nd edition. Edited with Adam Sedgwick, 1883.

Editor of a series of three volumes, but only the first was published: *Text-book of Embryology. Volume 1. Invertebrata.* EW MacBride, London, 1914.

Jamestowne Bookworks
Williamsburg, Virginia

Recent titles

A Surgeon's Story — the Autobiography of Robert T. Morris. Roger Gosden & Pam Walker (2013).

In Vitro Fertilization Comes to America — Memoir of a Medical Breakthrough. Howard W. Jones Jr. (2014).

Various Verses by Gordon Burness — Complete Works of the Bard of Beckenham. Roger Gosden (Editor) (2015).

Howard & Georgeanna — Sixty Years of Marriage & Medicine. Howard W. Jones, Jr. (2015).

Forthcoming

This Old House in Appalachia. Roger Gosden

A Biologist in Paradise — Essays from Nature and Science. Roger Gosden.

Endnotes

CHAPTER 1

1. Birth Certificate. General Registry Office, United Kingdom. Registered 14 September, 1855.

2. Heape C and Heape R. Records of the Family of Heape, of Heape, Staley, Saddleworth, and Rochdale from circa 1170 to 1905. (Rochdale: Aldine Press, UK, 1905) 169.

3. South Australian Migrant Shipping. http://members.iinet.net.au/~perthdps/shipping/mig-sa1.htm#sa1

4. Legg JS (1972) Australian Dictionary of Biography. Volume 4.

5. Heape and Heape, Records of the Family of Heape.

6. Royal Collection Trust. Copyright © Her Majesty Queen Elizabeth II, 2016. Reproduced by permission.

7. Charles Darwin, The Life of Erasmus Darwin (1879) 1st Unabridged Edition, ed. Desmond King-Hele, Cambridge University Press, New York: 2003, 63.

8. Holt RV (1938) The Unitarian Contribution to Social Progress in England, Allen & Unwin, London.

9. Watt R (1988) Gender, Power and Unitarians in England 1760-1860. Longman, New York.

10. Heape and Heape, Records of the Family of Heape.

11. Ibid.

12. Ibid.

13. Robertson W (1877) The Life and Times of the Right Hon. John Bright. Published by the author, Rochdale.

14. Obituary, The Rochdale Observer and Standard. September 20, 1899.

15. RK Webb, Harriet Martineau. A Radical Victorian. Columbia University Press, New York, 1960. Wheatley V, The Life and Work of Harriet Martineau. London: Secker & Wartburg, 1957.

16. Elizabeth: Unitarian Chapel, Stand, nr. Manchester (20 August, 1885); Walter: Bedford Chapel, Bloomsbury, London (8 July, 1891). [Recorded in reference 2, also on Walter Heape's marriage certificate.]

17. Harmer S F Proc Linnean Soc Lond (1929-30) Session 102, 201.

18. Best G (1979) Mid-Victorian Britain 1851-75. London: Fontana, 181.

19. Desmond A (1994) Huxley: The Devil's Disciple. London: Michael Joseph, 14.

20. Charlton HB (1951) Portrait of a University, 1851-1951, to Commemorate the Centenary of Manchester University. (Manchester: Manchester UP).

21. Articles of Association. Companies House, Cardiff, UK.

22. Walter Heape unpublished diary.

23. Cassiope Report of Court No. 2524.22 April 1885. Port cities, Southampton. www.plimsoll.org.

24. Walter Heape unpublished diary.

25. Thompson, RD (1974) The Remarkable Gamgees. A Story of Achievement. Edinburgh: Ramsey Head Press.

26. S.V.F Butler, "Centers and peripheries: the development of British physiology, 1870-1914." J Hist Biol 21 (1988): 473-500.

27. Obituary Notice. Arthur Gamgee. The Lancet 173 (1909), 1141-1148.

28. Obituary notice, Marmaduke Alexander Lawson. J Bot 34 (1896), 191.

CHAPTER 2

1. Woollam DHM, "The Cambridge School of Physiology, 1850-1900," in Arthur Rook, ed., Cambridge and its contribution to medicine: Proceedings of the Seventh British Congress on the History of Medicine (London: Wellcome Institute, 1971).

2. Egremont M (1980) Balfour. A Life of Arthur James Balfour. Collins, London.

3. Alexander TE, PhD thesis. University Microfilms, Ann Arbor, MI, #70-2181.

4. Geison GL (1978) Michael Foster and the Cambridge School of Physiology. Princeton University Press, Princeton.

5. Foster M, Balfour FM (1874) Elements of Embryology. 1st ed. MacMillan, London.

6. Foster M (1882) Francis Maitland Balfour. Nature 26:313-314; Newton, A (1882) The Late Prof. Balfour. Nature 26, 342; Report of a Public Meeting Held at Cambridge 21 October 1882 to consider a Memorial to Professor

Balfour. Speech by Adam Sedgwick. Pp. 9-11. MacMillan and Bowes, Cambridge, 1882.

7. Osborn H. Impressions of Great Naturalists (Scribner, New York & London, 1924) 203-211. Reprinted with the permission of Scribner, a Division of Simon & Schuster, Inc., from Impressions of Great Naturalists by Henry Fairfield Osborn. Copyright ©1924 by Charles Scribner Sons. Copyright © renewed 1952 by Fairfield Osborn. All rights reserved.

8. Balfour FM (1881-2) A Treatise on Comparative Embryology. Vols. I and II. MacMillan, London.

9. E Ray Lankester, "Balfour's 'Comparative Embryology,'" Nature 25 (Nov. 10, 1881), 27.

10. Science 1 No. 9 (28 August 1880) pp. 97-98 (signed H.F.O.).

11. Anonymous (1881) Saturday Review. November 12, 609-610.

12. Osborn HF (1883) Francis Maitland Balfour. Science 2, 299-301.

13. Howes GB, Notes on a course of lectures delivered by Professor Balfour, Cambridge 1880. Handwritten notes preserved at the Cambridge University Library.

14. Haeckel E (1866) Generelle Morphologie der Organismen. Reimer, Berlin.

15. Haeckel E (1872) Anthropogenie. Engelmann, Leipzig. Quoted by: Dayrat B (2003) The roots of phylogeny: how did Haeckel build his trees? Syst Biol 52,515-527.

16. Quoted from Barnes, ME, "Karl Ernst von Baer's Laws of Embryology". Embryo Project Encyclopedia (2014-04-15). ISSN: 1940-5030 http://embryo.asu.edu/handle/10776/7821. See more at: http://embryo.asu.edu/pages/karl-ernst-von-baers-laws-embryology#sthash.yoFOSXVa.dpuf

17. Bowler PJ (1989) Development and adaptation: evolutionary concepts in British Morphology, 1870-1914. BJHS 22, 283-297.

18. Hall BK (2009) Embryos in evolution: evo-devo at the Naples Zoological Station in 1874.

19. Huxley TH (1849) On the anatomy and the affinities of the family of the Medusae Phil Trans Pt 2, p. 413.

20. Allman GJ (1853) On the anatomy and physiology of the Cordylophora, a contribution to our knowledge of the Tubularian Zoophytes. Phil Trans 143, 367-384.

21. Lankester ER (1873) On the primitive cell-layers of the embryos as the basis of genealogical classification of animals, and on the origin of vascular and lymph systems. Ann Mag Nat Hist 4 (fourth series), 321-338.

22. Haeckel E (1872) Die Kalkschwämme. Eine monographie. Verlag von Georg Reimer, Berlin.

23. Haeckel E (1873) On the Caleispongiae, their position in the animal kingdom, and their relation to the theory of descendence. Ann Mag Nat Hist Series 4 XI, 241-262. The term mesoderm is used twice on p 257 of this paper. (Translated by W.S. Dallas of the last two chapters of Haeckel's work on the Caleispongiae).

24. Cruikshank, W (1797) Experiments in which, on the third day after impregnation the ova of rabbits were found in the Fallopian tubes; and on the fourth day after impregnation in the uterus itself; with the first appearances of the foetus. Phil Trans 87, 197-214.

25. These words were not in use when Van Beneden, Kölliker and Heape published their papers.

26. Van Beneden E (1875) La maturation de l'oeuf, la fécundation et les premières phases du développement embryonnaire des mammifères d'après des recherches faites chez le lapin. Bull de l'Acad Roy de Sci de Belgique 40, 686-736.

27. Van Beneden E (1880) Recherches sur l'embryologie des mammifères. La formation des feuillets chez le lapin. Bull Acad Royal Belge.

28. Kölliker A (1882) Festschrift zur Feier des 300 Jährigen bestehens der Julius Maximilians-Universität zu Würzburg.

29. Rauber (1875) Die erste Entwichlung des Kaninchens. Sitzungsber. Naturfor Gesell. Leipzig. NO. 10, 103-109; Williams BS and Biggers JD (1990) Polar trophoblast (Rauber's layer) of the rabbit blastocyst. Anat Rec 227, 211-222.

30. Blackman HJ (2007) The natural sciences and the development of animal morphology in late-Victorian Cambridge. J Hist Biol 40, 71-108.

31. Trelfall R (1930) The origin of the automatic microtome. Biol Rev 5, 357-361.

32. Assheton R (1895) A re-investigation into the early stages of the development of the rabbit. Quart J Micr Sci 37, 113-164.

33. Hubrecht AAW (1905) Studies in mammalian embryology. II. The development of the germinal layers of Sorex vulgaris. Pp. 499-569.

34. Van Beneden E, Julin C (1880) Observations sur la maturation de l'oeuf chez les Cheiroptères. Arch Biol, Paris, 1, 551-571.

35. Lieberkühn N (1879) Über die Keimblätter der Säugethiere. Marburg: Universitäts-Buchdruckertei.

36. Asdell SA (1964) Patterns of Mammalian Reproduction. 2nd ed. Comstock Publishing Company, Ithaca, NY.

37. Huxley TH (1872) A Manual of the Anatomy of Vertebrate Animals. Appleton, New York; Huxley TH (1880) On the Application of the Laws of Evolution to the Arrangement of the Vertebrata and more Particularly of the Mammalia. Proc Zool Soc, London 43, 649-656.

38. Heape W. On the germinal layers and early development of the mole. Proc Roy Soc B Biol Sc 33:190, 1881.

39. Heape W. The development of the mole (Talpa europa). The formation of the germinal layers, and early development of the medullary groove and notochord. Quart J Micr Sci 23:412, 1883.

40. Heape W. The development of the mole (Talpa europa), the ovarian ovum, and segmentation of the ovum. Quart J Micr Sci 26:157, 1886a. Heape W. The development of the mole (Talpa europa). Stages E to J. Quart J Micr Sci 27:123, 1886b.Reproduced with permission.

41. Hertwig O (1912) Text-book of the embryology of man and mammals. Translated from the 3rd German edition by Marks EL. George Allen London; Swan Sonnenschein; Minot CS (1892) Human Embryology. Wood, New York.

42. Heape W. The development of the mole (Talpa europa). Stages E to J. Quart J Micr Sci 27:123, 1886b.

43. Council of the Senate, 27 March 1882.

44. Blackman, "Natural sciences and development of animal morphology in Late-Victorian Cambridge."

45. Sedgwick A (1882) Speech in a Report of a Public Meeting held in Cambridge on 21 October 1882 to consider a Memorial to Professor Balfour. Macmillan & Bowes, Cambridge.

46. Letter to the Vice-Chancellor from Humphry GM, Newton A, Foster M, Clark JW, dated 12 September 1882. Cambridge University Reporter, October 17, 1882.

47. Cambridge University Reporter.

48. Ibid.

49. Foster & Balfour: Elements of Embryology, 2d ed. by A Sedgwick & W Heape (London: Macmillan, 1883).

50. Ibid.

51. Blackman, "The natural sciences and the development of animal morphology in late Victorian Cambridge." J Hist Biol 40, 71-108.

52. Addo Elephant National Park. https://www.sanparks.org/parks/addo/

53. Sedgwick A (1885) The development of Peripatus capensis. Quart J Micr Sci 94, 449-468.

54. Report of the Special Board for Biology and Geology 12 March 1884. Cambridge University Library UA CUR 39.36. Item 11.

55. Report of the Special Board for Biology and Geology 26 May 1884. Cambridge University Library UA CUR 39.36. Item 12.

56. Cambridge University Reporter 15 December 1885, p. 284.

CHAPTER 3

1. Dohrn A (1872) The foundation of zoological stations. Nature 5, 277-280, 437-440.

2. Groeben C (1984) The Naples Zoological Station and Woods Hole. Oceanus 27, 60-69.

3. Report of the 40th Meeting of the British Association for the Advancement of Science held in Liverpool 1870. (1871) John Murray, London. P. lxi.

4. Dohrn A (1872) Report of the Committee for the Purpose of Promoting the Foundation of Zoological Stations in Different Parts of the World. In: Report of the 41st Meeting of The British Association for the Advancement of Science held in Edinburgh in August 1871. John Murray, London. P. lxxi; The British Association Meeting in Edinburgh. Nature 4, 317.

5. Lankester ER, "Summary of zoological observations made at Naples in the winter of 1871-72," Annals and Magazine of Natural History 11 (1873), 97.

6. Lankester ER, "An American Sea-side Laboratory," Nature 21 (1880), 497-499.

7. Notes, Nature 21 (1880), 596.

8. Huxley TH (1881) The herring. Nature 23, 607-613.

9. Huxley TH (1882) The salmon disease. Nature 25, 437-440.

10. Fryer CE (1883) A National Fisheries Society. Results of the International Fisheries Exhibition, London, England. Clowes and Sons, London.

11. Lankester CR (1883) The scientific results of the International Fisheries Exhibition, London 1883. International Fisheries Exhibition, London, England. Clowes and Sons, London; Lankester, CR (1883) Value of a marine laboratory to the development and regulation of our sea fisheries. Nature 32, 65-67.

12. Report of the Foundation Meeting of the Marine Biological Association. J Marine Biological Assn 1, 22-39, 1887. Marine Biological Association Archives.

13. Lester J, Bowles PJ eds. (1995) E Ray Lankester and the Making of Modern British Biology. British Society for the History of Science, Oxford.

14. An English Biological Station. The Times (London) 31 March 1884.

15. The Duke of Argyll, the Earl of Dalhousie, Lord Arthur Russell, the Lord Mayor, the prime warden of the Fishmongers' Company, the President of the Royal Society (Professor Huxley), the Presidents of the Linnean (Sir John Lubbock), Zoological (Professor Flower), and Royal Microscopical Societies (Dr. Dallinger), Dr WB Carpenter, CB, FRS, Mr WS Caine, MP, Mr Frank Crisp VP and Treasurer, Linnean Society, and Secretary of the Royal Microscopical Society, Mr Thomas Christy FLS, Mr Thiselton Dyer FRS, CMG, Mr John Evans (Treasurer of the Royal Society), Dr Albert Güntherm FRS, Sir Joseph Hooker KCSI, Professor Michael Foster (Secretary of the Royal Society), Professor E Ray Lankester FRS, Professor Ewart FRSE, Professor Milnes Marshall, Professor Moseley FRS, Mr John Murray FRSE, the Rev Dr Norman FLS, Sir Lyon Playfair KCB, Mr George J Romanes FRS, Professor Burdon Sanderson FRS, Dr Sclater FRS, Mr Adam Sedgwick, Mr Percy Sladen FLS, Dr HC Sorby FRS, Mr Charles Stewart FLS.

16. Report of the Foundation Meeting of the Marine Biological Association, J Marine Biol Assoc. 1 (1887) 22-39. Marine Biological Association Archives.

17. E Ray Lankester to Anton Dohrn, 7 August 1884. Copyright © Stazione Zoologica Anton Dohrn di Napoli, Archivio Storico A. 1884.

18. Anton Dohrn to Ray Lankester, 15 August 1884. Copyright © Stazione Zoologica Anton Dohrn di Napoli, Archivio Storico A. 1884.

19. Anton Dohrn to E Ray Lankester, 27 August 1884. Copyright © Stazione Zoologica Anton Dohrn di Napoli, Archivo Storico A. 1884.

20. Report of the Council of the Marine Biological Association for the year 1887-1888 in J Marine Biol Assoc (OS) ii, 116-124. Marine Biological Association Archives.

21. Minutes of the Council of the Marine Biological Association. 13 May 1885. Marine Biological Laboratory Library. Marine Biological Association Archives.

22. Minutes of the Council of the Marine Biological Association. 12 June 1885. Marine Biological Laboratory Library. Marine Biological Association Archives.

23. Walter Heape to Alfred Newton, 12 December 1886. Cambridge University Library. Add. 9839/1H/542.

24. Report of the Commissioner of Fish and Fisheries, USA. 1885.

25. Woods Holl is the old name of Woods Hole. Also the Fisheries Laboratory should not be confused with the Marine Biological Laboratory, Woods Hole, which was not founded until 1888.

26. Minutes of the Council of the Marine Biological Association, 27 October 1885. Marine Biological Laboratory Library. Marine Biological Association Archives.

27. Minutes of the Council of the Marine Biological Association, 14 December 1885. Marine Biological Laboratory Library. Marine Biological Association Archives.

28. E Ray Lankester to TH Huxley, 8 December 1885, 9n Huxley papers, Vol. 21, 90, Imperial College Archives.

29. E Ray Lankester to Thiselton-Dyer, 14 November 1885, in Thistleton-Dyer papers, Kew.

30. Minutes of the Council of the Marine Biological Association, 14 December 1885. Marine Biological Laboratory Library. Marine Biological Association Archives.

31. Lankester to Council of the Marine Biological Association, 28 January 1886. Marine Biological Association Archives.

32. Minutes of the Council of the Marine Biological Association, 14 December 1885. Marine Biological Association Archives.

33. Bericht über die Zoologische Station Würhrend der Jahre 1885-1892.

34. E Ray Lankester to Anton Dohrn, 9 April 1886. Copyright © Stazione Zoologica Anton Dohrn di Napoli, Archivio Storico A. 1886.

35. Meeting of the Council. 19 March 1886. Marine Biological Laboratory Library.

36. Walter Heape to Alfred Newton, 12 December 1886, Cambridge University Library Add 9839/1h/542.

37. Meeting of the Council 7 June 1886. Marine Biological Laboratory Library. Marine Biological Association Archives.

38. Heape to Newton, 18 July 1886. Cambridge University Library Add. 9839/1H/540.

39. Heape to Newton, 9 October 1886. Cambridge University Library Add. 9839/1H/541.

40. Walter Heape to Anton Dohrn, 20 November 1886. Copyright © Stazione Zoologica Anton Dohrn di Napoli, Archivio Storico A. 1886.

41. Anton Dohrn to Walter Heape, 26 November 1886. Copyright © Stazione Zoologica Anton Dohrn di Napoli, Archivio Storico A. 1886.

42. Walter Heape to Anton Dohrn, 2 December 1886. Copyright © Stazione Zoologica Anton Dohrn di Napoli, Archivio Storico A. 1886.

43. Meeting of the Council 27 May 1887. Marine Biological Laboratory Library. Marine Biological Association Archives.

44. From bulter, a word from the Cornish fisheries, referring to: "...strong lines 500 feet long, with 60 hooks, each 8 feet asunder..." Oxford English Dictionary.

45. Heape W, "Notes on the Fishing Industry of Plymouth," Journal of the Marine Biological Association 1 (1887) 45-95. Marine Biological Association Archives.

46. Currency used in the United Kingdom before 1971. A shilling (s) contains 12 pennies (d) and one pound (£) contains 20 shillings. A maund is a measure of capacity varying with the locality and the commodity to be measured (Oxford English Dictionary). The variability of this measure is shown by Heape's estimate that a maund of flatfish is about 70 lbs, while a maund of round fish is only 6 lb.

47. Heape W, "Notes on the fishing industry."

48. Ibid. Heape W. Notes on the fishing industry of Plymouth. J Marine Biol Assn 1:45, 1887.

49. Day F (1887) National Fish Culture Association for 1887. Pp. 274-282.

50. Heape W (1887) Description of the Laboratory of the Marine Biological Association at Plymouth. J Marine Biol Assn Issue 1, 96-104. Marine Biological Association Archives.

51. Report of the Council of the Marine Biological Association for year 1887-1888. Held on 27 June, J Marine Biol Assoc (OS) ii, 116-122. Marine Biological Association Archives.

52. TH Huxley to Michael Foster, 30 September 1887. Medical History, Suppl 2009 (28) 166-190. No. 233: ALS H356. Wellcome Library, London.

53. TH Huxley to Michael Foster, 1 February 1886. Medical History. Suppl 2009 (28) 153-165. No. 188: ALS H324. Wellcome Library, London.

54. Anton Dohrn to Lankester, 12 December 1886. Copyright © Stazione Zoologica Anton Dohrn di Napoli, Archivio Storico A. 1886.

55. E Ray Lankester to TH Huxley, 10 January 1888. Archives Imperial College London. Huxley Papers. Vol.21, 111.

56. Walter Heape to Anton Dohrn, 26 January 1888. Copyright © Stazione Zoologica Anton Dohrn di Napoli, Archivio Storico A. 1888.

57. Plymstock Radford is an electoral ward of the City of Plymouth bordering on Plymouth Sound.

58. Report of the Resident Superintendent 5th December 1887. J Marine Biological Association (OS) II, 142-152. Marine Biological Association Archives. The Challenger Expedition (1872-1876) was made possible by the loan of a ship from the Royal Navy refitted for scientific research. It is credited with laying the foundation of the science of oceanography.

59. Report of the Council of the Marine Biological Association for 1886. 24 June 1887. J Marine Biol Assoc 1, 40-43.

60. Boswarva J (1861-2) A Catalogue of the Marine Algae of Plymouth. Trans Plymouth Institute. Pp.67-86. Report of the Council of the Marine Biological Association for 1886. J Marine Biol Assoc 1 (OS) (24 June 1887), 40-43.

61. Obituary. Parfitt, Edward 1820-1893. Trans Devon Assoc 25, 159-162.

62. Cunningham JT (1888) Preliminary enquiries at Plymouth into the marine fauna and the ova of fishes. J Marine Biol Assoc OS 11, 194-201. Marine Biological Association Archives.

63. Report of the Resident Superintendent, 5 December 1887. Marine Biological Association Archives.

64. Report to MBA Council, 27 June 1888. Marine Biological Association Archives.

65. Walter Heape to Anton Dohrn, 30 January, 1887, 26 January, 1888, 4 November, 1890. Copyright © Stazione Zoologica Anton Dohrn di Napoli, Archivio Storico A. 1887.

66. Ethel Heape to Anton Dohrn, 28 December 1898. Copyright © Stazione Zoologica Anton Dohrn di Napoli, Archivio Storico A. 1898.

CHAPTER 4

1. Part of this chapter is based on Biggers JD (1991) Walter Heape FRS: a pioneer in reproductive biology: Centenary of his embryo transfer experiments. J Reprod Fertil 93, 173-186.

2. Heape C, Heape R (1905) Records of the Family of Heape, of Heape, Staley, Saddleworth, and Rochdale from circa 1170 to 1905. p. 169. Aldine Press, Rochdale (England).

3. In the 19th century cleavage was called segmentation.

4. Heape W. Preliminary note of the transplantation and growth of mammalian ova within a uterine foster-mother. Proc Roy Soc B Biol Sc 48:457, 1890.

5. Heape W (1897) Further note on the transplantation and growth of mammalian ova within a uterine foster-mother. Proc Roy Soc Lond 62, 178-183.

6. Ibid.

7. Locke FS (1901) Die Wirkung der Metalle des Blutplasmas und verschiedener Zucker auf das isolierte. Saugetierherz Zentralbl Physiol 14, 670-672.

8. Heape W. Preliminary note of the transplantation and growth of mammalian ova within a uterine foster-mother. Proc Roy Soc B Biol Sc 48:457, 1890.

9. Ibid.

10. The Plymouth Institution was founded in 1812, for the promotion of Literature, Science, and the Fine Arts, in the town and neighbourhood.

11. Heape W (1887) Recent proposed modifications of the Darwinian Theory. Rep. Trans. Plymouth Institution 9, 389-391 (abstr.).

12. Bowler PJ (1983) The Eclipse of Darwinism. Johns Hopkins University Press.

13. Application from Walter Heape to the Balfour Memorial Fund submitting his candidacy for the 1890 Balfour Studentship, 26 September 1890. University Archives, University Library, Cambridge.

14. Romanes GJ (1895) Darwin, and after Darwin. Vol. II. Pp. 145-148. Chicago, Open Court Publishing Co.

15. Ibid.

16. Heape W. Further note on the transplantation and growth of mammalian ova within a uterine foster-mother. Proc Roy Soc B Biol Sc 62:178, 1897.

17. Darwin C (1868) The Variation of Animals and Plants under Domestication. Chapter 11. Johns Hopkins paperback edition (1998), Baltimore. Maryland.

18. Leonard JA, Rohland N, Glaberman S, Fleischer RC, Caccone A, Hofreiter M (2005) A rapid loss of stripes: the evolutionary history of the extinct quagga. Biol Letters 1, 291-295.

19. Earl of Morton (1821) A communication of a singular fact in natural history. Phil Trans Roy Soc Lond 111, 20-22.

20. Raboud Etienne (1914) Telegony. J Hered 5, 389-399.

21. Flint A (1883) A Text-book of Human Physiology. Appleton, New York.

22. Amphimixis is a term introduced by August Weismann to denote the fusion of two cells, such as a spermatozoon and an ovum. In this case it is equivalent to fertilization.

23. Weissman A. (1893) The germ plasm: a theory of heredity. (Translation by William N Parker) Scott, London.

24. Heape W. Further note on the transplantation and growth of mammalian ova within a uterine foster-mother. Proc Roy Soc B Biol Sc 62:178, 1897.

25. Ewart JC (1899) The Penycuik Experiments. London, A & C Black.

26. "The Penycuik Experiments," editorial reprinted by permission from Macmillan Publishers Ltd: Nature 60 (1899) 272-274.

27. Liu YS (2010) Telegony, the sire effect and non-Mendelian inheritance. Anim Reprod Sci 46, 338-343; Crean, AJ, Kappa, AM, Bonduriansky, R (2014) Revisiting telegony: offspring inherit an acquired characteristic of their mother's previous mate. Ecology Letters 17, 1543-1552.

28. Heape and Heape, Records, 169.

29. Obituary (1910) Samuel Buckley. The Lancet 1 (June 25), 1793.

30. Jaina Sutra, Trans. Jacobi H (1964) In: Muller MF (Ed.) Sacred Books of the East, vol. 22. Motilala Banarsidass, Delhi, pp. 217-270.

31. Niemann H, Kues WA (2003) Application of transgenesis in livestock for agriculture and biomedicine. Anim Reprod Sci 79, 291-317.

32. Biggers JD (2012) In vitro fertilization and embryo transfer: historical origin and development. Reprod Biomed Online 25, 118-127.

CHAPTER 5

1. Sutton JB. Menstruation in monkeys, British Gynaecological Journal (later Proc Roy Soc Med) 2 (1886) 289.

2. Balfour Memorial Fund. Cambridge University Reporter. June 12, 1883, p. 832.

3. Letter from Walter Heape to Professor Alfred Newton, 6 December, 1889, University Archives, University Library.

4. Letter by Walter Heape to the Balfour Memorial Fund submitting his candidature for the 1890 Balfour Studentship. 26 September 1890. University Archives, University Library, Cambridge University.

5. Heape, W (undated) Letter to the Royal Society of London.

6. Letter from Walter Heape to the Balfour Memorial Fund submitting his candidature for the 1890 Balfour Studentship. 26 September 1890. University Archives, University Library, Cambridge University.

7. Minutes of the Selection Committee for the Balfour Studentship. 24 October 1890; Letter from Walter Heape to the Secretary of the Balfour Memorial Fund accepting the 1890 Balfour Studentship University Archives, University Library, Cambridge.

8. Chanda S, Caulton E (1999) David Douglas Cunningham (1843-1914): a biographical profile. Aerobiologia 15, 255-258.

9. Report to the Managers of the Balfour Studentship by Walter Heape, 5 November 1893. University Archives, University Library, Cambridge University.

10. Jacks LP (1917) Life and letters of Stopford Brooke. Scribner, New York.

11. Heape W. The menstruation of Semnopithecus entellus. Phil Trans Roy Soc B Biol Sc 54:169, 1893.

12. Heape W. The menstruation of Semnopithecus entellus. Phil Trans Roy Soc B Biol Sc 185:411, 1894.

13. Heape W. The menstruation and ovulation of Macacus rhesus. Proc Roy Soc B Biol Sc 60:202, 1896.

14. Heape W. The menstruation and ovulation of Macacus rhesus, with observations on the changes undergone by the discharged follicle. Part II. Phil Trans Roy Soc B Biol Sc 188:135, 1897.

15. Sutton, "Menstruation in monkeys," 289.

16. Heape W. The menstruation and ovulation of Macacus rhesus. Proc Roy Soc B Biol Sc 60:202, 1896.

17. Heape W. The menstruation of Semnopithecus entellus. Phil Trans Roy Soc B Biol Sc 185:411, 1894.

18. Minot CS (1892) Human Embryology. William Wood and Co., New York.

19. Heape W. The menstruation and ovulation of Macacus rhesus, with observations on the changes undergone by the discharged follicle. Part II. Phil Trans Roy Soc B Biol Sc 188:135, 1897.

20. A Milnes Marshall, Vertebrate Embryology (London: GP Putman's Sons, 1893) 457-465.

21. Obituary Notice (1894-95). Arthur Milnes Marshall. Proc Roy Soc Lond 57, i-v.

22. Heape W. On the menstruation of monkeys and the human female. Trans Obstet Soc 40:161, 1898.

23. Johnstone AW (1895) The relation of menstruation to the other reproductive functions. Am J Obstet 32: 33-48.

24. Heape W. On the menstruation of monkeys and the human female. Trans Obstet Soc 40:161, 1898. Heape W. On menstruation and ovulation in monkeys and the human female. Brit Med J 21 (1982):1868, 1898.

25. Hitschmann F, Adler L (1908) Der Bau der Uterusschleimhaut des geschlechtsreifer Weibes mit besonderer Beruücksichtigung der Menstruation. Monatsschrift fuür Geburtshuülfe u. Gynäkologie 27, 1-82.

26. Tabibzadeh S (1996) The signals and molecular pathways involved in human menstruation, a unique process of tissue destruction and remodelling. Mol Hum Reprod 2, 77-92.

27. Salamonsen LA (2003) Tissue injury and repair in the female human reproductive tract. Reproduction 125, 301-311.

28. Heape W. The "sexual season" of mammals and the relation of the "pro-oestrum" to menstruation. Quart J Micr Sci 44:1, 1900.

29. Heape W. Ovulation and degeneration of ova in the rabbit. Proc Roy Soc B Biol Sc 76:260, 1905.

CHAPTER 6

1. Lazzaro Spallanzani, Dissertations relative to the natural history of animals and vegetables, Vol. 2, Thomas Beddoes, Trans. (London: J. Murray, 1784; Gale ECCO, Print Editions, 2010) 79-80.

2. Asdell SA (1964) Patterns of mammalian reproduction. Cornell University Press, 2nd ed. Ithaca, NY.

3. Heape W. The menstruation of Semnopithecus entellus. Phil Trans Roy Soc B Biol Sc 185:411, 1894.

4. Heape W. The menstruation and ovulation of Macacus rhesus, with observations on the changes undergone by the discharged follicle. Part II. Phil Trans Roy Soc B Biol Sc 188:135, 1897.

5. Wiltshire A (1883) The comparative physiology of menstruation. Brit Med J 1 395-400, 446-448, 500-502; Veterinary J & Ann Comp Path 16, 257-266, 349-353; 17, 16-27.

6. Heape W. The "sexual season" of mammals and the relation of the "pro-oestrum" to menstruation. Quart J Micr Sci 44:1, 1900. Reproduced by permission of the Company of Biologists.

7. Ibid.

8. Ibid.

9. Asdell SA (1931) Estrus. Nature 73, 341-342. Tyson SL (1931) Oestrus. Nature 74, 512-513. Asdell SA (1932) Oestrus. Nature 75, 131-132. Corner GW (1937) Etymology and pronunciation of the word "oestrus" and its derivatives. Nature 85, 197-198.

10. Review: Simmer HH (1977) Pflüger's nerve reflex theory of menstruation: The product of analogy, teleology and neurophysiology,Clio Medica 12, 57-90.

11. Müller J (1843) Elements of Physiology.Book 8, 828. (Lea and Blanchard, Philadelphia (Translated from the German).

12. Retterer E (1892) Sur les modifications de la muqueuse uterine a l'époque du rut. Comptes rendu Soc de Biol 44, 637-642.

13. Hartman CG (1929) The homology of menstruation. Science 92, 1992-1995.

14. Hartman CG (1928) A readily detectable sign of ovulation in the monkey. Science 68, 452- 453.

15. Pouchet FA (1842) Thèorie positive de l'ovulation spontanée et de la fecundation des mammifères et de l'espèce humaine. Roret, Paris.

16. Bischoff TLW (1847) Proofs that the periodic maturation and discharge of the ova are, in the Mammalia and the human female independent of coition, as a first condition of their propagation. (Translated from the German by CR Gilman and T Tellkampf). Rare Books, Harvard 24.c.1847.1

17. Dalton JC (1851) On the corpus luteum of menstruation and pregnancy. Trans AMA 4, 548-624.

18. Editorial (1968) John C. Dalton, Jr. (1825-1889) Experimental Physiologist. JAMA 203, 155-156.

19. Heape W. The menstruation and ovulation of Macacus rhesus. Proc Roy Soc B Biol Sc 60, 202, 1896.

20. Heape W. The "sexual season" of mammals and the relation of the "pro-oestrum" to menstruation. Quart J Micr Sci 44, 1, 1900.

21. Marshall, FHA (1904) The oestrous cycle in the common ferret. Quart J Micr Sci 48, 323-345.

22. Marshall FHA (1903) The oestrous cycle and the formation of the corpus luteum in the sheep. Phil Trans B 47-96.

23. Marshall FHA (1904) The oestrous cycle in the common ferret. Quart J Micro Sci 48, 323.

24. Marshall FHA, Jolly WA (1905) Contributions to the physiology of mammalian reproduction. Part I. The oestrous cycle in the dog. Part II The ovary as an organ of internal secretion. Phil Trans B 99-121.

25. Evans HM, Cole HH (1931) An introduction to the study of the oestrous cycle in the dog. Memoirs of the University of California 9, No. 2, 65-101.

26. Marshall FHA. The Physiology of Reproduction (London: Longman, Green and Co., 1910).

27. Parkes AS ed. Marshall's Physiology of Reproduction, 3d ed. (London: Longmans, Green & Co., 1960) p. ix.

28. Letter from Walter Heape to Professor Alfred Newton, 6 December, 1889, University Archives, University Library.

29. Review: Hartman CG, Leathem JH (1963) Oogenesis and ovulation. In: Mechanisms concerned with Conception. Hartman, CG ed. Macmillan, New York.

30. Heuser, CH, Streeter, GL (1941) Development of the macaque embryo. Carnegie Contrib Embryol 29, 15-55.

31. Hertig AT, Rock J, Adams EA (1956) A description of 34 human ova within the first 17 days of development. Amer J Anat 98, 435-493.

32. Sengoopta C (2000) The modern ovary: constructions, meanings, uses. Hist Sci 38, 425-488.

33. Martin C. (1893) The nerve theory of menstruation. Brit Gyn J 9, 271-283.

34. Starling EH (1905) The Croonian Lectures on the chemical correlation of the functions of the body. The Lancet, Aug 5, 339-341.

35. Heape W. Ovulation and degeneration of ova in the rabbit. Proc Roy Soc B Biol Sc 76:260, 1905.

CHAPTER 7

1. Walter Heape to Francis Galton, 1 July 1894, Special Collection, University College, London.
2. Walter Heape to Francis Galton, 3 July 1894, Special Collection, University College, London.
3. Moore-Colyer R (1995) Aspects of horse breeding and the supply of horses in Victorian Britain. Agr Hist Rev 43, 47-60.
4. Sidney S (1893) The Book of the Horse. New Edition. Cassell & Company, London. p. 98.
5. Galton F, unpublished document, 1894, Special Collection, University College, London.
6. Spallanzani L (1789) A dissertation concerning the artificial fecundation of certain mammals. Trans. by Thomas Beddoes. Gale Ecco Print Edition, Vol. 2, 143.
7. Spallanzani L (1789) Part of a letter from Abbé Spallanzani to the Marquis Lucchesini, Chamberlain to the King of Prussia, Trans. Thomas Beddoes. Gale Ecco Print Edition. Vol 2, 475.
8. Home E (1799) An account of the dissection of an hermaphrodite dog. To which are prefixed some observations on hermaphrodites in general. Phil Trans Roy Soc 89, 157-178.
9. Poynter FNL (1968) Hunter, Spallanzani, and the history of artificial insemination. In: Medicine Science and Culture. Ed Stevenson LG & Multhauf RP. Johns Hopkins Press, Baltimore.
10. The Réaumur temperature scale was widely used in Europe. The French adopted the Celsius scale in 1790. To convert from the Réaumur scale to the Celsius scale multiply by 5/4.
11. Spallanzani L, Dissertation concerning artificial fecundation.
12. Spallanzani L, Dissertation concerning artificial fecundation.
13. Hunter J (1792) Observations on bees, Phil Trans Roy Soc 128-195.
14. Charles Bonnet to Spallanzani. In A dissertation concerning the artificial fecundation of certain mammals, Vol. 2, 284.
15. Spallanzani L, Part of a letter from Spallanzani to the Marquis Lucchesini.
16. Schellen AMCM (1957) Artificial Insemination in the Human. Elsevier, Amsterdam. Pp. 7-24.
17. Sims JM (1866) Clinical notes on uterine surgery, with special reference to the management of the sterile condition. London: Hardwicke.

18. Poynter, "Hunter, Spallanzani, and the history of artificial insemination."

19. Gérard J (1888) Nouvelles causes de stérilité dans les deux sexes. Fécondation artificielle comme moyan ultime de traitment. Marpnet and Flammarion, Paris.

20. Rambaud Y, de Laforest D (1884) Le Faiseur d'Hommes avec une preface de M. George Barral. Marpnet and Flammarion, Paris.

21. Richards M (2008) Artificial insemination and eugenics: celibate motherhood, eutelegenesis and germinal choice. Studies in History and Philosophy of Biological and Biomedical Sciences 39, 211-221.

22. Lee RB (1897) A history and description of the modern dogs of Great Britain and Ireland. Sporting Division. Vol II, Ch XIX. Horace Cox, London.

23. The details of Millais' experiments were published in 1897 by Heape. See also "A Dog Breeder" (1884) Artificial insemination. Veterinary J 18, 256-258.

24. Heape to Galton, July 1894, Special Collection, University College, London.

25. Heape to Galton, 31 July 1894, Special Collection, University College, London.

26. Heape to Galton, 14 October 1894, Special Collection, University College, London.

27. Heape to Galton, 5 May 1895, Special Collection, University College, London.

28. Heape to Galton, 11 May 1895, Special Collection, University College, London.

29. Galton F (1897) The average contribution of each several ancestor to the total heritage of the offspring Proc Roy Soc 61, 401-413.

30. Heape to Galton, 1 December 1895, Special Collection, University College, London.

31. Heape W. The artificial insemination of mammals and subsequent possible fertilization or impregnation of their ova. Proc Roy Soc B Biol Sc 61:52, 1897.

32. Heape W. On the artificial insemination of mares. Veterinarian 71:202, 1898.

33. J Reprod Fertil 3 (1) 8, from 'Sir John Hammond CBE, FRS, an interview' with Professor AS Parkes. Reprinted by permission.

34. Iwanoff E (1907) De la fecundation artificielle chez les mammifères. Archive des sciences biologique. St Petersburg 12, 277-503.

35. Iwanow E (1930) Artificial insemination of mammals. Vet Rec 10, 25-30. (Trans. H Fox).

CHAPTER 8

1. Walter Heape, The Breeding Industry: Its Value to the Country and its Needs, Cambridge: Cambridge University Press, 1906.

2. Wallace AR (1889) On the tendency of varieties to depart indefinitely from the original type. Proc Linn Soc 3, 53-62.

3. A detailed fascinating description on Galton's work assembling this large data base and its analysis is given by Gillam NW (2001) A Life of Sir Francis Galton. Oxford University Press.

4. Galton F (1889) Natural Inheritance. Macmillan London.

5. Obituary. Walter Frank Raphael Weldon, 1860-1906. Biometrika 5, 1-52.

6. Weldon WFR (1890) The variations occurring in certain decapod crustaceans, I. Crangon vulgaris. Proc Roy Soc 47, 445-453.

7. Weldon WFR (1892) Certain correlated variables in Crangon vulgaris. Proc Roy Soc 51, 1-21.

8. Weldon WFR (1893) On certain correlated variations in Carcinus moenas, Proc Roy Soc 54, 318-329.

9. Report of the Committee, consisting of Mr Galton (Chairman), Mr F Darwin, Professor Macalister, Professor Meldola, Professor Poulton, and Professor Weldon, "for the conduction of statistical enquiries into the Measurable Characteristics of Plants and Animals." Part I. "An attempt to measure the death-rate due to the Selective Destruction of Carcinus moenas with respect to a particular dimension." Drawn up for the Committee by Professor Weldon, F.R.S. Proc Roy Soc 57, 360-379 (1894).

10. Grant from the Donation Fund of the Royal Society. (1894) Proc Roy Soc 57, 60-68.

11. Weldon WFR (1894) Remarks on variation in animals and plants. To accompany the First Report of the Committee for conducting Statistical Inquiries into the Measurable Characteristics of Plants and Animals. Proc Roy Soc 57, 379-382.

12. Bateson W (1894) Materials for the Study of Evolution, Treated with Especial Regard to the Discontinuity in the Origin of Species. MacMillan, London.

13. Weldon WFR (1894) Review of Bateson. Nature 50, 25-26.

14. Minutes of a Meeting at the Royal Society January 14, 1897.

15. Minutes of a Meeting at the Royal Society February 11, 1897.

16. Lord Walsingham was the 7th Baron who owned an estate in Merton, Norfolk.

17. Heape to Galton, 16 December 1896, Special Collection, University College, London.

18. Heape to Galton, 5 January, 1897, Special Collection, University College, London.

19. Heape to Galton, 7 January, 1897, Special Collection, University College, London.

20. Heape to Galton, 11 February, 1897, Special Collection, University College, London.

21. Heape W. Note on the fertility of different breeds of sheep, with remarks on the prevalence of abortion and barrenness therein. Proc Roy Soc B Biol Sc 65:99, 1899.

22. Heape W. Abortion, barrenness and fertility in sheep. J Roy Agric Soc Ser III:10, 1899.

23. Minutes of the meeting at the Royal Society February 11, 1897.

24. Minutes of the meeting at the Royal Society February 26, 1897.

25. The Royal Society, draft of circular.

26. Galton to Pearson, February 1897, in K Pearson, Life and labours of Francis Galton.

27. Minutes of a Meeting at the Royal Society, January 25 1900.

28. Francis Galton to Karl Pearson, in Pearson K, The life and labours of Francis Galton, V. 3A, Cambridge University Press, 1930, 287.

29. Walter Heape to William Bateson, 1 February, 1900, Special Collection, Queen's University, Kingston, Ontario, Canada.

30. Walter Heape to William Bateson, 3 February, 1900, Special Collection, Queen's University, Kingston, Ontario, Canada.

31. Minutes of a Meeting at the Royal Society July 6, 1909.

32. Olby RC (2000) Horticulture. The font for the baptism of genetics. Nature Rev Genet 1, 65-70.

33. Weldon WFR (1902) Mendel's laws of alternative inheritance in peas. Biometrika 1, 228-254.

34. Bateson W (1902) Mendel's Principles of Heredity. Cambridge University Press.

35. Walter Heape [Letter to William Bateson] 2 June, 1902, Queen's University Special Collection.

36. Heape W (1906) The breeding industry: its value to the country and its needs. Cambridge University Press.

37. The Royal Society Year Book 1909.

CHAPTER 9

1. Heape to Galton 27 March, 1897. Special Collections University College, London.

2. Heape to Galton 26 May, 1897. Special Collections University College, London.

3. Galton to Heape draft letter 18 June, 1897. Special Collection University College, London.

4. Francis Galton. Notes summarizing a meeting with Walter Heape. Special Collection University College, London.

5. Heape to Galton, 29 June 1897, Special Collection, University College, London.

6. Galton to Heape draft letter 30 June 1897. Special Collection, University College, London.

7. Ibid.

8. Heape to Galton, 4 July 1897, Special Collection, University College, London.

9. Minutes of a meeting, Royal Society, 16 November 1897.

10. Heape W (1899) Abortion, barrenness, and fertility in sheep. J Roy Agric Soc Ser 3 10, 1-32.

11. Heape W (1899) Note on the fertility of different breeds of sheep, with remarks on the prevalence of abortion and barrenness therein. Proc Roy Soc 65, 99-111.

12. Kotz S, Johnson NL (1988) Encyclopedia of Statistical Sciences. Vol. 8. Pp 77-81.

13. Marshall FHA (1905) Fertility in Scottish sheep. Proc Roy Soc B 77, 58-62. Marshall FHA (1904) Fertility in Scottish sheep. Trans Highland Agricultural Society 16, 34-48. Marshall FHA (1908) Fertility in Scottish sheep. Trans Highland Agricultural Society 20, 139-151. Marshall FHA (1908) The effects of environment and nutrition upon fertility. Science Progress 7, 369-377.

14. Marshall FHA (1910) The Physiology of Reproduction. Longmans, Green and Co, London. pp. 586-622.

15. Wentworth EN, Sweet JB (1917) Inheritance of fertility in Southdown sheep. Amer Nat 51, 662-682.

16. Walter Heape, The Breeding Industry: Its Value to the Country and its Needs (Cambridge: Cambridge University Press, 1906).

17. Russell J (1966) A history of agricultural science in Great Britain. Allen and Unwin, London.

18. Pearl R (1916) The animal breeding industry. Scientific Monthly 3, 23-30.

19. Biffin HR (1906) The application of Mendel's laws of inheritance to breeding problems. J Royal Agric Soc 67, 46-63.

20. Grundy J (2002) The Hereford Bull; his contribution to New World and domestic beef production. Agr Hist Rev 50, 69-88.

21. Russell EJ (1966) A history of agricultural science in Great Britain, 1620-1954. Allen and Unwin, London.

22. Marshall FHA (1903) III. The œstrous cycle and the formation of the corpus luteum in the sheep. Phil Trans B 196, 47-96. Marshall FHA (1904) The œstrous cycle in the common ferret. Quart J Micro Sci 48, 323-345. Marshall FHA (1905) V. Contributions to the physiology of mammalian reproduction. Part 1. The œstrous cycle in the dog. Part II. The ovary as an organ of internal secretion. Phil Trans 198, 99-121.

23. British Medical Journal, March 12, 1904.

24. Letter from Heape to Ewart 17 October 1910. Ewart papers, University of Edinburgh.

25. Olby R (1991) Social imperialism and state support for agricultural research in Edwardian Britain. Ann Sci 48, 509-526.

26. Dale HE (1956) Daniel Hall. Pioneer in Scientific Agriculture. Murray, London.

27. Development Commission. National Archives UK T1/11386.

28. Appendix D (from Parliamentary Papers "Third Report of the Development Commissioners' (1911) 15, 910. (Quoted by Olby 1991).

29. Marshall FHA (1906) Review: The Breeding Industry (Walter Heape) Nature 74, 101.

30. Editorial review (1906) The livestock of the nation. Saturday Review. 14th April. Pp 464.

31. DeJager T (1993) Pure science and practical interests; The origins of the Agricultural Research Council, 1930-1937. Minerva 31, 129-150.

32. Marshall FHA, Hammond J (1946) The Science of Animal Breeding in Britain. Longmans Green, London.

33. Harvey N (1954) Walter Heape and the British stockbreeder. Agriculture 61, 381-385.

CHAPTER 10

1. Edward Blair & E Richard Churchill. Everybody Came to Leadville, (Leadville, CO: Timberline Books, 1971).

2. Spence CC (1958) British Investments and the American Mining Frontier 1860-1901. Ithaca, NY: Cornell University Press.

3. Prospectus of the Elkhorn Mining Company. Guildhall Library, London.

4. Memorandum of Association of the Elkhorn Mining Company, 3 February 1890. Guildhall Library, London.

5. Summary of Capital and Shares, Elkhorn Mining Company, 17 June 1890. National Archives, Kew, Surrey, UK.

6. Spence, British Investments and the American Mining Frontier 1860-1901.

7. Registration No. 30756. Directors: Hon. AG Brand (Chairman), JW Hart, WA Lindsay, Hon. WC Pepys, JG Smith.

8. Weed WH (1900) USGS 22nd Annual Report 1900-1901. Pt II. Geology and Ore Deposits of the Elkhorn Mining District, Jefferson County, Montana. Pp. 399-549.

9. Address by the Chairman of the New Elkhorn Mining Company, 4th Annual General Meeting, Summarized in The Mining World and Engineering Record, Dec. 22, 1900, 964-967.

10. U.S. Mineral Survey No. 1207.

11. U.S. Mineral Survey No. 684.

12. "New Elkhorn—the Leadville property," editorial, Mining World and Engineering Record, Copyright © The British Library Board, April 4, 1896, 585.

13. Memorandum of Association of the Elkhorn Mining Company Limited, dated 3 December, 1895. National Archives, Kew, Surrey, UK.

14. Registration No. 46157. National Archives, Kew, Surrey, UK.

15. Summary of Share Capital and Shares of the New Elkhorn Mining company. The Companies Acts 1862-1900. The National Archives, Kew, UK.

16. Recorded in The Courthouse, Leadville, CO, Book 169, p.102; Report at the First Annual General Meeting, 8 April, 1897.

17. Report of the Resident Superintendent (Mr. Robbins) to the First Annual General Meeting.

18. Herald Democrat, Leadville, CO, May 14, 1896.

19. Detailed accounts of the strike are given by Report of the Joint Special Legislative General Assembly on the Leadville Strike.

20. Denver Times. 2 February 1899, p 8, col 2.

21. Report of the 2nd Annual General Meeting held 4 May, 1898, Supplement, The Mining World and Engineering Record, 7 May, 1898, 883-885.

22. Editorial (1898) A costly Colorado venture. Anglo-Colorado Mining and Milling Gazette 28 May, 1898, 1(4), 51.

23. A historical United Kingdom inflation and price conversion. Salfalra.com/other/historical-uk-inflation-price-conversion.

24. Blair E (1980) Leadville: Colorado's Magic City. Ch XIV Pruett Publishing co., Boulder, Colorado.

25. Kelley's Report, incorporated in the Directors' Report, presented at the 4th Annual General Meeting of the Shareholders, 19 December, 1900.

26. Heape's Report, incorporated in the Directors' Report, presented at the 4th Annual General Meeting of the Shareholders, 19 December, 1900.

27. Directors' Report, 4th Annual General Meeting of Shareholders, 19 December, 1900.

28. Discussion 4th Annual General Meeting. The Mining World and Engineering Record, Copyright © The British Library Board, 22 December, 1900, pp. 964-967.

29. Denver Times. 11 January, 1901, p 11, c 3; 13 February, 1901, p11, c 2; 20 February, 1901, p 11, c 4; Anglo-Colorado Mining and Milling Guide, 4 (30 March, 1901), 37, Copyright © The British Library Board.

30. The Courthouse, Leadville, CO, Book 191, p. 477.

31. Anglo-Colorado Mining and Milling Guide 4 (27 April, 1901), 101. Copyright © The British Library Board.

32. Anglo-Colorado Mining and Milling Guide 4 (31 July, 1901), 101. Copyright © The British Library Board.

33. Discussion 5th Annual General Meeting. The Mining World and Engineering Record (30 December, 1901), pp. 32-34. Copyright © The British Library Board.

34. Anglo-Colorado Mining and Milling Guide, 6 (30 December, 1903), 179. © The British Library Board.

35. 5th Annual General Meeting, Mining World and Engineering Record, © The British Library Board.

36. Carbonate Weekly Chronicle, Leadville, 18 February, 1918.

37. Southwold: town, map and museum. http://www.southwoldandson.co.uk/site/South%20Green/South%20Green.htm

38. With thanks to Paul Scriven, MBE, Southwold Historical Museum.

39. Census record.

CHAPTER 11

1. Mittwoch U (1985) Erroneous theories of sex determination. J Med Genet 22, 164-170.

2. Mittwoch U (2000) Three thousand years of questioning sex determination. Cytogenet Cell Genet 91, 186-191.

3. Bull JJ (1983) Evolution of sex determining mechanisms. Benjamin/ Cummings Publishing Company, Menlo Park, California.

4. Parkes AS (1926) The mammalian sex-ratio. Biol Rev 2, 1-50.

5. Forbes TR (1947) The crowing hen: early observations on spontaneous sex reversal in birds. Yale J Biol Med 19, 955-970.

6. Morgan TH (1907) Sex-determination in animals. Science 25, 382-384.

7. Maienschein J (1984) What determines sex? Isis 75, 457-480.

8. Painter TS (1921) The Y chromosome in mammals. Science 53. Painter TS (1923) Studies in mammalian spermatogenesis. II. The spermatogenesis of man. J Exp Zool 37, 291-336.

9. Heape W (1907) Notes on the proportions of the sexes in dogs. Proc Camb Phil Soc. 14, 121-151.

10. Ibid.

11. McClung CE (1902) The accessory chromosome—sex determinant. Biol Bull 3, 43-84.

12. Bateson W, Saunders ER (1902) Experimental studies in the physiology of heredity. Reports to the Evolution Committee of the Royal Society. Report I, 1-160.

13. Castle WE (1903) The heredity of sex. Bull Mus Comp Zool Harvard 40, 189-218.

14. Wilson EB (1905) The chromosomes in relation to the determination of sex in insects. Science 22, 500-502.

15. Brush SG (1978) Nettie M Stevens and the discovery of sex determination by chromosomes. Isis 69, 163-172.

16. Stevens NM (1905) Studies in spermatogenesis with especial reference to the "accessory chromosome". Carnegie Institute of Washington, Washington, DC. Publication No. 36.

17. Wilson EB (1905) Studies on chromosomes. I. The behavior of idiochromosomes in Hemiptera. J Exp Zool 2, 371-405.

18. Doncaster L (1906) On the maturation of the unfertilized egg and the fate of the polar bodies in the Tenthredinidae (sawflies). Quart J Micro Sci 490 new series, 561-589.

19. Punnett RC, Bateson W (1908) The heredity of sex. Science 27, 785-787.

20. Heape, Notes on the proportions of the sexes in dogs.

21. Heape W (1909) The proportion of the sexes produced by whites and coloured people in Cuba. Phil Trans B 200, 271-330.

22. Russo published three papers on his results. The first is: Russo A (1907) Modificazioni sperimentali dell' element epitheliale dell' ovaia dei mammiferi. Atti R acad Lincei, Roma 16. A summary of the work is presented in Russo A (1909) Studien uber die Bestimmung des weiblischen Geschlechtes. Fischer, Jena.

23. Punnett RC, Bateson W (1908) The heredity of sex. Science 27, 785-787.

24. Castle WE (1910) Russo on sex-determination and artificial modification of the Mendelian ratios. Am Nat 44, 434-439.

25. Heape W (1908) Note on Russo's attempt to show differentiation of sex in the ovarian ova of the rabbit. Proc Camb Phil Soc 14, 609-612.

26. Punnett RC (1909) On the alleged influence of lecithin upon the determination of sex in rabbits. Proc Camb Phil Soc. 15, Pt. II, 92-93.

27. Wilson EB (1900) The Cell in Development and Inheritance. MacMillan, London.

28. Wilson EB (1907) Sex determination in relation to fertilization and parthenogenesis. Science 25, 376-370.

29. Punnett RC (1903) On nutrition and sex determination in man. Camb Philos Soc 12, 262-276.

30. Heron D (1906) On the inheritance of the sex ratio. Biometrika 5, 79-85.

31. Woods FA (1906) The non-inheritance of sex in man. Biometrika 5, 73-78.

32. Heape, Notes on the proportions of the sexes in dogs.

33. Heape to Dohrn, 14 and 30 September 1903, Copyright © Stazione Zoologica Anton Dohrn di Napoli – Archivio Storico.

34. Heape to Dohrn, 31 October 1903, Copyright © Stazione Zoologica Anton Dohrn di Napoli – Archivio Storico.

35. Darwin C (1871) On the Descent of Man Vol 1. P. 304. John Murray.

36. The proportion of the sexes produced by whites and coloured people in Cuba. Phil Trans B 200, 271-330.

37. Tedor JB, Reif JS (1978) Natal patterns among registered dogs in the United States. JAVMA 172, 1179-1185.

38. Glücksmann A (1951) Cell death in normal vertebrate ontogeny. Biol Rev 26, 59-86.

CHAPTER 12

1. Downie, RA (1940) James George Frazer: The portrait of a scholar. Watts & Co., London.

2. Heape W. The menstruation of Semnopithecus entellus. Phil Trans Roy Soc B Biol Sc 54:169, 1893.

3. Heape W. The "sexual season" of mammals and the relation of the "pro-oestrum" to menstruation. Quart J Micr Sci 44:1, 1900. Reproduced with permission.

4. James George Frazer, Totemism and Exogamy (London: MacMillan and Co., Ltd., 1910). Also available in facsimile editions.

5. Frazer, Totemism and Exogamy, 3-4.

6. Walter Heape to JG Frazer, 20 January, 1910, by permission, The Master and Fellows of Trinity College, Cambridge. Quoted by Frazer in Totemism and Exogamy, Macmillan (1910) Vol. IV, pp. 65-66.

7. Walter Heape to JG Frazer, 24 January, 1910, by permission, The Master and Fellows of Trinity College, Cambridge. Quoted in part by JG Fraser in Totemism and Exogamy, Vol. IV, 66-67.

8. Frazer, Totemism and Exogamy, p. 61.

9. Frazer, Totemism and Exogamy, 8.

10. Walter Heape to JG Frazer, 17 December, 1909, by permission, The Master and Fellows of Trinity College, Cambridge. Quoted by Frazer in Totemism and Exogamy, 162-163.

11. Frazer, Totemism and Exogamy, Vol IV, 168-169.

12. Heape W, Sex Antagonism, 131.

13. Heape W, Sex Antagonism, 200-203.

14. Heape W, Sex Antagonism, 207-208.

15. The Suffragette, 13 Dec. 1912, Vol. 1, No. 9. p. 1. Cambridge, MA: Schlesinger Library papers.

16. Heape W, Sex Antagonism, 101.

17. Gilbert, SM & Gubar S. No Man's Land, The Place of the Woman Writer in the Twentieth Century. Vol. 1, The War of the Words. (New Haven: Yale University Press, 1988), 8-29.

18. The Lancet (1913) Sex Antagonism. 181, 1607-1608.

19. British Medical Journal (1913) Dec. 27. P. 1631.

20. Lichtenberger JP (1914) Annals of the American Academy of Political and Social Science 52, 248-249.

21. The Atheneum. 21 June, 1913 (no. 4469), p. 675.

22. Saturday Review (1913).

23. Wolfe AB. Review, American Journal of Sociology 20, no. 4 (1915), 551. www.jstor.org/stable/2762921.

24. New York Times, Review, October 19, 1913.

25. Colquhoun E (1913) Modern feminism: and sex antagonism. Quarterly Review London. July, No. 436, 63-71, 105-110.

26. With kind permission of Ava Helen and Linus Pauling Papers, Oregon State University Archives.

27. Gilbert and Gubar, No Man's Land, The Place of the Woman Writer in the Twentieth Century. Vol. 1, The War of the Words, 30.

28. The Declining Birth-Rate: Its Causes and Effects (1916) Dutton, New York: vi.

29. Heape W (1914) Preparation for Marriage. Cassell, London.

30. Heape to Frazer, 17 December 1909, by permission, The Master and Fellows of Trinity College Cambridge.

CHAPTER 13

1. Heape W (1923) The Heape and Grylls Rapid Camera. Nature 111, 881.

2. ADM 186/244. July 1920. The National Archives, Kew, UK.

3. Annual Report of the President, Ordnance Board for the year 1914. SUPPL 6/169. The National Archives, Kew, UK.

4. Taylor EW, Wilson JS, Maxwell PD. At the Sign of the Orrey. The Origins of the Firm of Cooke, Troughton and Simms, Ltd. Published privately by the Company, p. 49.

5. Chesterman WD (1951) The Photographic Study of Rapid Events. Clarendon, Oxford; Lunn GH (1951) High-speed photography. Nature 291, 617-619.

6. Connell WH. The Heape and Grylls machine for high speed photography. J Sci Instr 4 (1926), 84-87. IOP Publishing. Reproduced with permission.

7. Patent Specification. No. GB156, 811. The National Archives, Kew, UK.

8. O'Dell TH (1994) Inventions and official secrecy. Clarendon Press, Oxford.

9. Patent specifications: GB126, 673; GB128,057; GB128,234;GB131,028. National Archives, Kew, UK.

10. ADM 186/244. July 1920. The National Archives, Kew, UK.

11. Eric Cussans, interview by JDB and Professor Henry Leese, University of York, 15 December, 1981.

12. Progress in Gunnery Material, July 1920. ADM 186/244, The National Archives, Kew, UK.

13. United States Patent Office. Apparatus for obtaining photographic records. No. 1,488,542.

14. Progress in Gunnery Material, 1921. ADM 186/251, The National Archives, Kew, UK.

15. 11 October, 1922. WO 186/6. The National Archives, Kew, UK.

16. Progress in Gunnery Material, 1922 and 1923. ADM 186/259. The National Archives, Kew.

17. Clippings of all these reports are in a scrapbook shown to me by Alexandra Heape, Heape's daughter-in-law: London Times 17 May, 1923; Manchester Guardian 17 May, 1923; Engineering 18 May, 1923; British Journal of Photography 25 May, 1923; The Electrician 25 May, 1923; Electrical Review 25 May; Nature 26 May, 1923.

18. Clippings from the scrapbook: London Illustrated News 16 June, 1923; Engineering 22 June, 1923; Rochdale Observer 23 June, 1923; The Field 16 August, 1923.

19. Heape W (1923) The Heape and Grylls rapid cinema. Nature 111, 881.

20. Hadfield R (1923) The history and progress of metallurgical sciences and its influence on modern engineering. Birmingham University.

21. Anthony J Marder, From the Dreadnought to Scapa Flow, Vol. III (Oxford University Press, 1979; repr. Seaforth Publishing and U.S. Naval Institute Press).

22. Hadfield R (1925) Filming a 15-inch gun. The Graphic. 2 February.

23. Edgerton HE, Germeshausen JK, Grier HE (1937) Photographic methods of measurement. J Appl Physics 8, 2-9.

24. WHD Clarke to Monsieur le Marquis de Chasseloup Laubat, MUN 7/298, The National Archives, Kew, UK. The 240 mm trench mortar was a heavy piece of equipment widely used in the second half of the conflict.

CHAPTER 14

1. Marshall FHA, Preface, Migration, Emigration and Nomadism, Heffer, Cambridge, 1931.

2. Baker J R (1932) A physiologist looks at wild animals. Nature 130, 380-381.

3. Review (1932) Spectator. 27 February, p. 28.

4. Spinage CA (2012) The springbok. African Ecology. Chapter 12 571-614. Springer, New York.

5. Collett R (1895) Myodes lemming its habits and migrations in Norway. Christiana Videnskabs-Selskabs Forhandlinger. No. 3 pp 4-62. AW Brøgger's Printing Office. (Google ebook).

6. Stenseth, NC (1995) The long-term study of voles, mice, and lemmings: homage to Robert Collett. Trends Ecol Evol 10, 512.

7. MacLean SF, Fitzgerald BM, Pitelka FA (1974) Population cycles in arctic lemmings: winter reproduction and predation by weasels. Arctic and Alpine Research 6, 1-12; Millar JS (2001) On reproduction in lemmings. Ecoscience 8, 145-150.

8. Kausrud KL et al (2008) Linking climate change to lemming cycles. Nature 456, 93-97.

9. Skinner JD (1993) Springbok (Antidorcas marsupialis) treks. Trans Roy Soc South Afr 48 part 2, 291-305.

10. Liversidge R (1978) It was all exaggeration. Afr Wildlife 32, 26-27.

11. Scully WC (1898) Between Sun and Sand. A Tale of an African Desert. JC Juta, Cape Town.

12. Roche C (2008) The fertile brain and inventive power of man: Anthropogenic factors in the cessation of springbok treks and the disruption of the Karoo ecosystem (1865-1908). Journal of the International African Institute. 78, 157-188.

13. http://www.nda.agric.za/vetweb/History/H_Diseases/H_Animal_Diseases_in%20SA8.htm

14. Skinner JD (1993) Springbok (Antidorcas marsupialis) treks. Trans Roy Soc S Afr 48 pt 2, 291-305.

15. Parkes AS (1929) The internal secretions of the ovary.

16. Semba RD (2012) The discovery of the vitamins. Int J Vit Nutr Res 82, 310-315.

17. Evans HM, Burr GO (1925) The anti-sterility vitamin fat soluble E. Proc Natl Acad Sci USA 11, 334-341.

18. Evans HM, Bishop KS (1922) On the existence of a hitherto unrecognized dietary factor essential for reproduction. Science 56, 650-651.

19. Elton C (1927) Animal Ecology. 1st ed. London, Sidgwick and Jackson.

20. Review (1932) Emigration, migration and nomadism. Geological Mag 69, 87.

21. Myers GS (1949) Usage of anadromous, catadromous and allied terms for migratory fishes. Copeia Nr.2 (June30), 89-97.

22. Skinner JD (1993) Springbok (Antidorcas marsupialis) treks. Trans Roy Soc Afr 48 (Part 2), 291-304.

23. Spinaje CA (2012) Other abundant populations. In: African Ecology. Ch.12, pp 571-614.

24. Shaw AK, Couzin ID (2013) Migration or residency? The evolution of movement behavior and information usage in seasonal environments. Amer Nat 181,114-124.

CHAPTER 15
1. Marshall FHA. Nature 124 (12 Oct 1929) 588-589.